MW00812798

Southeast Asia in China

Southeast Asia in China

Historical Entanglements and Contemporary Engagements

Ying-kit Chan and Chang-Yau Hoon

LEXINGTON BOOKS
Lanham • Boulder • New York • London

Published by Lexington Books
An imprint of The Rowman & Littlefield Publishing Group, Inc.
4501 Forbes Boulevard, Suite 200, Lanham, Maryland 20706
www.rowman.com

86-90 Paul Street, London EC2A 4NE

Copyright © 2023 by The Rowman & Littlefield Publishing Group, Inc.

All rights reserved. No part of this book may be reproduced in any form or by any elec-
tronic or mechanical means, including information storage and retrieval systems, without
written permission from the publisher, except by a reviewer who may quote passages
in a review.

British Library Cataloguing in Publication Information Available

Library of Congress Cataloging-in-Publication Data

Names: Chan, Ying-kit, 1983– author. | Hoon, Chang-Yau, author.
Title: Southeast Asia in China : historical entanglements and contemporary engagements
 / Ying-kit Chan and Chang-Yau Hoon.
Description: Lanham : Lexington Books, [2023] | Includes bibliographical references and
 index. | Summary: "This study examines the power asymmetry between China and
 Southeast Asia from the perspective of the latter. The authors analyze how Southeast
 Asia has historically assumed a peripheral position when juxtaposed against the power
 of the Chinese state"— Provided by publisher.
Identifiers: LCCN 2022045630 (print) | LCCN 2022045631 (ebook) | ISBN
 9781793612144 (cloth) | ISBN 9781793612151 (epub)
Subjects: LCSH: Southeast Asia—Relations—China. | China—Relations—
 Southeast Asia.
Classification: LCC DS525.9.C5 C425 2023 (print) | LCC DS525.9.C5 (ebook) | DDC
 327.59051—dc23/eng/20221020
LC record available at https://lccn.loc.gov/2022045630
LC ebook record available at https://lccn.loc.gov/2022045631

∞™ The paper used in this publication meets the minimum requirements of American
National Standard for Information Sciences—Permanence of Paper for Printed Library
Materials, ANSI/NISO Z39.48-1992.

*This book is dedicated to Professor Wang Gungwu,
who has inspired generations of scholars in the
study of China and Southeast Asia*

Contents

Preface

In his latest monograph, *China Reconnects*, Professor Wang Gungwu (2019, 66) contends that "China's transformation to a modern nation-state is still [a] work in progress." The Chinese concept of nation was historically based on the "emperor-state," where an absolute authority ruled over all things under heaven (天下 *tianxia*) through a centralized bureaucracy. Embedded in the political system of ancient China, the concept of *tianxia* is essentially a "political philosophy that justifies the emperor's rule over the kingdom . . . [which] . . . helped to bind the separate localities of the domain under one boundary" (Babones 2020, 134). Such spatial imagination was extended to the borderlands at the periphery of the empire, which include societies or civilizations outside its boundary. For instance, many Southeast Asian countries or the so-called "China's south" (Wang 2019) had historically played a subservient role in their tributary relationships with ancient China. They recognized ancient China as a powerful kingdom due to its immense size and technological advancement and its capability of making long voyages reaching the shores of its southern neighbors using a large fleet of ships, such as during the Ming dynasty.

The deep structure of the notion of *tianxia* that gave shape to the Chinese civilization continues to dominate the psyche of key Chinese leaders and thinkers in how they deal with external powers in the modern international order (Wang 2008). Nonetheless, the way in which the Chinese state's modality assumed its authority over *tianxia* has transformed over time—from coercive war to ideological revolution, hegemonic diplomacy, and eventually comprehensive economic cooperation today. While tributary offerings have long been discontinued, the return of a formidable China with the Communist regime had confronted Southeast Asian nations for several decades in the mid-twentieth century. During this period, many of these newly independent Southeast Asian nations were forced to decide which side of the Cold War to support. Furthermore, the Communist insurgencies across Southeast Asia supported by Mao's China, led by local Communist parties and some ethnic

Chinese, had caused suspicions and anxieties of Southeast Asian governments toward China and the Chinese minority in their countries. China had
only gradually withdrawn its support for Communist movements in Southeast
Asia after Deng Xiaoping's Reform and Opening-Up Policy when it re-estab-
lished diplomatic relations with the Southeast Asian region. China's rejection
of dual citizenship for Chinese nationals through its Nationality Law promulgated in 1980 was a welcome gesture that significantly reduced the anxieties of Southeast Asian governments over the loyalty of their ethnic Chinese
population. In the next decade, the end of the Cold War had witnessed the
normalization of relations between China and Southeast Asian countries.

As China's largest trade partner today, ASEAN's engagement with
China has been active but cautious for the past three decades. On one hand,
ASEAN has actively engaged China in multilateral organizations such as the
ASEAN Regional Forum, Asia-Pacific Economic Cooperation, ASEAN+3,
ASEAN-China Dialogue, and China-ASEAN Free Trade Area. On the other
hand, ASEAN has been hedging with other big powers, such as the United
States, Japan, Russia, and India, by establishing defense and security relations to counterbalance Chinese influence (Wu 2009, 22). As the bilateral ties
between China and ASEAN strengthened, China has also become accustomed
to the "ASEAN Way," which describes a system of non-confrontational consultation to reach consensus (Acharya 1998). In 2013, President Xi Jinping
announced the colossal global infrastructure development project known as
the Belt and Road Initiative (BRI), which is fated to play a crucial role in
driving the economy of Southeast Asia. Babones (2020, 138) argues that the
tianxia notion came back to the fore in the BRI as the project seeks to establish an international order that places China at the center.

Scholarly volumes on the relations between China and Southeast Asia
were scarce until more than a decade after the Cold War and the normalization of bilateral ties between China and ASEAN when such literature began
to proliferate. After the monograph titled *The Political Economy of China's
Changing Relations with Southeast Asia* (Wong 1984), there was a lacuna
for almost two decades before a series of volumes on China and Southeast
Asia relations, focusing on overlapping issues about international relations,
political economy, and regional security, began to flood the bookshelves.[1]
The literature has been further expanded as new developments on China's
BRI in Southeast Asia arise, which has raised questions on the changing geopolitical dynamics in the region with encroaching Chinese economic interests.[2] However, the attention paid to historical and socio-cultural exchanges
between China and Southeast Asia remains scant and is limited to a few
substantial volumes published in the past two decades.[3]

As part of "China's south," Southeast Asia has historically assumed a
peripheral position when juxtaposed against the giant Middle Kingdom. The

power asymmetry is reflected in the apparent bias in the literature where most studies are about China's presence in or engagement with Southeast Asia rather than the reverse. Studies on the presence or influence of Southeast Asia in China have been a marginal enterprise. The present volume, a collaboration between a China historian and a Southeast Asian specialist, aims to fill this void by exploring Southeast Asia's historical entanglements and contemporary engagements in China through a Southeast Asian perspective; the authors are of Southeast Asian origins. As China seeks to understand Southeast Asia's presence in the country on its terms, it is also engaged in the process of self-discovery and defining where and how it should stand in relation to the region. Southeast Asia has been commonly identified as being peripheral to China's rise, supporting (or strategically accepting) the BRI and playing second fiddle to China in whatever the latter does. However, individual Southeast Asian countries possess and exercise their agency. They can manipulate the power struggle between China and the United States in the Asia-Pacific region to their advantage for maximum economic and strategic gains.

Furthermore, Weiming Tu's (2005) concept of "periphery as center" in his take on "cultural China" (which he defined as culturally and ethnically Chinese societies in Hong Kong, Singapore, Taiwan, and other similar communities in the rest of the world) proposed seeing Southeast Asia as an important source of inspiration and lessons for China as well as the *center* of exchanges between China and the outside world. Hence, departing from the discourse of China as the *a priori* center dominating the scholarship on China–Southeast Asia relations, the present volume hopes to subvert such power relations to bring fresh perspectives on the historical and contemporary contributions of Southeast Asia(ns) in China.

We agree with Emmerson (2021, xxi) that both China and Southeast Asia are complex; a scholar, "however steeped in expertise and broadened by learning, would struggle to do justice to the heterogeneity of Southeast Asia—multiple states with different histories, cultures, languages, economies, and polities behaving differently for different reasons." Hence, instead of providing a survey of each country in Southeast Asia, the book, which could well be one of the first books to explore the presence of Southeast Asia in China, examines a selection of countries in the region, focusing on Thailand and Indonesia. Besides the fact that both countries are important founding members of ASEAN and have large economies and populations, they also represent two different divisions of Southeast Asia—mainland and maritime—which gives voice to both. Furthermore, as significant participants of BRI hedging against China and the United States for decades, both countries can help either make or break the Americans' Pacific Rim of encirclement.

This book begins with an investigation into the little-known history of thousands of male laborers who left Nanyang for southwestern China in support of the Allied war effort during the Second World War. Although often translated as "Southeast Asia," it is more accurate to regard Nanyang as "China's south," especially since the Chinese migrants assumed the region and its Sinocentric existence as being south of China. Due to their fluid and fragmented identities, these nationalist transnational volunteers had liminal belonging to both China and Nanyang. They were regarded as neither "Chinese" nor "Southeast Asians" when concepts of citizenship and nation-states were still in the process of creation. The fact that the identities of these returnees had transformed from sojourners who did not become permanent settlers in their host societies before the war to settlers in Southeast Asia after the war show the constructedness and malleability of identity. Through the discussion of the narratives of the Nanyang volunteers, the chapter incites a rethinking of the issues of citizenship, identity, and nationhood in postwar and contemporary China.

Chapter 2 continues the interrogation on the contested notion of national identity by examining ethnicity and frontier studies in Southwest China in light of Pan-Thai nationalism. When the political base of the Nationalist government led by Chiang Kai-shek moved to Sichuan in Southwest China in 1937, it faced political tensions motivated by cultural and ethnic differences in Southwest China. Adjacent to Sichuan were Guizhou and Yunnan, two of China's most ethnically diverse provinces, whose sense of belonging to the Zhonghua minzu (中華民族; variously translated as "the Chinese nation," "Chinese race," or "the various races of China") was unconfirmed. In addition to this domestic concern, there was the external threat to China's southwestern border—namely, Pan-Thai nationalism, which was an aggressive, militant, and radical ideology perpetuated by the Thai state to reclaim its "lost territories" of the Malay sultanates in northern Malaya, the Shan States in Burma, the French protectorates of Cambodia and Laos, and parts of Guizhou and Yunnan that were populated by the Tai (傣 Dai), whom Thailand claimed as a branch of the Thai race. This situation forced Chinese intellectuals to determine the nature of Tai minorities and clarify the Tai peoples' status in the Chinese nation. By suppressing any overt display of ethnic identity by the Tai, the Chinese state treated them as "immature" but unquestionably "Chinese" citizens to be educated and developed.

The next chapter looks at how the idea of the migrant's corridor, which linked Chinese sojourners in Southeast Asia with their kinsmen back at home, extended from China to the Sinophone spheres of Singapore and Thailand. It examines the appointment of respected Chinese business migrants-turned-citizens, who had a strong affinity with China, as Singapore's first ambassadors to Thailand. The ways that these Sino-Singaporean businessmen maintained cultural and commercial ties to their ancestral homeland and other diaspora members in locales such as Thailand is a case in point of how they traversed the migrant's corridor and created favorable outcomes in both business and diplomacy. Cognizant of the sensitivity being situated in the Malay world, Singapore consciously rejected being a culturally Chinese state or a replica of mainland China. However, its Chinese merchants possessed the social capital for Singapore to tap into the bamboo networks of trade, commerce, and compatriotism with Thailand's Sino-Thai capitalist elites and cultivate diplomatic relations with Thailand.

Part II of the book explores contemporary engagements of Southeast Asia(ns) in China, encompassing the knowledge production of Southeast Asia in China, responses to Chinese soft power and people-to-people exchange, and Southeast Asian capital in China. As a strategic region to China, Southeast Asia is also home to transnational Chinese capitalists who have helped accelerate and sustain China's economic growth since the 1980s. Therefore, knowledge of Southeast Asia is imperative to China as it seeks to defend and expand its influence over the region's constituent nation-states in a global rivalry for consumer markets and diplomatic allies. Nonetheless, Southeast Asian studies in China remain subpar, and this situation has hardly improved over the past few decades. While the Chinese government has invested more resources into academic research on Southeast Asia in recent years, the discipline can be described as primarily defined by policy-relevant research dominated by economics, law, and political science, with the marginalization of humanistic subjects. After surveying the history of Southeast Asian studies in China, chapter 4 explores how Southeast Asian studies has become a niche discipline in China. Universities and research institutes that provide this niche discipline also offer the state expert advice for policymaking and geopolitical outlook in the context of China's increasingly complex interactions with contemporary Southeast Asia. The chapter also examines the case of Thai studies in China, which is arguably one of the most thematically diverse and geopolitically relevant subfields of Southeast Asian studies in China. This chapter lays the foundation for deeper discussions into the implications of producing knowledge about Southeast Asia for business and people-to-people cultural exchanges between China and Southeast Asia in the following two chapters.

With its momentous rise in the past two decades, the Chinese state has increased its investments in soft power promotion as part of its public diplomacy strategy. As one of the key elements of the BRI, education exchanges form an essential part of the advancement of people-to-people ties. The Chinese government has been generously offering scholarships to attract international students to study in China. Such efforts began to bear fruit a decade after the normalization of China-ASEAN diplomatic relations in 1990 as the number of Southeast Asian students in China, driven by economic impetus and promising job prospects in their home country, proliferated. Chapter 5 discusses how China has also calibrated international higher education as a statecraft through the case of Indonesia, which has experienced soaring demands for Mandarin proficiency since 1998. As Indonesia is a country with a troubled and tumultuous relationship with China and its Chinese minority, the chapter demonstrates how nonstate actors such as students can play a role in bridging the cultural gulf between Indonesia and China and influence the public perception of China in Indonesia by offering counter-narratives to negative media representations.

Southeast Asian Chinese conglomerates were among the first to invest in China in the early period of the Opening-Up Policy. These investments laid the foundation for their China operations and helped build trust and a local network with Chinese authorities and businesses. As pioneers in establishing companies and production during China's transition into a socialist market economy, Southeast Asian capitalists were also instrumental in knowledge and technology transfer to China. In their host country, many Chinese conglomerates engage in patron-client relationships with indigenous power elites, who provide license and protection in return for material gains. In recent years, they have also played a reverse role in facilitating China's outward investment into Southeast Asia, using their social capital and knowledge of the local market and becoming conduits in promoting the BRI in the region. In light of this situation, chapter 6 explores the role of Southeast Asian capital in China, focusing mainly on the ethnic Chinese conglomerates and how they respond to the dynamic geopolitical contexts of China and Southeast Asia. Specifically, the chapter examines the case studies of Myanmar, Singapore, Indonesia, Malaysia, and Thailand because of the significant role the ethnic Chinese play in these economies. Studying the investment of older-generation Chinese migrant entrepreneurs such as Liem Sioe Liong, Mochtar Riady, Robert Kuok, and Dhanin Chearavanont, the chapter observes a shift in Southeast Asian business investments from being motivated by the importance of patrimony to being driven by profit, especially among the subsequent generations who have little emotional affinity to China. With an increasingly assertive China that expects its diaspora to serve the interests of the "ancestral land," it remains a challenge for Southeast Asian Chinese capitalists to negotiate and balance their national identity with their cultural identity.

We are grateful for the research grant (UBD/RSCH/1.10/FICBF(b)/2020/008) provided by Universiti Brunei Darussalam to hire a copyeditor and a research assistant to help us with the preparation of the manuscript. We would particularly like to acknowledge our copyeditor, Dr. Najib Noorashid, for his tireless efforts in handling the copyediting of this volume, and our research assistant, Westly Lo, for helping us with the literature search and review. The impetus for our book came when we spoke to Eric Kuntzman and Kasey Beduhn at Lexington Books, Rowman & Littlefield, who saw the potential in our book and guided us through the publication process. Our gratitude goes to them for their expertise and patience. We also thank Rachel Kirkland for shepherding our raw manuscript into a fine book.

Earlier versions of two chapters were previously published in the following places and included in this volume. The authors and publisher gratefully acknowledge the permission granted to reproduce the copyrighted material in this book: "Ethnicity and Frontier Studies in Southwest China: Pan-Thai Nationalism and the Wartime Debate on National Identity, 1932–1945," *Twentieth-Century China* 44, no. 3 (2019): 324–344, and "Traversing the Migrant Corridor: Singapore's First Ambassadors to Thailand, 1965–1990," *Asian Perspective* 44, no. 3 (2020): 487–511. The authors would like to thank Johns Hopkins University Press and the editors of *Twentieth-Century China* and *Asian Perspective* for their permission to reuse the material here. This is also an opportunity to clarify the choice of using traditional Chinese characters for the book. Although the use of simplified Chinese characters might appeal to readers who are more accustomed to reading in them, many of the chapters are historical case studies derived from archival texts and primary sources, which have been written in the traditional script. In order to reproduce the quoted writings in their original form and standardize the characters that appear in the book, the traditional font is adopted.

Ying-kit Chan,
Singapore
Chang-Yau Hoon,
Bandar Seri Begawan
March 2022

NOTES

1. See Chen and Liao (2005), Ho and Ku (2005), Saw et al. (2005), Wong et al. (2006), Yip (2006), Lai and Lim (2007), Goh and Simon (2008), Yeoh et al. (2009), Li and Kwa (2011), Pradt (2016), Diokno et al. (2019), Emmerson (2021), and Shambaugh (2021).

2. See Dittmer and Ngeow (2017), Blanchard (2019), Lim and Chibulka (2019), Hiebert (2020), and Strangio (2020).

3. See Evans et al. (2000), Stuart-Fox (2003), Tagliacozzo and Chang (2011), Wade and Chin (2019), and Hoon and Chan (2021).

PART I

Historical Entanglements

Chapter 1

At the Crossroads of Empire and Nation

Nanyang Volunteers in Wartime China

During China's war with Japan from 1937 to 1945, now widely acknowledged as a major theater of the Second World War (Mitter 2013), thousands of male laborers left Nanyang, or Southeast Asia, for southwestern China to support the Allied war effort. To be sure, Nanyang is not exactly synonymous with Southeast Asia. Chinese educators in colonial Southeast Asia had tried to give "Nanyang" exact geographical definition. Their nationalistic narratives promoting the sovereign Chinese nation-state regarded Nanyang as less an abstract or symbolic entity than one that was grounded in objective reality, which assumed a concrete, territorial, and Sinocentric existence as the region south of China. In their imagination, the Chinese in this Nanyang region were co-ethnics who remained loyal to their so-called ancestral Chinese motherland—they were projected as "nationalized transnationals" in the name of the nation-state (Sai 2013). The vision of these educators finally materialized when the Burma Road came into being. The Burma Road had been constructed to convey supplies—mostly gasoline and oil (G.E.T. 1942, 59)—from British India to the embattled Chinese republic, which lost access to the sea following Japan's conquest of the southern coasts. To fully deliver the road's military potential, China needed to recruit more skilled drivers and mechanics from abroad (Webster 2003). In response, from March to October 1939, the Nanyang China Relief Fund (南洋華僑籌賑祖國難民總會 *Nanyang huaqiao chouzhen zuguo nanmin zonghui*), based in the British colony of Singapore and chaired by philanthropist Tan Kah Kee 陳嘉庚 (1874–1961), helped dispatch approximately 3,200 drivers and mechanics to the front line. The drivers and mechanics, collectively known as Nanyang volunteers, operated and repaired the trucks that transported materiel and sustained China's only supply line at the time. They also received some military

3

training prior to their deployment in outposts along the Burma Road, blurring the distinction between civilians and soldiers during China's war with Japan (Chen 2006, 38). Anti-Japanese efforts were not limited to Malaya, but because a number of drivers and mechanics volunteered there, Malaya became synonymous with Nanyang. In fact, by 1940, almost half of all financial contributions from Southeast Asia originated in Malaya alone, dwarfing those from the rest of the world (Tay 2015, 47).

Until recently, the story of these semi-militarized Nanyang volunteers, like China's role in securing the final Allied victory, has been forgotten, relegated to autobiographies, oral histories, and private writings that enjoy limited circulation (Tan 2016). National histories of China and Southeast Asian states have difficulty categorizing the Nanyang volunteers, whose fluid—if not fragmented—identities at a time when citizenship had yet to become an important qualification of the nation-state meant that they were neither "Chinese" nor "Southeast Asians" in contemporary vocabulary (Zhou 2019). Indeed, national histories are processes of "othering" or struggles of claiming ownership over events, groups, individuals, memories, and even entire societies to singularize and legitimize the nation-state. War memory and commemoration are particularly useful in constructing the identity of a nation-state. They build a sense of solidarity on retrospectively shared experiences of defense, oppression, and trauma and strengthen a nation-state's contemporary resolve to prevent their future occurrence. However, despite state mobilization of substantial resources to domesticate or suppress popular expressions and public memories of the past, war experiences have remained plural in China and Southeast Asia, and a single emblematic event can yield different understandings independent of state interpretations (Yoshida 2006; Blackburn and Hack 2012; Wang 2012). Although this chapter discusses the memories of Nanyang volunteers in national histories, it also focuses on the internationalization of Malayan Chinese—a fluid amalgamation of people coming from different native-places and of different cultural and language backgrounds (Yen 1986)—vis-à-vis the volunteers' participation in an almost forgotten theater of a global war. By contextualizing the Nanyang volunteers in the labor regimes of colonial Asia, the chapter examines how these skilled drivers and mechanics circumvented restrictions imposed on their volunteerism and war contributions, helped transfer technological knowledge to China, and negotiated their transnational identities during and after the war. The chapter also contextualizes the volunteers in the waves of returnees during the prewar (sojourners who did not become permanent settlers in their host societies), war (they and others who physically defended China at war), and postwar (settlers in Southeast Asia, some of whom had been Communist revolutionaries in Malaya, who chose to re-migrate to China and take up Chinese citizenship) periods. Ultimately, by discussing the representations of these historical events and the politics involved, the chapter suggests that the Nanyang volunteers, albeit being active only at war, inadvertently prompted a rethinking of the issues of citizenship, identity, and nationhood in postwar and contemporary China.

Emigration creates diaspora when people move, settle elsewhere, but retain a sense of belonging to the countries they left, often referred to as the homeland (Ho 2018, 4). Given that diasporic imaginaries are given to chauvinistic—or nationalistic—agendas, diasporas are better examined conceptually from a historically informed perspective rather than as a primordial condition (Brah 1996). In this context, especially in instances where written records are scarce, stories, testimonies, and oral histories become important. As the diasporic Chinese communities in Southeast Asia, especially in Malaysia and Singapore, also strove to create a shared past of resistance with mainland China, they produced, consumed, and modified the stories and popular memories of China's war with Japan. The interplay between history and story has been a worldwide phenomenon; the distinction between history and popular memory is as routinely blurred in China and Southeast Asia as in other parts of the world. Given the universality of this interplay, it is easy to miss the versatility of stories as a source of inspiration and hope, whether or not they are serving state agendas. In a series of books, historian Paul A. Cohen highlights both the universality and the versatility of stories in the writing and reconstruction of history, setting the accounts of historians against the range of popular myths that have been fashioned about characters, events, and experiences of the past. For Cohen, the "insider cultural knowledge" that has rendered understandable the many stories of China's traumatic past, of its war with Japan, or otherwise, is composed of idioms, metaphors, and vocabularies familiar only to those who grow up in Chinese culture. Notwithstanding the exceptionalism and cultural determinism that are normally associated with such renderings, Cohen has gainfully suggested that people who speak the languages of China and spend time in China can take for granted and, more important, individualize or customize stories of the past to suit the culture, politics, and society that they have collectively constructed (Cohen 1997; 2009; 2017). To integrate the different dimensions of Nanyang volunteers in wartime China, then, this chapter applies the tripartite analytical framework that Cohen has deployed to study the Boxer Rebellion (1899–1901): the past experienced (experience), the past reconstructed (event), and the past mythologized (myth) (Cohen 1997, xv). The Nanyang volunteers have yielded changing, multifaceted interpretations over time, both from their own experience and as contemporary observers who lived through it, and as a myth fashioned by subsequent generations of commentators, historians, and politicians who sought to make sense of their own circumstances. Political rhetoric in China and Southeast Asian countries has also oscillated between seeing them as resources for nation building (or for fighting a war), co-ethnics deserving protection by the ancestral land, and foreign threats to the prevailing political ideology (Ho 2018, 5). China's attempts to reengage the Chinese in Southeast Asia capitalize on the transnational identifications of Chinese overseas to claim an extraterritorial hold over the Chinese diaspora. In the transnational politics of remembrance, and commemorated by monuments and war memorials in China, Malaysia, and Singapore, the figure, or memory, of Nanyang volunteers is, in death, deployed for life.

Monuments and war memorials commemorating the dead fall under the purview of what we may call necropolitics, broadly defined as a form of biopower and an "ultimate expression of sovereignty that resides in the power and capacity to dictate who is able to live and who must die" (Mbembe 2019, 66). Specifically, necropolitics, or necropower, refers to the subjugation of life to the power of death, which reconfigures relations between resistance, sacrifice, and terror. Necropolitics also accounts for how "death-worlds" or unique forms of social existence subject people to "living conditions that confer upon them the status of the living dead" (Mbembe 2019, 92). The concept of necropolitics in terms of how power and sovereignty are exercised relates to how the Nanyang volunteers are commemorated, compensated, and conciliated in China, and the logic of erecting monumental structures responds to the state's exercise of sovereignty associated with necropower and generating sites of inclusion and exclusion.

Necropolitics yields the concept of necrocitizenship, involving militarization imposed by the state and its manifestations within local cultural practices and subjectivities (Diaz-Barriga and Dorsey 2019, 11). In communities traumatized by conflict, fear, and war, necrocitizenship can assume the forms of martyrs' shrines and military cemeteries that connect citizens' loyalty or sense of belonging to the nation (Vu 2021). In the context of the Nanyang volunteers, state policies of glorifying and compensating the loyal dead through commemoration and war memorials, implemented over time by the Nationalist and Communist regimes in mainland China, have the lasting impact of celebrating rather than lamenting violence (Edwards 2016; Vu 2021). The war with Japan is now considered a bloody victory, a "founding myth for a people destined to shape the global order" (Mitter 2020). The opening of archives has allowed scholars and the public in China to discuss controversial aspects of the war, including the Nationalists' once-dismissed role in battling Japanese forces and the wider implications for China's Cold War and contemporary geopolitics (Mitter and Moore 2011). During the long period of silence from the late 1940s to the reform era, war veterans were hardly heard in mainland Chinese politics, despite the colorful portrayals of military-related themes in mainstream films and television. Attributable to the absence of a genuinely national army (during the war with Japan) and veteran associations, the conspicuous silence of the war veterans and wartime generation resulted in a somewhat simplistic, even artificial, rendering of the past (Diamant 2011). Party veterans (the few who had not been purged in the years leading to the reform era), rather than war veterans, benefited from holidays and laws established elsewhere to commemorate wartime contributions. As the Chinese state assumed almost complete control of necropower, war veterans were either forgotten or, worse, vilified as stooges of the Nationalist regime and foreign imperialists. It was only when the war veterans were no longer perceived as threats to party rhetoric that they were finally celebrated and rehabilitated. The legacy of the Nanyang volunteers underwent a similar trajectory, and they became retro- and necro-citizens only after the Chinese state felt sufficiently secure to accept, embrace, and honor them as martyrs and war veterans. For the state, they must disappear from memory and endure the violence of erasure before their descendants and local communities placated and resuscitated them from a silenced past.

VOLUNTEERING FOR WAR

In October 1938, with the fall of Guangzhou, China lost its last major seaport, as well as access to tons of materiel in Hong Kong. In response, the Chinese Nationalist (Kuomintang; KMT) government devoted its full attention to developing the Burma Road as a key supply route for war. It set up the Southwest Transport Agency (西南運輸處 Xinan yunshu chu), which quickly founded a branch in Singapore. The Nationalist government also dispatched a telegram to the Nanyang China Relief Fund for assistance in recruiting skilled drivers and mechanics to volunteer for war, confident that its well-calibrated appeals, via its outreach programs throughout the 1920s and 1930s, to the patriotism of Malayan Chinese would finally pay off (Yong and McKenna 1990). Moreover, although many ethnic Chinese were born in Malaya, they received a Chinese-medium education that fermented their sense of attachment to China. Aroused by daily newspaper reports of the war and angered by accounts of Japanese atrocities committed in their home provinces, they were eager to find ways to help their so-called motherland (Leong 1979, 301–302). True to the Nationalist government's projection, the reality of a weak China bullied by an aggressive Japan did instill patriotic feelings among overseas Chinese communities, which became a ready war resource for China (Tan 2016, 78).

The Nationalist regime's attempt to tap Malayan Chinese as a war resource introduced them as key—albeit soon forgotten—players in a global military conflict. Their contributions during China's war with Japan, which China eventually won and which led to its inclusion as one of the "Big Four" powers (along with Britain, the Soviet Union, and the United States), helped reverse China's fortunes and transform it into a stronger, eventually victorious nation. Although situated in the wider history of Chinese overseas labor since the nineteenth century, the story of Nanyang volunteers differs from that of the coolie trade. Until early in the twentieth century, most Chinese immigrants to Malaya were young men from impoverished villages in the southern provinces of Fujian and Guangdong. With family support, they paid their own passage to work as coolies, or unskilled laborers, but they lacked capital and relied on loans in the "credit ticket" system. Under this arrangement, an agency, usually based in a Chinese town, financed the coolies' transportation, which would be borne by their employers in Malaya. To repay their headman, who was typically a member of the coolies' home clan, they labored for little (if any) salary for a specified period until the debt was paid off. Although some coolies succeeded in sending money home in the form of remittances, the bulk of their savings went to those who had financed their passage, and many laborers remained trapped in a system of debt peonage, either to their employer in Malaya or to the agency that had arranged their passage (Powell 2016, 466). According to historian Wang Gungwu, most Malayan Chinese belonged to two groups: laborers (工 *gong*) and merchants (商 *shang*) (Wang 1981, 162). But for other historians, such as Yen Ching-hwang, the social order in Malaya closely mirrored that in China, composed of scholars (士 *shi*), farmers (農 *nong*), laborers, and merchants, with a small but not entirely negligible coterie of writers, who were active in literary expression and production, and laborers or former coolies who moved to the hinterland as cultivators, gambier and pepper planters, and rubber tappers (Yen 1986, 141–142). Historian Lynn Hollen Lees outrightly rejects the portrayal of Malayan societies as divided into only the rich (or elite) and the poor (or masses), arguing that as the Malayan economy developed, occupational structures became more differentiated among not only the Chinese but also other ethnicities, and towns or port cities such as Singapore became centers for new jobs in administration and commerce (Lees 2017, 137). Imported technology helped develop the colonial economy and create new professions, and unbonded agents or laborers in Malaya could learn how to operate newly invented machines and technologies (Goh 2013). Coolie and menial jobs that commanded meager salaries became unattractive, and Chinese immigrants and settlers alike preferred to acquire technological skills to work as drivers and mechanics in service of the entrepot of Singapore and plantations in the hinterland of the Malay Peninsula.

For the Nationalist government, the new surge of patriotism and a new sense of national unity among Malayan Chinese for its cause was comforting—so was the relatively high level of mechanization of the colonial economy and transport system. In 1936, for example, China had approximately

1,630 trucks, while Malaya had 29,273 registered trucks; most truck drivers in Malaya were ethnic Chinese (Xia 2015, 97). Malaya also had 6,106 licensed (or skilled) drivers, 4,031 of whom were ethnic Chinese (Xia 2015, 98). Although estimates for motor-vehicle mechanics are unavailable, they were reckoned to be at least in the thousands (Xia 2015, 98). The financial expenses of clothing, retraining, and transporting the skilled drivers and mechanics from Malaya to southwestern China were to be met by local relief fund associations, such as the Nanyang China Relief Fund (NCRF), which also greatly aided the cash-strapped Nationalist government (Koh 2013, 75). Singapore was particularly crucial not only as a key port of departure for the Nanyang volunteers but also as a staging area, or training ground, for other skilled drivers and mechanics in the Southeast Asian region. That drivers and mechanics were tested for their skills in Singapore—drivers were required to verify their ability to operate trucks along its relatively well-paved roads, and mechanics were required to demonstrate their knowledge by identifying vehicle components and assembling engine components—reveals the island's importance as a major center of Western science and technology (Koh 2013, 75–76). Singapore acted as a seaport for Nationalist China, albeit one that was further afield and not under direct control.

The hard infrastructure of machines, ports, roads, and vehicles was matched with the soft infrastructure of China salvation associations scattered across the world at the time; the NCRF was merely one of them, albeit the most influential and resourceful in Malaya, if not Southeast Asia. The salvation associations made substantial donations. In 1939 alone, they contributed an estimated sum of 1.3 billion Chinese dollars, constituting approximately 72 percent of the Nationalist government's war budget (Yang and Xu 2015, 435). But the British colonial government of Malaya was a potential obstacle to their efforts. In the late 1930s, Britain had sought to maintain its neutrality over the Sino-Japanese war, and colonial officials in Malaya restricted overt displays of Chinese patriotism and anti-Japanese sentiments, including boycotts and street demonstrations. In response, the NCRF, founded in October 1938 as an amalgamation of the China salvation associations in Southeast Asia, promoted its fundraising activities under the banner of humanitarianism, whose supposed purpose was to aid civilians trapped in war rather than to help China resist Japan—hence its emphasis on "relief funds" (籌賑 *chou-zhen*) and "war refugees" (難民 *nanmin*) in its manifesto and slogans. But the fundraisers, donors, and even the colonial authorities shared a tacit understanding of what the activities meant, and "humanitarian" aid to Nationalist China went unabated without significant disruption or interference (Yang and Xu 2015, 435).

At its inception, the NCRF launched a call for volunteer skilled drivers and mechanics to support malnourished and impoverished civilians in southwestern China through the transport of materials—rather than materiel. Approximately five thousand people answered the call, and almost 3,200 were selected. Due to the preference for young, able-bodied men—a result of the longstanding belief that men could better survive harsh conditions than women—female volunteers had to falsify their age and gender to pass the selection, keeping their identities hidden even after selection (Tan 2016, 79). To strengthen the corps of skilled drivers and mechanics who would be dispatched to China, the NCRF urged local Chinese organizations such as the Chinese Chamber of Commerce to set up training centers to prepare the candidates for adverse wartime conditions. After approximately five months of military and professional training, the volunteers were sent off—the first batch in March 1939—in farewell ceremonies sponsored by the NCRF, Chinese philanthropists, and even Buddhist monasteries and temples (Chan 2009, 52). Upon their arrival in Kunming, the volunteers were received warmly by the local inhabitants and soldiers, who identified them as fellow compatriots willing to enter the front line and die for the Chinese motherland. For their part, the volunteers also felt for the locals who had been distressed by war, despite having hailed from southeastern rather than southwestern China (Tan 2016, 80).

The Nationalist government's welcome disguised its reservations about the Nanyang volunteers. Shortly after their arrival, the volunteers had to undergo further education to gain familiarity with the local terrain and roads, with familiarity being a metaphor for that with the nation. They also continued their military training under their supervisors, who wanted to instill discipline and a deeper sense of mission in them. For the officials of Yunnan, the volunteers, steeped in the ways of the tropics, were different from them and the people of the motherland: the Malayan authorities exploited only the labor of these volunteers and, unlike them, expected little else. Driven by such stereotyping of the volunteers, Yunnan officials emphasized the value of hardship—over the creature comforts they imagined the volunteers to be enjoying "back" in Malaya—and collective living, hoping to organize them into reliable subordinates. Remaining suspicious of the volunteers' intentions, given confidential reports that Wang Jingwei's 汪精衛 (1883–1944) agents had infiltrated their ranks, the Yunnan officials monitored their movements and reiterated their resolve to mold the volunteers into model citizens, transporters, and workers under their charge and direction (Xia 2016, 147–148). The biopolitical power of the Nationalist state thus contradicted itself—while it regarded Chinese overseas as a pillar of national survival, it also viewed them as the suspicious "Other" and privileged natal ties, rendering their belonging as secondary to that of those who remained in China (Ho 2018, 12).

The volunteers had to endure more than just constant officiousness and surveillance; dire conditions, composed of fatigue, hunger, and sleep deprivation compounded by incessant air raids and machine-gun fire, proved to be a deeply harrowing experience for most survivors. The drivers had to navigate mountain passes and treacherous terrain, and the mechanics had to work around the clock to service trucks and military vehicles worn out by long hours on rocky roads. The mechanics warrant special mention for introducing the technique of magnetic particle inspection (MPI), a nondestructive method now widely used for ferromagnetic materials testing in which a tested material is magnetized by a magnetic field of sufficient magnitude (Stanek and Skvor 2019, 1) to detect stress corrosion and fix cracks and leaks (Zhong 2009, 65–66). Given the nonetheless difficult circumstances, it was a miracle, as contemporary observers put it, that the drivers and mechanics could still maintain and put to work approximately a thousand out of the three thousand trucks that plied the Burma Road. The Burma Road continued running until May 1942, when Burma fell to the Japanese. The volunteers had aided British troops in resisting the Japanese invasion by transporting Chinese materiel and soldiers to Burma. They helped to destroy the trucks and various installations that remained in Rangoon as American and British forces made a strategic scorched-earth withdrawal from the Indian province (Tan 2016, 80–81). By then, a thousand volunteers had perished from accidents, bombing, and disease (Yang and Xu 2015, 436). For those who survived, their cross-border experiences constituted a different set of war memories vis-à-vis that of the people, Chinese or otherwise, who remained in Southeast Asia throughout the global war (Tan 2016, 81).

NEGOTIATING IDENTITIES

After the NCRF dispatched the Nanyang volunteers to southwestern China, Tan Kah Kee and other local Chinese leaders in Southeast Asia continued to monitor the wartime situation and well-being of the volunteers there. Recognizing that the Nationalist government might be unable to offer its frontline personnel adequate support, the NCRF sent winter clothing, medical supplies, and other daily essentials to Yunnan, hoping that they would reach the volunteers. Tan Kah Kee wrote to the director of the Southwest Transport Agency seeking his assistance in ensuring the health and safety of the volunteers. Although the supervisors and trainers in Yunnan assured the Southwest Transport Agency that the volunteers were in excellent shape, letters from the volunteers to their families in Nanyang continued to suggest otherwise. The Nationalist state bureau, the Republic of China Overseas Chinese Affairs Commission (中華民國僑務委員會 *Zhonghua minguo qiaowu weiyuanhui*), set up in 1926 as a cabinet-level unit to cultivate and strengthen relationships with overseas Chinese (To 2014, 65), was also concerned about the living conditions on the war front and the negative press they might garner for China. Rumors about corruption and harsh conditions on the front lines also hurt the NCRF's recruitment drive back in Malaya (Tan 2016, 81). By July 1939, sixty-two mechanics reportedly deserted their posts due to ill-treatment (Akashi 1970, 114). Calling Nanyang volunteers "technical talents" (技術人才 *jishu rencai*), the Overseas Chinese Affairs Commission emphasized that they, having sacrificed their comfortable lives and successful careers to serve their embattled motherland, deserved respect and better treatment under their trainers and supervisors (Xia 2016, 262–263). Despite the reassurance and official reports, the NCRF decided to conduct its own investigation. With the help of Malayan journalists, the NCRF sent a comfort delegation to Yunnan and uncovered the woeful neglect and appalling conditions suffered by the drivers and mechanics. The delegates quickly telegrammed Tan Kah Kee, requesting that urgent supplies be sent to the volunteers (Xia 2016, 266). The telegram indicated that the blankets, cash, and medicines had been siphoned off by corrupt officials (Mitter 2013, 277). It also mentioned that volunteer drivers had to transport luxury items and female entertainers for these officials, which was irrelevant to the war effort (Qin and Tang 1989, 100).

Upon receipt of the telegram, Tan Kah Kee phoned Soong Mei-ling 宋美齡 (1898–2003), the wife of Nationalist president Chiang Kai-shek 蔣介石 (1887–1975), for her assistance in transferring fifty thousand Chinese dollars directly into the hands of the Nanyang volunteer corps (Xia 2016, 267). Tan Kah Kee eventually realized that corrupt and incompetent officials were causing the volunteers to suffer and die, and he petitioned Chiang Kai-shek to punish the culprits and remedy the situation (Xia 2016, 269). The Southwest Transport Agency was displeased with Tan Kah Kee's bypassing of the chain of command, however, and maintained that wartime exigencies and pressures, rather than government indifference and negligence, had resulted in the volunteers' hardship (Xia 2016, 269–270). Tensions arose on the ground as well. Jealous of the Nanyang volunteers for the supplies they continued to receive from Malaya, soldiers and workers who came from other mainland Chinese provinces discriminated against them, many of whom did not identify them as fellow compatriots. They looked down on the Nanyang volunteers, somewhat inaccurately, as "jobless people from abroad" (海外失業者 *haiwai shiyezhe*) who should feel grateful to the Chinese motherland for their sense of purpose (Xia 2016, 271). Paradoxically, then, the Nanyang volunteers felt more foreign (as an abstract group of Malayan Chinese) than local (as a uniform team of Chinese fighters and patriots), and their sentiments challenged the assumed cultural compatibility of migrant co-ethnics (Ho 2018, 3). To complicate matters, the Southwest Transport Agency ceased to function after the fall of Burma, while Malayan Chinese leaders, such as Tan Kah Kee, were either hiding or captured by the Japanese after the fall of Singapore in February 1942. The Nanyang volunteers came to be remembered as victims of Nationalist malfeasance, and this narrative came to subsume earlier stories of bravery, patriotism, and personal sacrifice for the Chinese motherland (Tan 2016, 82).

Under no effective institution or leader henceforth, the Nanyang volunteers were exposed to further exploitation and uncertainty. Some two hundred drivers joined British forces in India, while a group enlisted in the Chinese Communist army as militants to continue the fight against the Japanese (Qin and Tang 1989, 128). A handful of volunteers underwent training by Allied agents and partook in espionage missions in Thailand and Vietnam (Tan 2016, 83), becoming anti-imperialistic "global revolutionaries" who would help liberate Southeast Asian nations from colonial rule (Harper 2021). Most volunteers, however, were simply laid off and left to fend for themselves, unable to join regular armies or return to Malaya amid the chaotic situation. The more fortunate ones settled in Burma and the uplands of mainland Southeast Asia, joining the stateless societies of Zomia or Southeast Asian Massif (Scott 2009). Others remained under the auspices of retraining centers in Yunnan, with little assistance from local communities. Chinese newspapers reported that some volunteers were reduced to begging in the streets: "[The Nanyang volunteers] did not let their ancestral home down. It was the country that had failed them" (Tan 2016, 83). Dispersed and assuming different identities across Asia, the Nanyang volunteers ceased to function as a collective group. By then, most volunteers had lost their patriotic zeal and were demanding demobilization and repatriation, eager to return home to Malaya even though the war was not over (Gao and Kou 2011, 78–79).

The repatriation of the volunteers took shape in stages and across different provinces in China. While Tan Kah Kee was out of formal action himself, his aides resettled many displaced volunteers in the border towns of Yunnan, eventually forming the Yunnan Overseas Chinese Mutual Aid Association. Supported by philanthropists and charitable organizations in Fujian, Guizhou, and Yunnan, the association located volunteers lost in the chaos of war and housed them in makeshift centers. Upon Japan's surrender in 1945, the Nationalist government entered talks with the British to repatriate the volunteers. But the British proposed a moratorium on the plan, citing that the situation in Malaya had not returned to a semblance of normality. To complicate matters, the Nationalist government lost the list compiled by the Yunnan Overseas Chinese Mutual Aid Association, which delayed repatriation by another few months. Finally, in June 1946, the Nationalist government approved the budget for repatriation, and in October 1946 the first batch of the 1,154 volunteers who had survived the war were on their way home, surer than before that home was Malaya (Tan 2016, 83–84).

HISTORIANS' RECONSTRUCTION OF
THE NANYANG VOLUNTEERS

For the surviving volunteers, home had changed. The Japanese occupation of
Malaya crippled the economy, and the colonial society was unprecedentedly
racialized and polarized. Racial identities carried ideological affiliations, and
Malayan Chinese, despite their divided loyalties between the KMT and the
Chinese Communist Party (CCP), were profiled as Communist sympathizers by the British authorities and Malay communities (Yong and McKenna
1990). In colonial Malaya, any celebration of erstwhile anti-Japanese war
efforts could be interpreted as being pro-Communist or anti-imperialist in
nature, and the Chinese downplayed their semi-militarized involvement as
Nanyang volunteers as a result. Even in China, which was taken over by the
Communists in 1949, the volunteers (and the KMT or Nationalist government,
at least initially) were ignored and missing from official narratives of China's
anti-Japanese or "anti-fascist" (反法西斯 *fan faxisi*) war because they had
returned to fight under the Nationalist banner (Tan 2016, 84–85), even though
whether the Nationalist regime had been fascist was debatable (Eastman
1974; Wakeman 1997). Anti-Communist policies in colonial Malaya and
postcolonial Malaysia and Singapore, combined with ethnonationalism in
decolonized Indonesia and Vietnam, expelled Chinese populations in these
countries. Such circumstances forced them to seek readmission to China as
"returnees" even though they might not have lived in China. The post-1949
Chinese state framed their move as the "return" of co-ethnics, resettled them
in farms, and offered economic and social entitlements (Peterson 2012; Han
2013; Ho 2015). The help and recognition extended to these "refugee returnees" were conditional on their cultural and political reintegration into socialist
China (Ho 2018, 15).

Seen in this context, the Nanyang volunteers postdated the sojourners
who, after accruing a reasonable sum of money, returned to their hometowns
and predated the refugee returnees who, after being compelled to leave their
countries of residence, were resettled in state-owned farms that might not be
located in their ancestral provinces of Fujian and Guangdong. Comparatively
speaking, the concerns of prewar sojourners were more personal and provincial, working in the hope of improving their immediate family's lot by remit-
ting the meager amounts they earned as apprentices, coolies, and plantation
laborers (Yen 1986; Hsu 2000). Although they had been "nationalized" or
politicized enough to support the overthrow of the Qing dynasty (1644–1912)
in favor of Sun Yat-sen's (1866–1925) republican leadership, the transnational Chinese nation-state remained an unfinished project throughout much
of the early twentieth century, with both Communist and Nationalist agents

having to build their understanding of the Chinese nation and translate their loyalty from nation to party (Yong and McKenna 1990). The internationalization of the Malayan Chinese, for instance, was truly complete when they participated directly in the defense of China during the Second World War, either through boycotts of Japanese goods and donations to the Chinese war effort or through voluntary labor by the Nanyang volunteers, no longer divided by party affiliations or ideologies. The new Communist government after 1949 continued the Qing and Republican approach of engaging the Chinese diaspora by establishing the Committee of Overseas Chinese Affairs (subsequently renamed the Overseas Chinese Affairs Commission [OCAC] of the People's Republic of China), which functioned until its abolition in 1970 at the height and amid the chaos of the Cultural Revolution. The Chinese government also formed the All-China Federation of Returned Overseas Chinese (中國全國歸國華僑聯合會 *Zhonghua quanguo guiguo huaqiao lianhehui*) to protect the rights of returned overseas Chinese (歸僑 *guiqiao*) and their dependents (僑眷 *qiaojuan*) from the socioeconomic effects of rural socialist transformation and use the expertise and wealth of Southeast Asian Chinese to develop and modernize agriculture (Ho 2018, 20). Resettled in state-owned farms, the refugee-returnees (歸國難僑 *guiguo nanqiao*) were allocated farming equipment to support their families through agricultural labor. In terms of nationality status, they, more than the Nanyang volunteers, posed complications for the Chinese government, because many of them had naturalized abroad or acquired the citizenship of a foreign country at birth—they had never lived in China before, so how could they have "returned" (Ho 2018, 22)? For decades, they were a stateless population in China until they were finally awarded registered residency (戶口 *hukou*) status in the years after the Cultural Revolution, when the merger of state farms with neighboring villages—the farms had become a financial burden and source of economic and social inequality and hence local resentment—and exposure of state farms to the outside world eroded the territorial bases of the farms for refugee-returnees (Han 2013). Like the Nanyang volunteers, the returnees were subject to cognitive taxonomies of the Chinese state that manifested as systematic modes of exclusion, repression, and stigmatization.

Since 1978, the beginning of China's reform era, the emphasis on co-ethnicity receded as the Chinese state's diaspora strategies prioritized economic contributions and scientific skillsets to promote national development. The CCP government thus shifted to highlighting primordial kinship ties to attract diasporic Chinese investments in the special economic zones concentrated in the ancestral provinces of Fujian and Guangdong (Kuah-Pearce 2011; Yow 2013). In response to the new state directive, mainland Chinese scholars began to reassess Nanyang volunteers' contributions to China's war with Japan positively. In 1989, Qin Qinzhi 秦欽峙 and Tang Jialin 湯

加麟 of the Yunnan Academy of Social Sciences, relying on interviews and oral histories, published the first-ever Chinese-language monograph on the volunteers, titled *The History of Nanyang Volunteers* (華僑機工回國抗日史 *Huaqiao jigong huiguo kang Ri shi*). Qin and Tang revised the conventional understanding of the volunteers by arguing that they were patriots rather than stooges of colonialism or fascism (Qin and Tang 1989). That the book was printed in none other than Yunnan pointed to the Chinese state's desire to establish a historical connection with the Chinese in Southeast Asia.

The book by Qin and Tang was popular and well received among mainland Chinese scholars, and a series of monographs were published in its wake, most of which emphasized the "positive" contributions of Chinese overseas in "resisting" the Japanese along with their mainland compatriots, even though they had supported the KMT; the Nanyang volunteers starred as supporting cast members in the epic stories on the heroism and patriotism of overseas Chinese communities as a collective (Ren 1993; Huang, Zhao, and Cong 1995). In subsequent years, the topic of Nanyang volunteers captured the attention of both editors of and contributors to scholarly journals themed on the "question" of Nanyang (南洋問題 *Nanyang wenti*) and the history of the CCP (黨史 *dangshi*). In their accounts, based on extensive anthropological and ethnographical research, the Nanyang volunteers became martyrs and accidental partners of the Chinese Communists, who were committed to liberating China from the Japanese imperialists (Xia 2016, 10). In Southeast Asia, particularly in Malaysia and Singapore, Chinese communities and organizations eager to rekindle their ancestral ties with China during the reform era were quick to respond with activities and projects that highlighted the role of Nanyang volunteers in winning China's war with Japan. As early as 1986, the South Seas Society (南洋學會 *Nanyang xuehui*), a pioneering scholarly association aimed at examining Nanyang through a Nanyang-centered rather than a China-centered perspective (Seah 2017), had sent a team of scholars and cultural enthusiasts to Kunming to trace the footsteps of the Nanyang volunteers. Assisted by the All-China Federation of Returned Overseas Chinese, the South Seas Society delegation met with local officials as well as with volunteers who had remained in Yunnan and their descendants. Relying on the interviews and testimonies compiled during the trip, the South Seas Society published a series of articles in its flagship journal that explored how the volunteers fought and survived China's war with Japan, with a focus on how the volunteers had perceived the war positively through their contributions and sacrifices (Lin 1994). Fortuitously, Chinese-language newspapers in Malaysia and Singapore also started to pay attention to the Nanyang volunteers, with periodic commentaries and opinion pieces seeking to remind readers of their involvement in China's victory over Japan (Xia 2016, 11).

In tandem with the rise of scholarly and public interest in the Nanyang volunteers across Asia, archives and research institutions based in mainland China began to collect and preserve accounts of their wartime contributions. The premier institution conducting such work was the Yunnan Provincial Archives (雲南省檔案館 *Yunnan sheng dang'an guan*), which published a selection of its historical sources on the Nanyang volunteers for both specialists and interested readers (Xia 2016, 12). As for the archives and museums in Fujian, where many volunteers had relocated, they were more active in compiling ethnographical data and produced oral accounts of heroic deeds by diasporic drivers and mechanics who remained bound to their motherland (Xia 2016, 12–13). Huaqiao University, with campuses in Quanzhou and Xiamen, where a substantial group of volunteer descendants continued to live, recorded testimonies of Nanyang volunteers about their encounters along the Burma Road and provided researchers with access to their physical holdings (Xia 2016, 13). Many scholars have since highlighted the contributions of Tan Kah Kee, hailing him as an exemplary figure who, despite having made his fortune overseas, had not forgotten his duties to China (Lin 1994). The growing accessibility of archival resources generated even more interest and scholarly work on the Nanyang volunteers, and appraisals of them became decidedly positive. In recent years, some volunteer descendants have gathered to publish their own recollections, which deviate little from the narrative that Nanyang volunteers had been unsung heroes in China's war with Japan (Chen 2010). In 2008, the State Archives Administration of China and the Yunnan Provincial Archives helped the National Archives of Singapore curate an exhibition on the "extraordinary story of Nanyang drivers and mechanics"; the Singapore leg of the exhibition was held in October 2009, following a preview in Yunnan in August 2009 and the exhibition's launch in Beijing in September 2009. The exhibition traveled to Hainan in December 2009 and Kuala Lumpur in August 2010. In the broader context of Sino-Singapore relations since the reopening of China during the late 1970s, these museum exchanges fostered not only bilateral ties but also ethnic links between China and the major Chinese societies of Southeast Asia. To seal the covenant, the National Archives of Singapore published a Chinese-language exhibition catalogue that stressed the historical significance and contemporary relevance of the Nanyang volunteers, whose role in China's war with Japan linked the Chinese of the past with those of the present (National Archives of Singapore 2010).

The Singapore Chinese Chamber of Commerce and Industry (SCCCI) has also been eager to rekindle ethnic ties and highlight Singapore's role as the spiritual home of the Nanyang volunteers. The SCCCI has aimed to help Singapore become an advisor, facilitator, and partner of economic exchange between China and the rest of the world (Visscher 2007, 276), and the emergence of public interest in the Nanyang volunteers offered an opportunity for the chamber to remind China of its links with Tan Kah Kee and its involvement in recruiting the volunteers who had gone to aid China in resisting the Japanese invasion. In the 1980s, the SCCCI championed the cause of establishing monuments to commemorate the volunteers. Since then, Yunnan has erected two war memorials. In 1980s Singapore, the state no longer viewed Chinese chauvinism as a national threat and had promoted a set of "Asian Values" to justify its soft authoritarianism and relate its economic success to its supposed adherence to Confucian ethics (Tan 2003), but it was only in the 1990s that it founded the Chinese Heritage Centre and restored the Sun Yat-sen Villa to acknowledge its historical ties with China and accommodate peripheral histories (Huang and Hong 2004). The SCCCI and Chinese Singaporeans took the cue and organized events such as a 35-day road trip from Singapore to Kunming to trace the route undertaken by the Nanyang volunteers and held public lectures by history professors from China and Singapore to educate Singaporeans about Malaya's role in securing China's eventual victory over Japan. Ministers and civil servants affirmed that the government endorsed these activities and initiatives, and a stone sculpture commemorating the Nanyang volunteers, obviously with the state's blessings, was erected inside the compound of Sun Yat-sen Nanyang Memorial Hall in March 2013. Historians based in Singapore were quick to note—and embrace—their state's enthusiasm for mobilizing ethnic ties and developing a "Big Singapore" that would loom larger than its geographical size and stretch further into the past beyond the colonial period (Huang and Hong 2004, 66). Like what happened in reform-era China, a dialectical relationship between historians' reconstruction of the past and the Singaporean state's scripting of national history existed, and the Nanyang volunteers became worthy of commemoration and manipulation in the age of China's rise and Singapore's "becoming (explicitly) Chinese" (Barr 2014).

CONCLUSION

Returning to the broader theme of Nanyang Chinese, this chapter has suggested that the Nanyang volunteers were situated within the labor regimes of colonial Asia and presented an example of the complex and multiple experiences of returnees to China. For several decades, the experiences of Nanyang volunteers had been subsumed under narratives of the Burma Road and China's war with Japan. Toward the end of the twentieth century, China's opening up to the world and warming up to ethnic Chinese communities in Southeast Asia led to greater access to the archives and historians' reconstruction of the volunteers' past. But despite their actual feelings of dislocation and exclusion on the ground, the volunteers were characterized in official Chinese rhetoric as unproblematic members of China's resistance force, with the implicit message that the solidarity that they had supposedly shared with their mainland compatriots should extend to the present and future of contemporary China's rise. Wielding not only regional—if not global—clout but also the necropower to decide who from the past should be celebrated or rehabilitated, the Chinese state directly influences the direction and prospects of scholarly research and makes relevant or irrelevant the geopolitical focus of individual nations in Southeast Asia. That said, as the historical record has suggested, the Nanyang volunteers circumvented restrictions imposed on their volunteerism and war contributions and transferred technological knowledge to China. Most revealing of all, their historical presence pointed to inconvenient truths and irresolvable dilemmas about citizenship, memory, and nationhood that the erection of monuments and war memorials can only hope to assuage but never fully reconcile.

Chapter 2

Ethnicity and Frontier Studies in Southwest China

Pan-Thai Nationalism and the Wartime Debate on National Identity, 1932–1945

With the outbreak of full-blown war with Japan in 1937, the Nationalist Chinese government under Chiang Kai-shek evacuated from its strongholds and major cities in East China. The Nationalist government had two choices for military retreat: Northwest China and Southwest China. In Northwest China, the loyalty of ethnic minorities to the Nationalist state was tenuous and nominal at best. The Japanese supported the Mongolian Federated Autonomous Government and other puppet regimes that ruled parts of Gansu, Ningxia, and Qinghai. The Soviet Russians, who supported the Chinese war effort (and whom Chiang Kai-shek nonetheless never fully trusted), controlled much of Qinghai and Xinjiang, then ruled by Muslim warlords who barely recognized Chinese suzerainty. Despite Northwest China's developmental potential and abundance of unexploited natural resources, Chiang Kai-shek was unwilling to expose his regime to the Japanese threat and Russian control (Tighe 2009). He thus moved his political base to Sichuan in Southwest China (Lin 2011).

Chongqing, a city in Sichuan, became the wartime capital of China. Shrouded in a blanket of fog that limited Japan's summertime air-raid operations, Chongqing was well connected to the overland supply routes used to bring in relief goods from British India, ensuring that the Nationalist government remained well provisioned throughout the war.[1] Although the Nationalist government had pacified the bandits, warlords, and secret societies in the Sichuan region before relocating, the situation remained volatile in Southwest China, the region unoccupied by Japanese forces during the war and known as the "Great Rear" (大後方 *dahoufang*). While temporarily (but not entirely, as we shall see) safe from the foreign threat (外患 *waihuan*), the Nationalist government based in Sichuan faced the domestic concern (內憂 *neiyou*) of political tensions motivated by cultural and ethnic differences in Southwest China. Adjacent to Sichuan were Guizhou and Yunnan, two of China's most ethnically diverse provinces, whose peoples remained unconvinced that they unequivocally belonged to the *Zhonghua minzu* (中華民族; variously translated as "the Chinese nation," "Chinese race," or "the various races of China"). Speaking for the Nationalist government, academics whom historian James Leibold has called "racial nationalists" emphasized the Han (漢) or Chinese characteristics of the *Zhonghua minzu* to the point that they became synecdoches for the Chinese race-nation (Leibold 2007, 113).

For the ethnic minorities in Guizhou, Sichuan, and Yunnan, the influx of Chinese refugees from Japanese-occupied territories constituted settler colonialism, which involved transplanting the Han people and/or removing native peoples with the justification that settlers could use the land more productively.[2] Yunnan-born ethnologist Jiang Yingliang 江應樑 (1909–1988), though writing for the state-affiliated Sun Yat-sen Institute for Culture and Education (中山文化教育館 *Zhongshan wenhua jiaoyu guan*), candidly noted the similarities between Chinese and Western colonialisms. He suggested that the Nationalist state learn from "imperialistic nations" (帝國主義國家 *diguo zhuyi guojia*) by sending academics to investigate the local conditions of Hunan, Guangxi, Guangdong, Guizhou, Sichuan, and Yunnan and, based on the academics' reports, develop these provinces to meet the wartime needs of the Chinese nation (Jiang 1938a, 42).[3] Lamenting the lack of a national consciousness among the ethnic groups in Southwest China, he advised the government to include the ethnic minorities in the "core of *minzu* unity" (民族大團結的核心 *minzu da tuanjie de hexin*) and, by educating them and developing the region into the "economic center for the war of resistance" (抗戰的經濟中心 *kangzhan de jingji zhongxin*), lift their cultural and economic levels to match those of the Chinese (Jiang 1938a, 14–20).[4]

Missing from Jiang Yingliang's book was an assessment of Southwest China's geopolitical environment, which many Chinese intellectuals (including Jiang Yingliang, albeit only in his other writings) attempted to produce in the 1930s and 1940s. This chapter examines how these intellectuals conceptualized a major threat to China's southwestern border—namely, Pan-Thai nationalism, an aggressive, militant, and radical ideology perpetuated by the Thai state that called for Siam (renamed Thailand in 1939) to reclaim its "lost territories" of the Malay sultanates of Kedah, Kelantan, Perak, and Terengganu, the Shan States in Burma (then ruled as a province of British India), the French protectorates of Cambodia and Laos, and, pertinent to this chapter, the parts of Guizhou and Yunnan that were populated by the Tai (傣 Dai), whom Thailand claimed as a branch of the Thai race.[5]

Pan-Thai nationalism forced Chinese intellectuals to determine the "nature" of Tai minorities and clarify the Tai peoples' status in the Chinese nation. Chinese social scientists, who had relocated with the Nationalist government to Southwest China, were particularly active in deconstructing the "myths" that American, European, and Thai intellectuals and statesmen perpetuated about the Tai or Thai race. Despite (or, perhaps, precisely because of) their intellectual constraints and wartime circumstances, they believed that they had applied "scientific" methods in creating an "objective" understanding of the Tai minorities and in rethinking ethnic relations in Southwest China. Through the mediation of Chinese intellectuals and social scientists, Pan-Thai nationalism played a crucial role in reinforcing what might retrospectively be considered "frontier studies" (邊疆學 *bianjiang xue*) in Nationalist China.

For the wartime Nationalist regime, domestic pressures included not only the economic imperatives of constructing a territorial base in the southwestern provinces to resist the Japanese invasion but also the collective opinion of concerned Chinese academics who suggested that the Nationalist government view Thailand as a credible threat to China's territorial sovereignty over Guizhou and Yunnan and devise effective strategies for defusing the situation. The Nationalist government had already been aware of the possible danger a "territorially voracious" Thailand posed; however, the emphasis of the academics made the significance of the Tai peoples apparent. In response, the government's main policy was to suppress, at least discursively or intellectually, any overt display of ethnic identity by the Tai, treating them as "immature" but unquestionably "Chinese" citizens to be educated, developed, or nurtured. In other words, despite the wartime regime's "crisis" reorientation of its geopolitical view to focus on developing the southwestern provinces, it required a degree of prompting and intellectual justification from Chinese scholars and social scientists to view the Tai peoples as potential threats. These scholars then received state support for their studies of the frontier and laid a discursive infrastructure for tying the southwestern minorities to the Chinese nation. This chapter, then, is about the dialectical relationship between Chinese academia and the Nationalist state in shaping frontier studies. Such an argument requires the blurring of James Leibold's otherwise useful distinction between racial nationalists and the cultural nationalists who had accepted the ethnic diversity in China and chosen to "locate the unity of the Chinese people in a subjective and emergent national consciousness that accompanied the natural evolutionary process of racial and cultural melding" (Leibold 2007, 145). Cultural nationalists might challenge official interpretations of the *Zhonghua minzu*, but they did not reject their government's claim that the ethnic minorities in Southwest China fell under the jurisdiction of the Chinese nation.

In the existing literature on the transformation of the Qing empire into a modern Chinese republic, the problem of Chinese nationalism is discussed primarily in terms of how the post-Qing, Han-dominated state tried, with limited success, to replace centuries-old ruling alliances and structures that were heavily and suitably customized for frontier conditions with Western-inspired bureaucratic institutions that discharged a more direct form of rule. The early Chinese republic, as historian Hsiao-ting Lin has suggested, had little idea of how the republic should treat Han relations with other ethnic groups other than the Manchus whom it had overthrown (Lin 2011). The dominant scholarly focus, as a result of tracing Qing imperial ideology and the geography of the Manchus' strategic concerns, has fallen on the ethnic tensions in Tibet and the northwestern borderlands, where political unrest has continued to challenge centralized rule in recent years.[6]

This "continuity narrative," which rightly connects Qing frontier administration with issues of ethnicity in the Republican Chinese state, has generally focused on the northwestern provinces, neglecting southwestern experience and the conceptualization of the Chinese nation and ethnic relations in Southwest China (Tai 2015; Jacobs 2017; Kinzley 2018).[7]

This chapter thus fills an important lacuna in the historical scholarship on the frontier ethnopolitics of Nationalist China by highlighting how, perhaps for the very first time in Chinese history, ethnic differences could threaten the stability of a centralized Chinese state, which, unlike previous dynastic regimes, claimed to rule all of China but was seated in Southwest China and surrounded by non-Han peripheries. The Nationalist government's project of transforming Qing imperial space into Chinese national space had continued into the 1930s and 1940s. The loss to the Japanese invasion, both literally and figuratively, of East China and the Northwest not only reoriented the wartime Chinese regime toward developing the Southwest (Kinzley 2018) but also concentrated the efforts of Chinese intellectuals and statesmen on resolving the ethnic tensions there to better manage China's last territories. This chapter comprises three main sections. The first section traces Chinese interest in understanding the Tai minorities to 1932, when a coup in Siam replaced the absolute monarchy with a constitutional government. The constitutional regime soon came under the control of Plaek Phibunsongkhram (1897–1964; known as Phibun) and Wichit Wathakan (1898–1962), who promoted Thai consciousness among not only Thai citizens but also the Tai peoples in Indochina and Southwest China.[8] The second section explores China's initial responses to Pan-Thai nationalism as seen in the wartime Nationalist government's correspondence with the provincial authorities of Yunnan, which was most exposed to Pan-Thai nationalism due to its geographical proximity to Thailand and substantial Tai population. It also revisits the debates on the *Zhonghua minzu* with reference to the Tai peoples in Southwest China.[9] The third section focuses, through the lens of three social scientists, on the role of emerging scientific disciplines, such as anthropology, ethnology, history, and sociology, in objectifying the Chinese interest in Thailand and in refuting Thailand's claim that Nanzhao, a kingdom that had existed in Yunnan during the eighth and ninth centuries, was Tai (or Thai). Chinese academics and university professors conducted field trips, compiled ethnographic data, and wrote articles to substantiate the Nationalist government's counterargument that the Tai peoples constituted part of the Chinese nation. Their efforts helped transform the Southwest from terra incognita into an ethnographically legible region for economic development and frontier studies, as suggested in the conclusion.

PAN-THAI NATIONALISM: PREMISES AND INITIAL RESPONSES

On June 24, 1932, as Siam slid into economic depression along with the rest of the world and political dissent mounted, a small coalition of civil and military bureaucrats known as the People's Party toppled the absolute monarchy and introduced constitutional democracy.

In the new official ideology, loyalty to the nation was expected to surpass (if not replace) loyalty to the king. As Phibun and his military coterie came to dominate the People's Party by claiming that only they could defend Siam against royalists and foreign intervention, the party leader was attracted to other states that emerged based on a strong, militarized version of nationalism. In 1938, Phibun became prime minister and, having assumed totalitarian powers, launched a campaign to construct, at least discursively, a Thai empire. During 1935 and 1936, the Ministry of Defense had published maps showing the imagined boundaries of Thai kingdoms from Nanzhao to the ruling Chakri realm; one map depicted the full extent of Siam and the territories lost to Burma, Britain, and France. In 1939, Siam was renamed Thailand to formalize the ethnonationalist bond between the majority Thai and the territorial state, and a map showing Thai-speaking peoples across Southeast Asia and southern China was distributed to schools and circulated in newspapers (Baker and Pongpaichit 2009).[10] On December 8, 1941, Japanese forces landed in southern Thailand, forcing the Thai government to conclude a pact of alliance with Japan, and in 1942, assured of Japanese support, the Thai military launched small-scale campaigns against the Shan States, Cambodia, and Laos. Thai troops in the Shan States clashed with Chinese forces sent to reinforce the British. In 1943, at Japanese urging, Thai forces resumed their advance and occupied Burmese territory up to the Yunnan border town of Daluo (打洛) (Murashima 2006).

By claiming that Indochinese peoples were branches of the Thai race and urging them to unite against French domination, the discourse of the irredentist Phibun regime was ethnocentric and anti-imperialist. By following the 1930s Nazi German example of claiming German-speaking peoples in Austria and Czechoslovakia as part of the Third Reich, the Phibun regime contested China's sovereignty over the Tai peoples in Guangxi, Guizhou, and Yunnan. The regime's conquest of the Shan States exposed Yunnan to a direct invasion from Thailand. Simultaneously, to assimilate the Thai Chinese for good, the Thai government closed Chinese-medium schools, arrested openly pro-Chiang Chinese leaders, and cowed Chinese clan associations into submission. It nationalized Chinese-registered companies and Chinese-dominated industries, effectively severing the flow of financial contributions from Thai Chinese businessmen to China's war effort. That the only Chinese newspaper licensed by the Thai government became a propaganda organ for the Japanese determined that the Thai Chinese, rendered silent and powerless, would play a negligible role in the Sino-Thai dispute over the spread of Pan-Thai nationalism in China (Skinner 1957).

Contemporary observers in China, Thailand, and elsewhere viewed Phibun's cultural and economic nationalisms as inspired by fascism. Ironically, China itself provided a secondhand source of fascist influence for Phibun. Chiang Kai-shek's New Life movement, which sought to militarize citizens' lives so that they could at any time sacrifice for their nation, offered Phibun a direct model for cultural mandates aimed at regulating proper behavior and dress. Chiang Kai-shek and Phibun were professional soldiers who wanted to change nations they perceived as lacking in cohesion and national spirit. The extent to which Nationalist China and Phibun's Thailand were fascist remains controversial—a topic well discussed elsewhere and beyond the scope of this chapter. The point is that Phibun appeared to have a more systematic program of racial nationalism than Chiang Kai-shek. In frontier or racial policies, the Nationalist government, as noted by Hsiao-ting Lin and others, was motivated by crisis management or regime security and survival rather than "deliberately orchestrated ethnopolitics predominated by revolutionary ideologies" (Lin 2011, xiv).[11]

Phibun and Wichit Wathakan did not invent the Thaicentric racial discourse. Instead, they appropriated what European and American writers had suggested—or mythologized—about the origins of the Thai race. Henry Rodolph Davies (1865–1950), a British military officer who helped survey the terrain of Yunnan for the construction of proposed railway lines from India to South China, claimed in his 1909 account that Thais were a southern offshoot of the Shan race that had ruled the Nanzhao kingdom (Davies 1909). William Clifton Dodd (1857–1919), an American missionary who was based in the northern Thai city of Chiang Mai, shared Davies's argument. Dodd toured Indochina, where he encountered various Tai groups and considered Thais one of these groups. Dodd helped popularize the claim of French orientalist Albert Terrien de Lacouperie (1844–1894) that the Tai groups emerged from seven waves of migration from Southwest China. Under Phibun, Dodd's writings, which were published in 1923, became a widely cited source in Thai school textbooks for depicting the Tai peoples as having venerable roots that could be traced back two millennia to the ancient state of Ailao (哀牢), in modern-day Yunnan—a history long enough for Thais to regard themselves as "the elder brother of the Chinese" until they were ousted from Nanzhao by Mongol invaders. As historian B. J. Terwiel has suggested, Dodd's writings "provided Thai chauvinists of the late 1920s and early 1930s with an easily accessible set of information that revealed a glorious past, just when they felt in need of establishing such credentials for their state" (Terwiel 1996, xvi).

A notable reference for the Phibun regime came from British diplomat W. A. R. Wood (1878–1970), who lived most of his life in Thailand. In his book, the first English-language history of the Siamese nation, he suggested that the people of Yunnan were more Thai than Chinese. He agreed with Dodd that Thais and Chinese were cognate races, Siam was a successor state to Nanzhao, and Siamese ancestors had migrated from Yunnan first to the Shan States and then to Indochina. Wood confessed that his book showed a pro-Siamese bias but maintained that the book was factually based on empirical research by Prince Damrong Rajanubhab (1862–1943), a self-taught historian who had endorsed Wood's work. Criticizing Chinese chronicles for their own biases, Wood argued that Thais were no less barbarous than Chinese. Had more Thai sources survived, he wrote, "We might perhaps find that the Chinese had as much to learn from the ancient Tai as their descendants have to learn from the Siamese of today" (Wood 1924, 37).

The initial response to Pan-Thai nationalism was Pan-Chinese nationalism, which historian Chen Bisheng 陳碧笙 (1908–1998) first proposed. By declaring that "the history of the *Zhonghua minzu* was a history of southward expansion" (中華民族的歷史, 是一部南進的歷史), Chen Bisheng anticipated what historian Herold Jacob Wiens would call the "southward penetration of China's culture" into the area south of the Yangzi River and mainland Southeast Asia (Chen 1938; Wiens 1954).

The Siamese, Chen Bisheng wrote, were "a division of the Chinese bloodline and culture" (中華血統文化的分支 *Zhonghua xuetong wenhua de fenzhi*), and thus Siam would inevitably "return to the embrace of the Chinese motherland" (重新回到祖國的懷抱 *chongxin huidao zuguo de huaibao*). Like Gu Jiegang 顧頡剛 (1893–1980), the intellectual leader who believed in the plurality of *Zhonghua minzu* as opposed to the official line of Chinese homogeneity, Chen Bisheng argued that ancestors of the Thais originated in Hunan, Guizhou, and Yunnan. He suggested that the distinction between Chinese and Thai was artificial because the Thai elite, including the royal family, had Chinese blood (炎黃的血液 *Yan Huang de xueye*). According to him, "The Thais wanted China to become powerful so that Thailand could be incorporated into China as a province" (暹羅日望中國強盛而內附為一省) (Chen 1938).

Chinese intellectuals acknowledged the danger of Pan-Thai nationalism to China's borders and sought to expose the "fallacies promoted by European and American scholars regarding the Thai race" (歐美學者關於泰族言論之謬誤) (F. Zhang 1939, 922). The so-called Thai race, as articulated by anthropologist Ling Chunsheng 凌純聲 (1901–1981) and others, was Sinicized (漢化 *Hanhua*) in Siam and Southwest China; the Thais were a major constituent of the *Zhonghua minzu* (Ling 1940).[12] This claim would form the basis for the wartime Nationalist government's sovereignty over much of Southwest China and for empirical and field research by social scientists working there.

THE REAR BECAME THE FRONT

For Nationalist China, Thailand was no less a threat than Japan or Russia. Unlike colonial Burma and Laos, for example, which also shared cultural, ethnic, and linguistic links with the inhabitants of Yunnan, independent Thailand could challenge China's territorial sovereignty and was supported by the Japanese in manipulating the national aspirations of non-Han minorities in Southwest China. As Jiang Yingliang recalled, the focus of the wartime Nationalist regime's frontier policies had been on the Northwest until it retreated to the western interior; henceforth, the security of Southwest China became its priority (Jiang 1948).

Before the Nationalist government retreated to Chongqing, newspaper editorials and opinion pieces such as those by Chen Bisheng and Ling Chunsheng prompted a rethinking of border priorities in wartime China. After the relocation to Chongqing was complete, Nationalist officials paid full attention to Pan-Thai nationalism and its threat to China's sovereignty over the Southwest. In 1940, the foreign ministry sent a telegram to the Yunnan provincial government, seeking more information on Tai groups and informing local officials that Nationalist leaders were wary of Thailand's territorial ambitions. The telegram noted the Phibun government's interest in the Tai groups of Yunnan and its slogan of Pan-Thaiism (大泰族主義 *da Taizu zhuyi*), which claimed that 19.5 million Thais (泰人 *Tairen*) were scattered across Southwest China. The Thai slogan, the telegram said, was reminiscent of Adolf Hitler's Pan-German ideology and his annexation of Austria and Czechoslovakia. The foreign ministry wanted to know whether Thais inhabited Yunnan and, if they did, the number and special activities (特殊活動 *teshu huodong*) of Thais in the province. The Nationalist government, or at least the foreign ministry, had little idea of who the Thais were and had no standard term for describing them—*Dai* (傣) was placed in parentheses after *Tai* (泰) in the telegram (*Yunnan shengzhengfu mi wai zi di 537 hao xinling* 1940).[13] In fact, as we shall see, Chinese social scientists had different terms for the Thais, variously referring to them as *Dai*, *Miao* (苗), or *Shan* (撣). Ethnic identities were indeed flexible (if not volatile) in wartime China.

The Yunnan provincial government reported that it had never measured the size of the Tai or Thai groups in the province but would compile the census as instructed. The Yunnan officials acknowledged the severity of the problem; they worried that China would lose half of its southwestern territories should the officials fail to find a solution soon. The situation was aggravated by Japan's instigation of the Phibun regime to invade regions allegedly populated by Thais (*Yunnan sheng minzhengting sansan zi di 4444 hao miling* 1940).[14] The provincial government then distributed questionnaires to the prefectural- and county-level officials who had Thai constituents living under their jurisdiction. After the surveys were concluded, the Yunnan provincial authorities appointed Jiang Yingliang to head the new Frontier Administration Design Committee (邊疆行政設計委員會 *Bianjiang xingzheng sheji weiyuanhui*).

Gu Jiegang had relocated from Beijing to Kunming, the capital of Yunnan Province, and was teaching at Yunnan University. His proximity to the varied ethnic groups in the province, coupled with his desire to save the Chinese nation through scholarship, resulted in his assuming a keen interest in frontier ethnopolitics. In Yunnan, he founded the *Bianjiang zhoukan* (邊疆周刊 *Frontier weekly*), a supplement to the popular *Yishi bao* (益世報 *Benefiting the world*), to alert educated Chinese to matters of China's frontiers.[15] Gu Jiegang proposed that Chinese should discard the term "China proper" (中國本部 *Zhongguo benbu*) because it was invented by the Japanese to distort Chinese history and claim Chinese territory that was populated by the Han race (Gu 1939a, 21–24). His friend (but intellectual rival) Fu Sinian 傅斯年 (1896–1950), who had insisted that the *Zhonghua minzu* possessed a single spoken language and written script, common culture, and collective ethic (with differences arising due to geography and the passage of time), urged Gu Jiegang to reconsider *Zhonghua minzu* as a single race that comprised the Han. The Japanese invaders, Fu Sinian wrote, capitalized on in-house differences and persuaded the Manchus and the Mongols to liberate themselves from Han domination. The Japanese were resorting to the same trick by publicizing that Guangxi and Yunnan were the ancestral homelands of the Thais, posing a grave threat to Southwest China's security (Fu 2003, 205).

In what appeared to be a response to Fu Sinian, Gu Jiegang argued that the *Zhonghua minzu* was one and that, amid wartime exigencies, all Chinese peoples should be integrated into a single Chinese nation; however, he continued to challenge the myth of a culturally or racially pure people descending from a single progenitor, be it the legendary Yellow Emperor or the archaeologically discovered Peking Man (Gu 1939b).[16] In a somewhat official intervention in the Gu-Fu debate, Zhang Tingxiu 張廷休 (1898–1961), a historian serving in the education ministry, cautioned against the impolitic use of *minzu* for the people of Yunnan. According to him, Japan was conspiring with Siam to claim that Yunnan and Guangxi were the original homeland of the Shan people and to recover the lost territories, and so the use of *Yunnan minzu* as a descriptor was aiding enemy propaganda (T. Zhang 1939).

Fu Shinian and Gu Jiegang represented the two dominant narrative strategies for dealing with the issue of ethnic diversity in China. One involved treating all the peoples of the former Qing empire who still resided within the bounded territory of Nationalist China as a unitary *Zhonghua minzu* who, despite notable differences in culture, physiognomy, and religion, were racially linked to a single progenitor and, despite dynastic changes and local variations, had been politically united by a single bureaucratic system since the beginning of recorded history. Such an argument (though its proponents did not acknowledge it as such) was akin to the Pan-Thaiism against which it was reacting. The other narrative strategy entailed accepting the cultural and racial diversity of China and believing that the nation-building project would successfully weld together the majority Han and the frontier minorities (Leibold 2007). Such a narrative, however, was considered politically incorrect in the milieu of wartime nationalism, in which educated Chinese were expected to save the nation through scholarship; Gu Jiegang had to acknowledge the unity of the *Zhonghua minzu* before proposing his controversial argument that China was racially heterogeneous. In principle, cultural and racial nationalists agreed that "the *Zhonghua minzu* was one" but differed on the methods for unifying the Chinese nation.

NANZHAO WAS NOT THAI

The Second Sino-Japanese War forced many Chinese academics to reexamine their commitment to self-liberation and intellectual freedom and postpone the enlightenment project for national survival.[17] As Leibold has suggested, patriotic "faith" became more important—or politically acceptable—than the self-indulgent pursuit of pure intellectual "reason" (Leibold 2007, 137).

Anthropologists, ethnologists, historians, and sociologists who retreated with the Nationalist government to Sichuan produced data and advised officials on how to integrate the southwestern provinces into the Chinese nation. In Yunnan, the professors of Peking University, Tsinghua University, and Nankai University set up the National Southwest Associated University (國立西南聯合大學 *Guoli xi'nan lianhe daxue*), or Lianda (聯大) for short, where they continued to strike a balance between academic objectivity and wartime patriotism (Israel 1998).

As Yunnan-born ethnologist Fang Guoyu 方國瑜 (1903–1983) reported, "inland academics congregated in Kunming to discuss frontier administration" (內地學人多來集昆明, 尚論邊政), and the study of non-Han peoples became part of *bianzheng* (邊政 frontier administration) (Fang 2001, 2–3). Cut off from much of China during the war, Chinese scholars conducted extensive ethnological research in Guizhou, Sichuan, and (especially) Yunnan and produced voluminous literature on frontier minorities. The wartime Nationalist regime in Chongqing founded new academic institutions (of which Lianda was the most prominent) and expanded existing ones to accommodate the scholars who had fled to the Southwest. Other institutions involved in the study of frontiers included the Institute of History and Philology, Academia Sinica, the Humanities Institute of Sun Yat-sen University, the sociology department of Yenching University, the sociology and economics research institute of Lingnan University, the economics department of Nankai University, and the Sun Yat-sen Institute for Culture and Education. Nationalist officials relied on the academic reports generated from field research to study how they could develop the impoverished southwestern frontier into a center for wartime defense and counterattack.

This dependence on academic reports might explain why the education ministry, despite its dire financial state, was willing to fund these institutions and their academic fieldwork. The scholars' findings and recommendations laid out the blueprint for frontier administration—more specifically, economic development and rural reconstruction—in the southwestern provinces.[18] No distinct discipline called "frontier studies" (邊疆學 *bianjiang xue*) existed then; for most Chinese at that time, frontier studies involved applying the concepts derived from anthropology, economics, ethnology, and sociology to frontier administration.[19]

During this golden age of ethnological research and what was subsequently considered frontier studies (Ma 2006, 26), particularly as it pertained to the Tai peoples, Chinese academics took issue with the claim that Nanzhao was a Thai kingdom. By consulting Tang dynasty (618–907) materials, Ling Chunsheng had ascertained that Nanzhao was founded not by the Tai but by the Bai (白) and Yi (彝) (Ling 1938).[20] Fang Guoyu depended on other Chinese texts to suggest that Nanzhao was established by the highly Sinicized

Bai. He and Ling Chunsheng were colleagues at the Institute of History and Philology, and they wanted to inspire other social scientists to prove the historical record with empirical data derived from the minority groups of Yunnan. In October 1938, they founded the journal *Southwest Frontier* (西南 邊疆 *Xi'nan bianjiang*). Their aim, indicated in the inaugural issue, was "to introduce the southwestern frontier to the Chinese and convey knowledge that might contribute to fighting the war and building the nation" (把西南介紹於 國人, 期於抗戰建國政策的推行上有所貢獻) (Luo 2014, 38–39).

Southwest Frontier became a major vehicle for the publication of work that dispelled the myth of Thai origins, which involved tracing the Thai nation back to the Nanzhao kingdom.[21] Jiang Yingliang, using data collected from his fieldwork in Tai-populated areas of Yunnan, contributed one of the journal's first articles. Like Fang Guoyu, Jiang Yingliang had been educated in China, having earned his doctorate in anthropology from Sun Yat-sen University (Jiang 2005).[22] In 1937, he received a fellowship financed by the Sino-British Boxer Indemnity Fund (中英庚款 *Zhong Ying gengkuan*) and moved to Yunnan, where he served as head of the Frontier Administration Design Committee. In Yunnan, he visited the Tai peoples in the remote borderlands, logistically supported by the education department of the provincial government. Although noting privately that he could understand why the Tai felt little loyalty to the Nationalist government (corrupt frontier officials exploited the Tai's labor and resources and made no attempt to improve their livelihood), he maintained that the Tai, whom he called the Shan (撣), shared the physiognomy and skin color of Chinese (中國人 *Zhongguoren*), which was synonymous with *Zhonghua minzu*. He wrote that in terms of blood (血 統 *xuetong*) and race (人種 *renzhong*), the Tai descended from the Baiyue (百越), who branched off from the *Zhonghua minzu*, suggesting that Nanzhao and all the kingdoms that were supposedly Tai were ultimately Chinese (Jiang 1938b).[23]

The Phibun government claimed that substantial populations of Thais resided in Guangxi, Guizhou, and Yunnan. Although Guangxi remained part of Free China, it was exposed to direct attacks by Japanese forces and hence was militarily vulnerable, as Japan's 1944 Ichigo offensive would reveal (van de Ven 2018). Chinese ethnologists and sociologists thus focused on Guizhou and Yunnan in researching ethnic communities as the basis for responding to Thailand's challenge. Cen Jiawu 岑家梧 (1912–1966) took up the challenge with his work on the frontier minorities of Guizhou. Born and raised in a poor family, he eventually enrolled in the sociology department of Sun Yat-sen University. In 1934, an elder cousin, who was a businessman in Southeast Asia, supported Cen Jiawu's transfer to Rikkyo University and then to Imperial University for his doctoral program. In Japan, he studied archaeology and anthropology and read the classic works of European, American, and Japanese scholars. His exposure to ethnographical approaches to studying and classifying people, used by Japanese academics to define the Yamato race and its "inferior" branches such as the Ainu and the Ryukyuan, alerted him to nontextual sources, such as dance, music, paintings, sculptures, and totems. His critically acclaimed *A History of Totemic Art* (圖騰藝術史 *Tuteng yishu shi*) used such materials to establish the dialectical relationship between art and totemism.[24] After the full outbreak of the Second Sino-Japanese War in July 1937, Cen Jiawu returned to China, where he also received an award from the Boxer Indemnity Fund to conduct field research in Yunnan. In 1940, he joined Lianda's economics department, then headed by sociologist Chen Xujing 陳序經 (1903–1967), and published his findings on the *Xi'nan minzu* (西南民族 southwestern races) at Lianda. In 1942, Cen Jiawu went to Guizhou University, where he taught sociology for two years (Feng 1992). His odyssey suggests that little distinction existed between anthropology, economics, and sociology in China at that time (Wang 2017).

Cen Jiawu's foray into ethnology and frontier studies dealt with the Miao (苗), who had resisted Qing imperial rule and, as recently as 1937, had rebelled in western Hunan against centralized Nationalist control (McCord 2011). In his writings on the Miao in Guizhou, he criticized the accounts by British and French travelers and suggested that these accounts, built upon hearsay and fragmented memories, could not be considered scientific (不能算是科學的著作 *buneng suan shi kexue de zhuzuo*). He thus urged Chinese social scientists to capitalize on the recent development of academic institutions related to anthropology, ethnology, history, and language and conduct truly scientific research (Cen 1992b).

Although Cen Jiawu studied the Miao rather than the Tai, he understood the implications of Pan-Thai nationalism for China's survival and territorial integrity. Like Gu Jiegang, Cen Jiawu argued that different races had intermarried to form the *Zhonghua minzu*. The raw materials of artifacts unearthed in northern China, he wrote, originated in the Southwest. For him, this meant that the southwestern peoples had interacted with the "Han race of the Central Plain" (中原漢族 *Zhongyuan Hanzu*)[25] and that they had migrated from northern China to the Southwest, where they had remained since (i.e., they did not move beyond China to become Thais or other Tai peoples). He used the concept of environmental determinism to explain the similarities rather than differences between the Han and non-Han, who had lived together in a fixed and bounded China in a single environment (同一的環境 *tongyi de huanjing*). The convergence of interests resulted not in competition but in the construction of a collective (利益共同的集體 *liyi gongtong de jiti*). In his words, "every race in China was an important member of the *Zhonghua minzu*" (各族都是中華民族重要的一員) (Cen 1992b, 31–32).

Cen Jiawu's sojourn in Japan allowed him to recognize the malleability of ethnic categories to suit political needs, but he apparently saw little contradiction in the use of such categories to explain the unity of the Chinese race-nation. Although he did not, like Fu Sinian, determine the progenitor of the *Zhonghua minzu*, Cen Jiawu insisted that the non-Han peoples, especially the Miao, were similar to the Han race in their costume, music, and dance. He observed the nuptials of chieftains (土司 *tusi*) in Guizhou and Yunnan and argued that they originated in a single culture thousands of years ago. Now that the Phibun regime was claiming the Miao in Indochina—where they were called the Hmong—as part of the Thai nation,[26] Cen Jiawu warned that Thailand might proceed to claim that the Miao minority in China were also a Tai-speaking race (泰語系民族 *Tai yuxi minzu*) and detach Miao territories from China. He encouraged "academics to strengthen the racial consciousness of the Chinese and expose the conspiracy of Pan-Thai ideology" (增强民族意識, 揭露大泰族主義者之陰謀) (Cen 1992a, 133–134).

Jiang Yingliang and Cen Jiawu were particularly known for their extensive fieldwork in the deepest reaches of Southwest China and for nationalistic awareness in their writings. By conducting field research in Thailand, partly funded by the Institute of Pacific Relations,[27] and by connecting Pan-Thai ideology to Thailand's internal dynamics, Chen Xujing distinguished himself from most Chinese academics during the war. Born on Hainan Island (then part of Guangdong Province), Chen Xujing traveled extensively during his childhood and received his early education in Singapore. After graduating from Fudan University, he received a doctoral degree in sociology from the University of Illinois in 1927. His father, a rags-to-riches merchant based in Singapore, funded his son's education. His sacrifices made Chen Xujing aware of the difficulties faced by sojourning Chinese when navigating their political conditions and assimilating into their host societies—he was sensitive to being a minority Chinese in the wider context of colonial Southeast Asia and the world.[28] His familiarity with Thailand, which he had used as a base when traveling in Southeast Asia and where he had several friends, may explain why he appeared to be more empathetic toward Thailand.

Chen Xujing's first book was his 1928 doctoral thesis "Recent Theories of Sovereignty," published by the Lingnan University Bookstore in 1929. His dissertation, composed of uncritical summaries of scholarly writings on sovereignty, considered the subject "purely Occidental," and he did not consult non-Western texts (Chen 1929, 5). In his concluding remarks, he wrote that "the sovereignty that [the state] possesses is not a right for doing what it pleases, but a power for developing human interests" (Chen 1929, 295–296). His position on the sovereign right of states to advance the interests of their own citizens would affect his perception of Pan-Thai nationalism.

Chen Xujing was not known for his work on sovereignty, however. In the 1930s, he became famous for advocating the "total Westernization" (全 盤西化 *quanpan xihua*) of China. He rejected the rural reconstruction program pioneered by intellectuals Liang Shuming 梁漱溟 (1893–1988) and Yan Yangchu 晏陽初 (1890–1990; also known as James Yen), who sought to modernize and transform villages and the countryside into a locomotive of reform and national development. Having little patience for Liang Shuming and others who wanted to transform China by sticking to rural institutions and traditions, Chen Xujing argued that only the complete Anglo-Americanization of China could save the nation. Although he recognized the depravity of capitalism and militarism that might follow the wholesale adoption of Western culture, he saw such depravity as the price that China must pay for real progress. Well versed in cultural anthropology and the concept of cultural holism—which suggests that any given culture constitutes an organic entity whose parts are so interrelated that modifying one will affect all others—he argued that it was impossible for China to Westernize by selecting only the desirable from the undesirable based on China's own cultural or moral judgments.[29]

Chen Xujing's positions on sovereignty and Westernization allowed him to view Thailand as a progressive nation that, despite its militant form of nationalism, had adapted to global trends (迎合世界潮流的趨向 *yinghe shijie chaoliu de quxiang*) and proactively adopted Western culture (自動 地去採納西洋的文化). By comparing China's quest for modernity with Thailand's development, he concluded that China was inferior (Chen 1941). He accepted the Western-imposed categories of identification and the West's denial of what historian Rebecca E. Karl calls "coevalness to the non-West," or "the view of modernity as synchronic uneven global space in a coeval temporality" (Karl 2002, 84). For Chen Xujing, China had fallen behind not only Japan and the West but also Westernizing but despised nations such as Siam. Unlike Jiang Yingliang and Cen Jiawu, Chen Xujing spoke some Thai and had watched Thai cultural performances in Thailand. Although he arrived at familiar conclusions about Thai culture (that it was similar to the customs and practices of Chinese in Chaozhou and Shantou, where many Sino-Thais had come from), Chen Xujing avoided the debate on the *Zhonghua minzu*, which assumed that the frontier minorities, including the Tai, were more culturally and economically backward than the Han (Chen 1941).

For Chen Xujing, China and Thailand were colonialized or imperialized spaces of the non-Western world. Unlike China, however, Thailand managed to earn the respect of Western nations, which abrogated their extraterritorial rights in Thailand. He admired Thailand's independence, which appeared more complete and more secure than China's, but he warned that Pan-Thai nationalism might antagonize Britain and France, whose Indochinese colonies were being claimed as Thai by the Phibun regime. Phibun, Chen Xujing wrote, should understand that Thailand existed as a buffer between the British and French colonies in mainland Southeast Asia—Thailand's independence had been granted rather than won. In *Siam and China* (暹羅與中國 *Xianluo yu Zhongguo*), published in 1941 as a collection of essays on Sino-Thai relations, Chen Xujing wanted not only to alert the Chinese to Pan-Thai nationalism but also to remind them "not to disdain their southern neighbor" (不要藐視我們的南鄰 *buyao miaoshi women de nanlin*) (Chen 1941, 101). By advocating Westernization rather than Sinicization, Pan-Chinese nationalism, or the idea of the *Zhonghua minzu*, and by seeking to awaken (喚醒 *huanxing*) the Chinese people to the possibility of friendly relations with the Thais, he was reacting against the nationalistic literature popular at that time for portraying Thais not only as an inferior branch of the *Zhonghua minzu* but also as an opportunistic people goaded by Japan into claiming parts of Southwest China as lost territories (Chen 1941, 1).

Like most Chinese social scientists, however, Chen Xujing took issue with the Thai claim that the Tai/Thai race originated in Nanzhao, which he argued had been based on incomplete and unreliable historical evidence. He believed the Phibun regime had not conducted its own historical or scientific research to validate the claims by European and American writers. Instead, it uncritically accepted the Western arguments as part of a national ideology because they anchored national pride to a glorious past of civilization and subsequently Westernization. In response to the argument that the Tai/Thai had migrated from Southwest China to Indochina, Chen Xujing suggested that Sichuan and Yunnan were scarcely populated by the Han until the modern period, and ethnic minorities faced little pressure to migrate southward: If no southward migration had occurred, how could the Thais in Sukhothai, Ayutthaya, and Siam be related to the inhabitants of Nanzhao? Challenging the European and American accounts of Thais' racial genealogy, Chen Xujing highlighted that Chinese chronicles had recorded the existence of various Thai kingdoms before Nanzhao was founded, thus dismissing the continuity between Siam/Thailand and the Thai kingdoms that were claimed to have existed in China (Chen 1941, 40–41).

Not satisfied with a mere repudiation of false claims, he strove to reconstruct a history of China's positive influence on Thais, which was thinly veiled as a tale of Sino-Thai cooperation and friendship. He cited the writings of W. A. R. Wood and Prince Damrong, suggesting that even skeptics would agree that Thais had adopted Chinese culture and measurement standards for centuries (Chen 1941, 41–47). Pan-Thai nationalism, Chen Xujing warned, could tear the Thai nation apart. If Thais were to rally the Thai race through nationalism, then the same could be done by China with the Chinese in Thailand, the French with Cambodians and Laotians, and the British with

Burmese and Malays. The national aspirations of non-Thai minorities, boosted by myths of racial origins similar to those of the Thais, might encourage separatism within Thailand (Chen 1941, 24–25).

Working in wartime Southwest China, Jiang Yingliang, Cen Jiawu, and Chen Xujing fused the approaches and insights from anthropology, ethnology, history, and sociology; institutionalized what would be considered frontier studies through fellowships, journals, and research institutes; conducted fieldwork in the remote borderlands (and, in Chen Xujing's case, outside China); and tested indigenous ideas such as *Zhonghua minzu* and European and American theories against the field. Attempting to relate various disciplines to the nation's needs, these academics disputed the Thais' origin myth and challenged Western support for the myth. Their diverse educational backgrounds meant that narrative strategies varied from the empirical to the theoretical. Among them, only Chen Xujing, perhaps because he was Western-trained and more independent of Chinese funding, acknowledged that nationalism, whether Chinese or Thai, was a double-edged sword. Although Chen Xujing might not have intended this, historical denial and distortion were endemic to both nationalisms, and a foreign national mythology could displace domestic loyalty and the indigenous past. Unlike Jiang Yingliang and Cen Jiawu, Chen Xujing did not invoke patriotic sentiments and the idea of *Zhonghua minzu*, preferring to deploy purer intellectual reasoning to make his case for greater—or more nuanced—Chinese awareness of Pan-Thai nationalism.

The discourse on Pan-Thai nationalism and Tai ethnicity forced the Nationalist state to acknowledge that the southwestern frontier, as well as the Northwest, was a hotbed of geopolitical conflict. The diversity of opinions on frontier issues, however, did not fall in line with the unitary nationalist message that state-affiliated and -supported institutes and journals were trying to convey. In 1943, Chiang Kai-shek broadcast a statement to the Thai people in which he stated that he intended no harm to the Thai people and harbored no territorial design on Thailand (Chinvanno 1992, 39);[30] however, his views on ethnicity published later that year instilled little confidence in the Thais. In his book *China's Destiny*, he reaffirmed the Nationalist government's one-nation creed by suggesting that the ethnic groups in China were "clan branches" (宗支 *zongzhi*) of the *Zhonghua minzu* (Chiang 1943, 1). Although his statement accorded to the frontier races equal status with the majority Han, it could serve as a pretext for declaring that Thais were part of the Tai branch of the *Zhonghua minzu* and for conquering Thailand. Clearly *Zhonghua minzu* was a euphemism for *Han*, and at the very least Chiang Kai-shek wanted to amalgamate non-Han identities within China (Liu 2015).

Nor did the intellectual diversity please some of China's frontier administrators. Yang Sen 楊森 (1884–1977), the governor of wartime Guizhou, complained that despite years of stressing the need to understand the frontier, the Chinese remained indifferent to the problem of southwestern peoples. He worried that Thais might join hands with frontier minorities to destabilize the Southwest—"a single spark could start a prairie fire" (星星之火可以燎原).[31]

After the war, Yang Sen requested that academics not only continue promoting knowledge of the frontier but also emphasize similarities rather than differences between the Han and non-Han. Academics and administrators, he wrote, should advocate that the *Zhonghua guozu* (中華國族) originated in one source (中華國族, 同出一源 *Zhonghua guozu, tong chu yiyuan*). Like most Chinese social scientists, he understood that getting ethnic minorities to accept their inclusion in the *Zhonghua minzu* required great ideological effort (Yang 1946, 353).

Yang Sen's use of *Zhonghua guozu* was a compromise. By 1946, the Nationalist government was eager to win the support of ethnic minorities, including those in the Southwest, against the Communists, who gained greater traction than either the Japanese or the Chinese Nationalists in the rural borderlands.[32] Reluctant to antagonize minorities on the ethnic issue, the Nationalist government rejected the racial nationalists' appeal to include *Zhonghua minzu* in the revised Chinese constitution and made a motion to acknowledge, on December 25, "the equality of all the *minzu* in the Republic of China" (中華民國各民族一律平等).[33] Yang Sen encouraged intermarriages and the intermingling of Han and non-Han, founded schools in Miao regions to transform non-Han into Han, and funded research on the "frontier compatriots" (邊胞 *bianbao*) to devise policies that would meld Han and non-Han. However, he admitted that fostering ethnic minorities' loyalty to the central government remained an uphill task (Yang 1972). Yang Sen's statements revealed that he thought scholarship should still serve national needs, that the Nationalist government's cultural and historical hold over Southwest China remained tenuous, and that a heightened sense of vulnerability was felt by the Chinese after the war—even little Thailand could threaten China's security and survival if ethnic differences were not explained away.

CONCLUSION

In 1930s and 1940s China, Thailand and Pan-Thai nationalism became subjects of academic study and intellectual discussion. By launching small-scale attacks on the Shan States and China's border positions in Yunnan and claiming that the Tai groups in Southwest China were more Thai than Chinese, Thailand finally received the full attention of Chinese academics and administrators. In response, Chinese social scientists portrayed a nation whose nationalist leaders were goaded by Japan into manufacturing the Thai race and circulating historically inaccurate ideas about its origins. For Chinese academics, who were themselves struggling to strike a balance between intellectual reason and wartime patriotism, the jingoistic Phibun regime was doing Japan's bidding and reproducing the narrative perpetuated by European and American writers of a singular cultural and racial tradition stretching back through Ayutthaya to the ancient Nanzhao kingdom. Although there were Chinese dissenters who studied the diverse cultures of China's southwestern frontier and concluded that the *Zhonghua minzu* should be plural rather than singular, those voices were drowned out by the mainstream of wartime Chinese scholarship, which dictated that academics should sacrifice a degree of academic objectivity and intellectual reason in favor of serving the nation's needs. The then-nascent field of frontier studies formed part of the scholarship that was subsequently consulted by the Communist government as officials developed strategies for ruling China's frontiers and produced scientific surveys and theories on which policies on nationalities were based.[34]

In retrospect, Chinese social scientists working on ethnic and frontier issues in 1930s and 1940s Southwest China were involved in what historian Tong Lam has called the Chinese "social science movement." European and American scholars had regarded China as a place without facts and accused the Chinese of having no credible or scientific knowledge of themselves. Consequently, as Lam suggests, Chinese intellectuals were "traumatized by this perceived national humiliation" and resolved to "overcome the alleged deficiencies by producing empirical facts about China themselves."[35] Although efforts by Chinese social scientists to study the southwestern frontier and debunk myths about Thai origins were loosely coordinated by the state, the efforts were tightly connected to the urgency to save whatever remained of a Chinese nation at war. In the end, whether the Chinese academics were cultural or racial nationalists, or whether they subscribed to the idea of *Zhonghua minzu* or *Zhonghua guozu*, they believed that frontier administration in the form of development, which meant primarily growth through state capitalism, could resolve ethnic differences and better integrate minority groups into the Chinese nation. The Communist government has, for the most part, inherited the developmental model, but it remains to be seen (to return to Jiang Yingliang's proposal to the wartime Nationalist regime) whether lifting the cultural and economic levels of frontier minorities, often implied to be low, can truly serve its purpose. Meanwhile, the colonial gaze and the assumptions of colonial social science nonetheless appear to be here to stay.

NOTES

1. For more on the Nationalist government's search for and consolidation of a territorial base in Southwest China, see Kapp (1973), Tetsuo (2009), Mitsuru (2011), and Tan (2013).

2. For settler colonialism as seen in the classic example of white missionaries and yeomen displacing Native Americans in the American West, see Conroy-Krutz (2015, 104).

3. In contrast to the lack of consensus on the boundaries of Northwest China well into the 1940s, the geographical extent of Southwest China was uncontroversial in Republican-era writings and endorsed by the state in official publications. See, for example, Yu (1938). Such early publications barely mentioned, let alone described, the ethnic composition of Southwest China.

4. All translations in this chapter are ours.

5. For studies that deal with Thai nationalism at some length, see Nuechterlein (1965), Vella (1978), Barme (1993), Winichakul (1994), Murashima (2005, 2006), and Strate (2015).

6. See Esherick (2006) and Leibold (2007). For Qing rule of its frontiers, see Hostetler (2001), Giersch (2006), and Guy (2010).

7. As Kinzley (2018) has suggested, the Nationalist government had prioritized central and eastern China over the southwestern provinces in economic or industrial development prior to the mid-1930s, and so the Southwest "remained largely terra incognita." See Kinzley (2012, 563).

8. With King Vajiravudh (r. 1910–1925), Phibun and Wichit Wathakan were the chief architects of Thai nationalism. See Barme (1993).

9. For a detailed treatment of the *Zhonghua minzu*, see Huang (2018).

10. See Reynolds (2004) and Subrahmanyan (2015).

11. For whether Nationalist China was fascist, see Eastman (1972), Kirby (1984), and Wakeman (1997). For a comparison of Thai and Chinese "fascisms," see Reynolds (2004, 11–16).

12. In Chinese writings at that time, *Hanhua* and *tonghua* (assimilated) were often used interchangeably, as seen in Ling's sentence "[Taizu] dai wanquan tonghua yu Han" ([The Tai race] was completely assimilated into the Han). See Ling (1940, 334).

13. Compare Ma (2006, 36–37).

14. Compare Ma (2006, 37–38).

15. For a sample list of academic institutions established in late 1930s Yunnan to conduct ethnographical research, see Leibold (2007, 134).

16. See also Leibold (2007, 139). Gu Jiegang revealed in his diary that his comments on the unity of the *Zhonghua minzu* were a response to Fu Sinian's letter. See Gu (2007, 197).

17. See Schwarcz (1986, 230–236).

18. For a list of the institutions and scholars involved in frontier studies, see Cen (1992b, 30–31).

19. There was also no clear distinction between anthropology and sociology. See Arkush (1981) and Di (2017).

20. As an anthropologist trained at the University of Paris, Ling Chunsheng also conducted field research (in northeastern China), but Yunnan lay outside his empirical concerns.

21. Another major journal was *Frontier Affairs* (*Bianzheng gonglun*), first published in August 1941. Although the journal facilitated frank and open dialogue between academics and administrators working in the frontier regions, it was not wholly devoted to frontier matters in Southwest China.

22. Jiang Yingliang studied history at Jinan University, which was located in Shanghai during the 1920s and 1930s. He blithely noted that for much of his tertiary education, he did not belong to any discipline or inherit the ideas of any intellectual master.

23. For Jiang Yingliang's field-trip preparations and private thoughts, see the biography by his son, Jiang (2005, 58–87).

24. For Cen Jiawu's life and educational background, see his wife's account, Feng (1992, 430–31).

25. As a term that means China proper, or the civilized area/place, *zhongyuan* is the opposite of *bianjiang*, understood in a similar sense as the nineteenth-century American frontier, on which a substantial scholarly literature existed for the Chinese social scientists' reference. See Matten (2016) and Gerstle (2017).

26. For Cen Jiawu, the Miao and the Yao were the same. See 岑家梧 (1992, 136).

27. Conceived by the founders to exchange ideas on how to improve relations between Pacific nations, the institute assumed an increasingly pro-China, anti-Japan stance during the war. See Thomas (1974) and Chiang (2001). Chen Xujing's fieldwork in Thailand formed part of his output for the institute. See Chen (1944).

28. For Chen Xujing's life experiences, see the work by his son, Chen (1999, 67–68).

29. For more on the "total Westernization" theory, see Cole (1979–1980) and Tian (2006). For more on the rural reconstruction project, see Alitto (1979) and Merkel-Hess (2016). Although mentored by Edward C. Hayes (1868–1928), a chief pioneer of American sociology and a founder of the American Sociological Association, Chen Xujing applied methodologies from different disciplines and could claim no academic genealogy for his writings.

30. The Nationalist government had been preparing its broadcast since 1942 to split Japan and Thailand, and so it had little to do with the 1943 Thai military advance to the Yunnan border. See Murashima (2006, 1091).

31. See Yang (1979, 68).

32. The Communists fought a more successful class and ideological war in the underdeveloped minority regions, having adopted the less discriminatory "various nationalities of China" formula, and maintained "a political edge over the [Nationalists] by implementing social and economic reforms among the minorities" (Liu 2004, 164).

33. Quoted in Huang (2018, 325). The major difference between *Zhonghua minzu* and *Zhonghua guozu* was that the former emphasized bloodline and disregarded the existence of multiple individual *minzu*, while the latter recognized the diversity of

ethnic communities residing in China and advocated their assimilation into the Chinese nation. For basic definitions of the two concepts, see Huang (2018, 325).

34. For how the Communist government was inspired by its Nationalist predecessor, see Mullaney (2011).

35. See Tong (2011, 3–4).

Chapter 3

Traversing the Migrant's Corridor

*Singapore's First Ambassadors
to Thailand, 1965–1990*

Singapore separated from Malaysia to become fully independent on August 9, 1965. Thailand was one of the first countries to recognize Singapore and upgraded Singapore's consulate general to an embassy on August 14, 1965. For more than fifty years, Singapore's bilateral relations with Thailand have been robust, but the contribution of Singapore's ambassadors, particularly those appointed during Lee Kuan Yew's premiership (1965–1990), remains little explored. This chapter examines the ways in which the earliest Singaporean ambassadors to Thailand were selected and the problems they faced maintaining the embassy in Bangkok. Chinese business migrants, the chapter argues, contributed to the development of these relations before Singapore had a full-fledged diplomatic service. Success in forging personal ties with the Thais became a source of pride for the ambassadors and their descendants, who published autobiographies, biographies, or recollections (which were, broadly speaking, from-rags-to-riches texts about how cultural loyalty had overcome class limitations, provided social mobility, and ensured success in business) to describe how the foundation for Singapore-Thailand relations was laid.

Singapore gained independence during the Cold War, when Malaysia ejected a heavily Chinese-populated Singapore from its federation and Britain felt assured leaving the Anglophile and staunchly anti-Communist Lee Kuan Yew (1923–2015) in charge of the strategic port city (Barr 2000a; Ang 2013a, 2018). With S. Rajaratnam (1915–2006), who served as Singapore's first foreign minister, Lee Kuan Yew developed the country's diplomatic mission. His favorite candidates for government service included journalists (such as Rajaratnam), lawyers (such as himself), and—particularly relevant to this chapter—businessmen who were clearly in favor of the American-led capitalist world order, to which Thailand also belonged under the Southeast Asia Treaty Organization (SEATO). Committed to the SEATO doctrine of containing the Communist threat in Southeast Asia, the right-wing Thai government dispatched troops to reinforce the US military and established itself as America's most important ally during the Vietnam War in return for American support of its economy and monarchy (Ruth 2011; Chua 2017). This chapter suggests that other than the emphasis on allying with America and defending against Communism shared by Singapore and Thailand, the ethnicity and cultural upbringing of Singapore's first ambassadors to Thailand actually allowed diplomatic ties between the two countries to take off and flourish during the Cold War.

The biographies and autobiographies of Singapore's first ambassadors to Thailand serve as this chapter's main sources. While historians may reject first-person accounts as subjective and factually unreliable, the ambassadors' autobiographies and biographies reveal how they arrive at their vocations, the difficulties of laying the foundation of Singapore-Thailand relations, and the extra- or non-bureaucratic appointment of Singapore's first ambassadors to Thailand. By going beyond official or national narratives and supposedly objective political analyses, these accounts suggest shifting definitions of Chineseness, migration, and citizenship in Southeast Asia during decolonization and state formation (Popkin 2005). The lives and activities of the ambassadors also provide a lens through which to examine the key features of Chinese migration—namely, voluntary labor export, seasonal sojourning, and the spatially dispersed family, which were either encountered or practiced by the ambassadors before they settled in Singapore and Thailand (Kuhn 2008).

The production of biographies and autobiographies discussed in this chapter was governed by the cultural discourse in Singapore, which developed in three key phases. In the first phase of cultural discourse, from 1965 to 1982, Singaporean officials promoted the values of "rugged individualism," which accentuated the cultivation of a disciplined, achievement-oriented work ethic. The second, from 1982 to 1990, saw the search for a specific Asian ethic, using indigenous ideologies and religions to promote an Asian mode of modernization. The third phase, from the 1990s on, focused on "Shared Values" to formulate a secular set of pan-ethnic social principles with which people could identify and on which a national identity could be constructed (Chun 2017). Taken together, the three phases generated the texts about the first Singaporean ambassadors to Thailand, which described their "rugged," "Asian," and "Singaporean" qualities encouraged by the government during Lee Kuan Yew's premiership (the autobiographies, biographies, and recollections were published shortly after Lee stepped down as prime minister, as if in celebration of his legacy). The Chinese values possessed by Singapore's first ambassadors were transferrable—in this case, from business to diplomacy—to ensure success no matter where they were applied, be it in the United States, China, Singapore, or Thailand. They became the "Shared Values" expounded by the Singaporean government in the 1990s, now deployed to explain success at the national level. Wherever relevant, the analysis of the biographies and autobiographies will integrate the sense of change over time implied by the three phases of cultural discourse vis-à-vis personal and state constructions of Chinese ethnicity and identity in Singapore.

CHINESENESS IN SINGAPORE AND THAILAND

The idea of Chineseness, or the production of Chinese identities, has been greatly contested in existing scholarship. While supporters contend that the concept has enabled the study of Chinese migrants' interactions with host societies and their partial assimilation into modern, non-Chinese nations, detractors charge that it produces a fiction of common origins, presumes cultural affinities, essentializes ethnic categories, and exaggerates the differences between Chinese and native populations. Nevertheless, the scholarly consensus is that the concept of Chineseness is both imagined (individuals adopt the explanations of primordiality—of bloodline and descent—to identify themselves as Chinese) and fluid (the very same individuals who identify with being Chinese can strengthen or discard their ethnic links based on what they see as advantageous in a situation and can also express their ethnic identity differently in terms of education, language, and religion). So far, in studies of Southeast Asia, the concept of Chineseness has been deployed to analyze only the domestic construction of Chinese communities and the rise of identity politics after decolonization. In Southeast Asian nation-states where Chinese migrants and settler descendants constitute a substantial minority (except for Singapore where ethnic Chinese form the majority), Chineseness creates a sense of the "other" against which new national identities are defined by political elites. This orientation may assume either an institutional form, as in Malaysia's affirmative policies toward the Malay majority, or a cultural form, in which it is portrayed as an alien culture compared to the dominant or majority culture, as in countries such as Indonesia and Vietnam.

In Singapore, the concept of diaspora is somewhat meaningless; Chinese Singaporeans, vis-à-vis colonial-era racial classifications and postcolonial social engineering, have dominated national culture and politics since independence. But as Philip A. Kuhn (2008) suggests, Singapore was not a culturally Chinese state; Chinese Singaporeans' domination of national culture did not result in a replica of mainland (China) or Greater Chinese (Hong Kong and Taiwan included) culture. Educated in Britain, Singapore's founding leaders felt little emotional attachment to Chinese culture or language and identified Chinese-medium education as a conduit for right-wing subversion (Kuhn 2008). They also understood that the domestic Chinese majority in Singapore was a regional minority in Southeast Asia and were well aware of Singapore's racialized geopolitical environment. Indonesia and Malaysia are Singapore's Muslim neighbors and subject the Chinese to varying degrees of cultural or institutional discrimination. Singapore was particularly sensitive to Indonesia's negative disposition toward China and did not want to be identified as a natural Third China; it only formalized relations with China in 1990, a year after Indonesia. Chineseness in Singapore thus assumes a significance that extends beyond domestic concerns to international relations (Tan 2003; Hoon 2006; Chia 2008; Tong 2010). That said, Lee Kuan Yew admired aspects of Chinese culture—its moral ideals, public service ethic, and respect for authority. His perception of Chinese culture served as the basis for Singapore's campaigns to first instill "Asian Values" (1980s) and then "Shared Values" (1990s) into Singaporean society—these essentially "Chinese" values were explicitly introduced as "Confucian" (Kuhn 2008).

Singapore's relations with Thailand were less complicated. In Thailand, Chinese laborers and merchants arrived in large numbers during the nineteenth century. Having few pretensions about themselves, they accepted the supreme power of the Siamese royalty and nobility and offered their economic expertise to maximize profit from commerce. As historian Lysa Hong (1984, 60) suggests, the Chinese were "suppliant and sought the patronage of the great and powerful in the kingdom. They did all they could to please the masters of the country in order to make money as conveniently as possible." The Siamese monarch ennobled Chinese tax farmers and considered them in the same light as his Siamese officials. Racial classification, or the idea that a person was "Chinese" by race, did not emerge until the early twentieth century as part of a surging Thai nationalism—a reaction to the privileges enjoyed by Chinese of rank and to an even greater wave of migration from China and perceived Chinese ties to republican and revolutionary movements in China, which threatened the Siamese monarchy. But the rise of Thai nationalism ultimately did not result in long-term Thai hostility to the Chinese. Unlike the indigenous elite in Indonesia and Malaysia, the Thai aristocracy was not subject to a colonial status hierarchy—the Chinese were not seen as collaborators of foreign rulers. Thai aristocracy had always been the dominant class, and Chinese elites could become part of it as a reward for services to the Thai monarchy. The Thais accepted commerce as a Chinese niche and did not seek to compete with the Chinese commercially; trade was ranked too low in their status order to be worth competing for. Criteria for acceptance were neither culture nor ethnicity, but rather submission to the Thai political system and loyalty to the Thai monarchy (Kuhn 2008, 298–299).

In 1957, anthropologist G. William Skinner published his influential *Chinese Society in Thailand: An Analytical History*, which revealed that by the late 1950s, the Chinese and Thai had become indistinguishable. Although the Thai government was also anxious about the possible spread of Communism and the loyalty of the Sino-Thai, the war economy of the Vietnam era enriched Thailand and expanded the ranks of the Sino-Thai urban middle class. The Sino-Thai used their newfound wealth to receive better tertiary education, cement their domination of the banking and business sectors, and seek high government positions, including those in the foreign ministry (Thak 2014). In sum, Thai tolerance, a partly shared Buddhist faith, and the old Siamese idea that the monarchy extended equal protection to all ethnic groups made for a fairly easy and flexible cultural adjustment (Kuhn 2008).

Nevertheless, Skinner's assimilationist model and characterization of Chinese-Thai interactions has simplified the process of Chinese integration into Thai society and is not entirely applicable to Thailand of the 1960s–1990s. The Sino-Thai's maintenance of dual identities (many of them, even today, observe Chinese customs among kinsmen and compatriots at home but publicly identify with being Thai among the Thai majority in schools and workplaces) has been ignored. To be sure, most Sino-Thai had, by the 1960s, adopted Thai names, attended Thai schools, and served in the Thai bureaucracy and military. The articulation of Thai nationalism by, among others, King Vajiravudh (r. 1910–1925), Plaek Phibunsongkhram (1897–1964), and especially Sarit Thanarat (1908–1963), who revived and invented the constitutional monarchy as a Thai tradition, had destabilized Chinese identity and compelled the Chinese to assimilate into Thai society (or to appear assimilated). Compared to perceptions of the Chinese in Indonesia and Malaysia, the Sino-Thai posed less of a threat to Thai national security and were perceived to be indispensable to economic development. The Thai government in the 1960s and 1970s rejected repressive measures, which might backfire by antagonizing the Sino-Thai and pushing them into the embrace of rural Communist forces, in favor of conciliatory policies that guaranteed the security of both the Chinese and the Thai. The relative ease of transforming the Chinese into Thai citizens created a more positive disposition toward the Chinese in Thailand than in Indonesia and Malaysia. Such circumstances allowed Singapore to tap into the preexisting networks of trade, commerce, and compatriotism between Singapore's Chinese merchants and Thailand's Sino-Thai capitalist elites and cultivate diplomatic relations with Thailand (Kaisan 1992; Wongsurawa 2008; Koning and Verver 2013; Thak 2014).

That said, the relationship between the ethnic Chinese community and the Thai political elite remained complex during the Cold War period. Only the elite capitalist Chinese in Bangkok enjoyed truly cordial relations with the right-wing Thai political elite. They forged alliances with the court, royalist political factions, and the armed forces. For the royalist ruling class, they were the "good Chinese" as opposed to the "bad Chinese," who allegedly sided with the Communists against the Thai monarchy and nation. Socioeconomic status, rather than ethnic background, thus determined the ethnic Chinese position in Thai society. The wealthy Chinese supported the Thais in positions of power and cooperated with the state in persecuting and suppressing working-class Chinese, some of whom allied themselves with Communist sympathizers and secret societies.[1] In other words, the political narrative vis-à-vis the ethnic Chinese during the Cold War remained similar to that of the early twentieth century. As historian Wasana Wongsurawat (2019, 141) has concluded, "The ethnic Chinese economic elite survived through its alliance with the conservative/royalist political elite while the working class and revolutionaries of all ethnic backgrounds were violently suppressed for the sake of national security." Having become successful businessmen by the time of their appointment, Singapore's first ambassadors to Thailand interacted with only the elite, capitalist Chinese in Bangkok. They thus fulfilled the image—or fitted the stereotype—of "good Chinese" in the Thai royalist ideal and could create favorable impressions among the royalty and political elite of Thailand.

Historian Philip A. Kuhn (2008) has introduced the concept of the "migrant's corridor," which can help explain how Sino-Singaporean businessmen maintained cultural and commercial ties to both their ancestral homeland and other members of the diaspora in places such as Thailand. The postcolonial Singaporean state would mobilize their connections to facilitate diplomacy, but only under certain conditions. According to Kuhn, migrants forced out of their poverty-stricken hometowns to seek survival elsewhere developed a set of native-place bonds, or compatriotism. Compatriotism required them to maintain links to the native place itself by sending remittances, helping kinsmen to join them in the venue society, and banding together for moral support and business opportunities. Migrants were not expected to settle permanently away from home; they were temporarily absent, or "sojourning," in another place of work. The concept of sojourning not only reinforced compatriot ties but also "sustained corridors to the *qiaoxiang* (hometown) from which migrant enterprises could attract fresh capital and labor" (Kuhn 2008, 43–44).

In Kuhn's formulation, the migrant's corridor that linked Chinese sojourners in Southeast Asia with their kinsmen back at home extended from China, which was already crisscrossed by such corridors: "busy channels of money, social transactions, and culture" (Kuhn 2008, 46). Corridors, then, served as extensions of the hometown that embraced compatriots far away, "a realm of interests and affections that linked people over great distances; they were both connective links and living cultural spaces" (Kuhn 2008, 46). A key element of the migrant's corridor is niche, an occupational specialty or social role in which a migrant population can survive because it is needed by the venue society and not filled by other groups. The concept of the migrant's corridor, while useful for illuminating how cultural and commercial bonds were maintained between ancestral homelands and venue societies, barely considers noneconomic goals or trends and the transformation of sojourners into citizens after regime change in both China and Southeast Asia during the Cold War. If the corridor was an extension of the migrant's old environment, how did connections change after the migrant broke with or reconfigured aspects of Chinese culture and political belonging? This chapter extends the use of the migrant's corridor as a concept to examine postcolonial Singapore's mobilization of sojourners-turned-citizens' commercial networks and cultural resources to forge diplomatic relations with Thailand. Under favorable conditions, including the free passage of culture, money, and people between Singapore and Thailand in the capitalist world order, the migrant's corridor broke with socialist China but became a diplomatic bridge that facilitated various exchanges between the two countries.[2]

The migrant's corridor, whether old or rebuilt, thus created communities and preserved their connections. The Chineseness of Singapore's first ambassadors to Thailand was both primordial and situational, operating to explain life's beginnings and successes and to resolve the dilemma between broken emotional ties with China and a newly acquired Singaporean citizenship (Tong 2010, 16). This understanding of Chineseness as being simultaneously primordial and situational and, therefore, discursively flexible and useful might complement and expand the concept of the migrant's corridor and its application to Singapore's early diplomacy with Thailand.

THE BIRTH OF ASEAN AND INITIAL SINGAPORE-THAILAND RELATIONS

The newly independent Singapore of the 1960s found itself in a precarious geopolitical landscape. Indonesia under Sukarno (1901–1970) had opposed the creation of Malaysia and had launched military attacks on Sabah and Sarawak. The Indochinese wars, which began in the 1950s, showed no signs of abating and threatened to spread Communism into the heart of mainland Southeast Asia. These tensions led to the formation of the Association of Southeast Asian Nations (ASEAN), composed of Indonesia, Malaysia, the Philippines, Singapore, and Thailand, in 1967. Singapore was initially unenthusiastic, fearing that ASEAN might become a vehicle for Indonesia's ambitions. Former Singaporean president S. R. Nathan (1924–2016), who had served as deputy secretary of the Ministry of Foreign Affairs, recalled that the first multilateral discussions about forming ASEAN did not mention Singapore, given Singapore's disputes with Indonesia and Malaysia.

Thailand was instrumental in including Singapore in ASEAN. The governor of the Bank of Thailand wrote to Lim Kim San (1916–2006), Singapore's finance minister, to ask whether the Singaporean government was inclined to join ASEAN. After consulting Lee Kuan Yew and S. Rajaratnam, Lim replied that Singapore would consider it. Thanat Khoman (1914–2016), Thailand's foreign minister, then met with Rajaratnam in Bangkok and allayed fears, explaining that ASEAN would be a purely cultural, economic, social, and technical group devoted to regional cooperation. Khoman promised that ASEAN, as a non-aligned association, would not support or partake in military operations of any kind. Khoman convinced Rajaratnam that Singapore would not be implicated in Cold War politics after joining ASEAN. Although Lee Kuan Yew and S. Rajaratnam were not easily given to persuasion, they liked the idea of regional economic cooperation that respected national sovereignty and permitted extra-regional arrangements (Nathan 2011).

Singapore proposed including Australia and New Zealand in ASEAN, but the proposal was never pursued. Singapore then insisted that the Australian and British military bases be kept in the region to keep the Communists at bay. Rajaratnam motioned to quit the negotiations unless Indonesia, which was most hostile to the bases' existence, agreed not to remove Australian and British bases from Singapore and the Malay Peninsula. With the support of the Philippines and especially Thailand, which would host substantial US forces during the Vietnam War, Singapore managed to alter the preamble of the ASEAN Declaration, which left the issue of foreign bases at the discretion of host nations. Nevertheless, Singapore and Thailand had their disagreements, especially over trade liberalization. While Singapore, a small economy, regarded Southeast Asia as a vital import and export market, Thailand sought to preserve its tariff autonomy after the formation of ASEAN, concerned that a free trade area might adversely affect the prices of Thai exports. The result was a compromise. Referenced in a separate press release after the ASEAN Declaration was made, the decision was that proposals for free trade agreements would be referred to the ASEAN Standing Committee for evaluation (Rajaratnam 2005; Nathan 2011).

The disagreements between Singapore and Thailand in the ASEAN negotiations revealed that Singapore's relations with Thailand did not begin on an easy footing. Lee Kuan Yew had referred to Thailand as the "organ grinder's monkey," the grinder being the United States. Thailand's leaders were not happy, particularly Thanat Khoman and the Thai foreign ministry (Nathan 2011, 427). But relations soon became cordial and constructive, with frequent communication between the foreign ministries. Throughout the Cold War period, Singapore viewed Thailand as a valuable bulwark against the spread of Communism from China and Vietnam (Ang 2009, 2013b). In August 1966, a year after Singapore's independence, Tan Siak Kew (1903–1977), whom S. R. Nathan (2014, viii) had described as "a scholar by inclination, a businessman by necessity, and a diplomat by duty," was appointed Singapore's first ambassador to Thailand.[3]

Tan Siak Kew was a Teochew born in the Chao'an district of Guangdong province. After receiving some elementary education, Tan moved to Singapore with his father and elder brother in 1910. He attended the Raffles Institution where he received the remainder of his formal education. After the death of his father, he quit school and started his own business (Visscher 2007).

Tan Siak Kew's first company traded in coffee, copra, and pepper. The shortage of staple goods in the years immediately after the Second World War enabled his business to grow due to his prewar networks, which included access to producers of scarce products, and to capital to finance trade deals. His connections to the Teochew rice millers in Thailand particularly stood him in good stead, and he was the longest-serving president of the Chinese Produce Exchange (1948–1967) (Visscher 2007). Fluent in English, Mandarin, and various Chinese dialects, he served two terms as president of the Singapore Chinese Chamber of Commerce (1952–1954, 1956–1958). In 1958, he was elected as a nominated member of the Legislative Assembly. As a business leader and politician, he criticized the British colonial government for its failure to devise policies that had clear, long-term benefits for Singaporean society. He strongly believed in the connection between trade and nation-building and opposed the intended removal of Chamber of Commerce representatives from the Legislative Assembly by the authorities. As he argued, "Without trade there is no Singapore, no government, no professions, no welfare or social services, no means of livelihood for the population" (*Straits Times* 1950, 9). His persistent belief in the importance of trade for Singapore was compatible with Lee Kuan Yew's economic pragmatism and vision for sustainable growth. Unsurprisingly, after Singapore's independence, Tan played a key role in the economy and politics of Singapore (Tan 2014).

As a Teochew community leader in Singapore, Tan Siak Kew's standing among the Thai business community had been well established since the 1950s. When Rajaratnam had to appoint the Singaporean ambassador to Thailand, Tan was an obvious choice. Tan had his reservations. The Thais, based on his understanding, preferred men of noble birth or high rank in the government to serve as diplomats; his mercantile class might not be welcome. The Thai preference stemmed from a Siamese court practice of exchanging correspondence with European aristocrats prior to the establishment of modern embassies. Rajaratnam went ahead with appointing Tan, however, and

Tan, who was unfamiliar with diplomatic protocols, accepted the assignment "out of a sense of public duty and as a grateful gesture to the government which has entrusted me, an amateur, with this appointment" (Liu 2005, 65).

As an unexpected nation, Singapore was unprepared to conduct diplomatic relations in the years immediately after independence (Lee 2008). Lee Kuan Yew embarked on an extensive tour of Asia, the Middle East, and Eastern Europe to seek recognition of Singapore. Singapore also had to build a diplomatic corps from scratch. Lacking career or professional diplomats, the government recruited personnel from the private sector. Several leaders of the Chinese Chamber of Commerce, such as Tan Siak Kew, were appointed to diplomatic positions. The Chamber as an institution was also recruited into national representational duties, encouraging trade with Singapore at overseas conferences and exhibitions and joining diplomatic visits for trade negotiations. The Chamber was particularly concerned about its interests in Southeast Asia, where the bulk of Singapore's external trade continued to take place. Chamber leaders even suggested that a trade research center be set up with other chambers of commerce in the region. Bypassing the foreign ministry, they dispatched a trade mission to Thailand, Burma (Myanmar), Cambodia, Hong Kong, and Japan in 1968. They hoped that the formation of ASEAN would facilitate cooperation among bankers, industrialists, and traders across Southeast Asia (Visscher 2007). Tan's appointment thus coincided with the economic aims of both the Singaporean government and the Chinese Chamber of Commerce.

The first Singapore "embassy" in Thailand was a hotel suite. Shortly after his arrival in Bangkok, Tan Siak Kew secured for the Singaporean government, at a discounted price, the residence of a former Italian ambassador at North Sathorn Road and made it the first permanent Singaporean embassy in Thailand. However, financial woes plagued the embassy because funds allocated for equipment and service purchases by overseas missions were tightly regulated by the Singaporean finance ministry, which overruled purchases made by ambassadors and their recruitment of local ancillary staff. Tan Siak Kew's engagement of a gardener for the chancery at a salary of $30 per month was overruled with instructions that he hire part-time gardeners as they do in places like London. Tan's proposed purchase of Thai teak furniture was turned down; he was instructed to buy furniture from a Singaporean retailer. But the furniture from Singapore developed cracks in the Bangkok heat within three months, and Tan had to stay at a hotel in the interim while the furniture was replaced. He paid for the new furniture and furnished the embassy from his own pocket. Already serving on a token allowance, he refused a renewal of his appointment after that humiliation and was replaced in September 1967 (Nathan 2011; Tan 2014).

Tan Siak Kew's successor was Ho Rih Hwa (1917–1999), another prominent businessman. Born in Singapore of working-class parents—his father
was "a simple, uneducated, humble middle-class man" (Ho 1990, 181)
working as a carpenter—Ho attended a private Chinese-medium elementary
school before moving, in 1928, to China for further education. This was in
effect a "reverse" migration back to the ancestral homeland where educational
prospects appeared more plausible than in the place of sojourn. His maternal
grandfather had worked and saved enough money in Singapore and decided
to take Ho and his brothers back to his home county in Guangdong Province.

In the 1930s, when Ho was studying at Lingnan University in Guangzhou,
war broke out between China and Japan. As Japanese troops were advancing
toward Guangzhou, Ho, along with Lingnan University staff and students,
evacuated to Hong Kong. However, the "young patriot" in Ho disliked the
"atmosphere of frivolity" in Hong Kong, and decided to transfer to Nanjing
University, which had relocated its operations to Chengdu in Sichuan Province
(Ho 1990, 59–60). In 1942, he graduated with a degree in agricultural economics. He became an assistant to his thesis supervisor, John Lossing Buck
(1890–1975), who helped secure his passage to Cornell University, where he
would receive a master's degree in economics.

At Cornell in 1946, Ho met and married his wife Li Lienfung (1923–2011),
a graduate student in English literature. Upon completing his studies, Ho
worked at Wah Chang Corporation for his father-in-law, Li Kuo Ching
(1887–1961), the "Tungsten King" who had discovered the first tungsten
deposits in his native Hunan Province. A naturalized American citizen, Li Kuo
Ching had contributed to the American war effort in the Second World War by
developing tungsten mines in California, Colorado, and Nevada (tungsten is
a key metal in electronics, steelmaking, and military technologies). He built
the world's largest tungsten refinery at Glen Clove, Long Island, New York,
and became one of the wealthiest Chinese Americans of his time (National
Mining Hall of Fame and Museum 2019). Because Ho was born in Southeast
Asia and "should know the conditions," Li decided to send him to Thai Wah,
a subsidiary of Wah Chang, in Bangkok (Ho 1990, 121–122). In the 1950s
and 1960s, Ho and his wife developed their own business interests in vermi-
celli, tapioca, and wheat flour while managing the import and export business
of Thai Wah (Ho 1990).[4]

Ho never thought he would become an ambassador. His initiation into
diplomatic life began when Singapore's Economic Development Board
(EDB) set up an office in Bangkok to facilitate trade between Singaporean
and Thai businessmen. Ho befriended the director of the EDB, who asked
him to serve as the EDB's honorary representative in Bangkok. In serving
the EDB, Ho was acquainted with Lim Kim San (1916–2006), then minister
of national development, and Hon Sui Sen (1916–1983), then chairman of

the EDB. Lim and Hon had discussed with Ho their concern for the economic future of Singapore. Ho was impressed and glad that these were the "kind of down-to-earth people" leading an independent Singapore (Ho 1990, 255). When Tan Siak Kew resigned, Ho was offered the post and became Singapore's new ambassador to Thailand.

The Thai government was apprehensive about Ho's appointment; Ho, like Tan before him, was an entrepreneur. According to what Ho knew about the situation in Thailand, "diplomats must be men of noble birth or of high rank in the government. The mercantile class was definitely excluded" (Ho 1990, 256). Ho was proud of Singapore "for not being so constricted by convention as to have a contempt for the 'mercantile' class." He consulted Rajaratnam on how to balance his dual responsibilities as a businessman and as a diplomat. Rajaratnam simply replied that he could do whatever he liked "as long as there is no conflict with Singapore" (Ho 1990, 256–257). Emulating Lien Ying Chow (1906–2004), Singapore's ambassador to Malaysia and another leader of the Chinese Chamber of Commerce, Ho served without remuneration in Thailand (Ho 1990). Rajaratnam told Ho that "Singapore is so young that we have as yet no cut-and-dried rules [as to how a diplomat should conduct himself]. Just be yourself and act naturally" (Ho 1990, 258). Ho purchased a residence at North Sathorn Road, which was near his Thai Wah office on South Sathorn Road, where the Singaporean government would build its own permanent chancery. He observed the royal protocols, called on the Thai king and ministers, attended luncheons and social functions, and participated in the annual Red Cross Fair, at which the Singaporean embassy sold commodities manufactured in Singapore, such as beer, biscuits, candies, cigarettes, and chocolates contributed by Thai Wah. Although Ho gradually learned to take his diplomatic work in stride and managed to enjoy his new social life, the "dual responsibilities of a businessman and a diplomat" took a toll on his health. Ho wrote to the foreign ministry, asking to be relieved. His request was approved. He and his wife then visited the Thai king and queen, had a lengthy conversation in which King Bhumibol praised Singapore for having a good government and leaders, and received autographed photos of the royal couple. Thanat Khoman gave Ho and his wife a farewell dinner, at which he recalled the days he had played golf with Li Kuo Ching when he was serving in the United Nations in New York (Ho 1990, 268–269).

As a senior staff member of the Singaporean embassy in Thailand later recalled, Ho, "a wealthy and highly respected businessman, with vast experience and connections in Thailand, Myanmar, and the U.S." and his "chirpy and talented wife . . . were a formidable team. We entertained every visiting Singapore delegation in style, mostly paid for from Mr. Ho's coffer" (Low 2005, 224). Nathan suggested that Ho's success as a diplomat lay with his longstanding business interests in Thailand and his connections to the Thai business establishment "of which an important part consisted of Sino-Thais." A quiet and unassuming man, Ho "never had a hard word to say about anything" and used his networks and wealth to complete his stint as a diplomat (Nathan 2011, 431).

"A MODEL OF THE IDEAL SINGAPOREAN"

Ho's successor was Chi Owyang (1897–1988), who spent one-third of his life in Thailand: sixteen years of his childhood and seventeen years as Singapore's third ambassador to Thailand. Born in the Longdu District in Chaozhou, Guangdong Province, Owyang was a Teochew. His parents brought him to Bangkok when he was a one-year-old. His father operated a small trading business for local products and had connections with timber businessmen in the mountainous areas. When his father died in 1906, his mother assumed responsibility for him and his younger sister.

In 1907, Owyang was ordained as a young novice at Wat Bopitpimook, where he began his formal education for three years. Then, in 1910, he enrolled at a private Chinese-medium school in Rajawong. After the overthrow of the Qing dynasty (1644–1912), his mother decided that "China was going to become strong again and that it would be good to be a Chinese" (Owyang 1996, 26).[5] She dismissed the advice of relatives and friends that she buy a boat for him so that he could quit school and transport merchandise for a living. Considering education an investment, she "emptied her hard-earned savings of 3,000 baht so that her son could go to study in China." As she put it, she was "emptying her purse on her son's head" (Owyang 1996, 28). In 1914, Owyang left for China and enrolled at the Anglo-Chinese College in Shantou—another instance of reverse migration when conditions in the homeland were perceived to have improved.

It was in Shantou that Owyang had his first opportunity to learn English, which became his third language, his first being Thai and the second Chinese. After completing high school, he went to Shanghai and majored in banking at Fudan University. In 1921, he graduated from Fudan with a Bachelor of Science degree in commerce and banking. He was the first overseas Chinese from Thailand to graduate from Fudan and was in the first batch of graduates from the Commerce and Banking Department of Fudan University. After graduation, he joined the Wuhan branch of the Industrial and Commercial Bank. After six months in Wuhan, he was transferred to the Hong Kong branch. Another six months later, however, he resigned to return to Bangkok, reuniting with his mother after a ten-year absence (Owyang 1996).

During the interwar period, the Thai banking industry was underdeveloped. The few Thai banks that existed with local capital were mainly custodians of funds for aristocrats and wealthy merchants. Foreign banks, notably British and French, performed the real banking functions. To both the Chinese and the Thais, the operations of modern banking remained a mystery. Owyang could not find a job in the foreign banks, which hired almost exclusively Western expatriates, and considered assuming the post of headmaster of a Chinese-medium school. He soon abandoned the idea, however, and returned to Hong Kong to rejoin the Industrial and Commercial Bank in 1923. In 1925, when the political situation in China was chaotic, he accepted the assignment of forming a branch in Guangzhou and became the branch's assistant manager (Owyang 1996). In 1927, he married a teacher, the daughter of a local official in Fujian Province. A year later, his first son—he would have four sons and one daughter in all—was born in Guangzhou. In 1930, the head office of the Industrial and Commercial Bank suffered a crippling monetary loss and was forced to close. Owyang started another career with the Guangzhou branch of the China State Bank, which had its headquarters in Shanghai. There he was promoted to manager, responsible for all Guangzhou operations of the China State Bank. He then bought a house in Bangkok for his mother and sister, which he described as practicing the Chinese virtue of honoring and caring for parents (Owyang 1996). He maintained a channel of connections that meaningfully related the migrant to the homeland and remained attached to Thailand.

In the fall of 1937, as war approached Guangzhou, Owyang's wife and children moved to Hong Kong. In October 1938, Guangzhou fell to the Japanese. Owyang managed to flee to Hong Kong, where he oversaw the exiled Guangzhou branch of the China State Bank. In 1941, Japanese troops occupied Hong Kong. Owyang became unemployed as the China State Bank was forcibly closed by the Japanese. Over the years, he moved his family to Zhanjiang, a port city under French jurisdiction serving as a transit point to Free China, then on to Chongqing, Guilin, and Guizhou, working for different banks in various capacities. When the war ended in August 1945, Owyang and his family returned to Guangzhou. With the collapse of the Nationalist government on the mainland, however, Owyang began to doubt the prospects of banking in China, where high inflation rendered proper banking almost impossible, and left for Singapore. There he founded the Overseas Union Bank with Lien Ying Chow in 1949 and became the bank's first general manager, which was, according to Owyang's son Hsuan, another display of his resilience and entrepreneurship (Owyang 1996).

Weary of the unsettled, war-torn environment in China, Owyang appreciated the favorable economic conditions of Singapore. Overseas Union Bank was the first bank established in postwar Singapore, which was already served by many foreign banks. Overseas Union Bank was also the first Chinese bank to set up business at Raffles Place, an "exclusive territory" in banking and business circles. As a new bank with limited funds, the options available to Overseas Union Bank were few. Owyang steered the bank toward international banking, which offered liquidity and low-risk profits. Well acquainted with the bankers and rice exporters in Thailand, Owyang enabled the bank to venture into rice import financing. As he explained, Singapore did not produce rice, a stable commodity that enjoys a constant demand regardless of economic fluctuations, and Thailand was the principal supplier of rice to Singapore. He visited Bangkok every month and called on the top executives and heads of the import-export departments of major Thai banks to acquire information. He also met with Thai rice exporters to establish contacts. His personal rapport with the Thais and knowledge of the rice trade allowed Overseas Union Bank's business with Thailand to flourish—almost all the Thai banks maintained a Singapore Dollar account with the bank. Thai rice exporters directed their bankers to channel all their business to Overseas Union Bank. Until the mid-1950s when the Bangkok Bank opened a Singapore branch, the Overseas Union Bank financed about 80 percent of rice imports into Singapore (Owyang 1996).

A few banks in Singapore sought to offer the same financing options to Thai banks, but Overseas Union Bank provided more—mail credit facilities. At Overseas Union Bank, the accounts of Thai banks would be credited immediately, as soon as cables were received indicating documents were on the way, instead of crediting the accounts only after documents had been received. Thai bankers and businessmen thus preferred to deal with Overseas Union Bank, and, by extension, Owyang (Owyang 1996). Owyang himself most admired Chin Sophonpanich (1908–1988) of the Bangkok Bank: "Mr. Chin . . . understands the business and he knows how to manage people . . . he spoke no English, but he was one of the smartest people in international banking and foreign exchange trading. He was a very positive person" (Owyang 1996, 118–119). Many Thai bankers were also personal friends of the Owyang family. For promoting close relations between Singapore and Thailand, Owyang was decorated by King Bhumibol with the "Companion of the Most Exalted Order of the White Elephant" (Owyang 1996, 136).

In 1971, Rajaratnam invited Owyang to be Singapore's ambassador to Thailand. A self-professed introvert who "hardly fitted the stereotype of a diplomat"—he did not drink, smoke, or play golf, and his proficiency in English, the "diplomatic language after the end of World War II," was merely adequate—Owyang did not expect to be the longest-serving Singaporean ambassador, not just to Thailand but to any country (Owyang 1996, 136–137). Before he was officially appointed, Owyang learned the ropes of diplomacy by attending briefings and reading files at the foreign ministry. In September 1971, he presented his credentials to King Bhumibol, who was impressed with his Thai language skills. In 1973, Lee Kuan Yew paid his first official visit to Thailand. After meeting with Thai ministers in Bangkok, Lee and his delegation, accompanied by Owyang, flew to Chiang Mai where they were granted an audience with King Bhumibol and Queen Sirikit. According to Owyang, the Thai king and queen had unprecedentedly hosted a foreign prime minister; such a reception was only accorded to monarchs and presidents (Owyang 1996). It was also during Owyang's stint that the permanent chancery of the Singaporean Embassy was established at 129 South Sathorn Road (Owyang 1996).

Owyang's appointment was opportune. The Thai government was then headed by Kukrit Pramoj (1911–1995), a member of the royal family, who was both a literary scholar and a banker. He served as the deputy chairman of the Bangkok Bank of Commerce and was well acquainted with Owyang before becoming prime minister. When Kukrit was visiting Singapore, the Overseas Union Bank held a dinner in his honor. Although Kukrit stepped down in 1976, Owyang's relations with Thai ministers remained cordial. Owyang facilitated Singapore's goodwill and trade missions to Thailand and helped Singapore become Thailand's most important ASEAN trading partner from 1965 to 1974. He worked to expand Singapore-Thailand economic relations beyond trade in primary commodities and refined petroleum products. He was supported in this vision by King Bhumibol, who was involved in more than 1,500 agricultural and educational projects for his people and was dedicated to sustaining the Thai economy. As Owyang told his son toward the end of his life, the king had contributed more than anyone to Thailand's economic success (Owyang 1996).

Hsuan Owyang recalled that for his father to serve in Thailand was "like going home." "It is human nature that childhood memories stay long and always occupy a place in a person's heart," Hsuan wrote (Owyang 1996, 150). Owyang felt completely at ease in Thailand. Hsuan noticed that every sound, sight, and gesture in Thailand conveyed a familiar, yet special, meaning to him that no foreigner or tourist could appreciate. Even Owyang's wife observed that "when it came to the Thais, they always had an edge [with him]" (Owyang 1996, 151). Owyang's feelings for the Thai people were reciprocated; Thai ministers and diplomats considered him one of their own, and one of the jokes in the Thai government was that when he finished his term, the Thais could appoint him as their ambassador to Singapore. In later years, Owyang would be seated with the royal family at banquets. Princess Maha Chakri Sirindhorn had sought his advice when she was contemplating studying engineering in Germany; he advised her to study Chinese instead because China was rising and would become an important player in international affairs.

Owyang's wife passed away in Bangkok in 1977, and attendees at her funeral included not only Thai dignitaries and merchants but also members of the Teochew community in Bangkok (Owyang 1996). After Thailand's normalization of relations with the People's Republic of China, Owyang also befriended the first Chinese ambassador to Thailand and helped him settle in Bangkok. For Owyang's assistance in setting up the Chinese embassy, he was invited to visit Beijing. In Beijing, he met the Chinese deputy foreign minister and the vice-president of the Chinese People's Association for Friendship with Foreign Countries. In 1983, King Bhumibol conferred the Knight Grand Cross of the Most Exalted Order of the White Elephant on Owyang, the first time he had conferred the award on an ambassador still in office.

In January 1988, Owyang turned ninety and wanted to retire. The foreign ministry announced that Tan Seng Chye, who was serving as the First Secretary of Singapore's embassy in Bangkok, would take over Owyang's duties. Tan Seng Chye and his successors were professional diplomats—Singapore's diplomatic service had developed fully by the 1980s. Owyang stayed in Bangkok to serve as Adviser to the Embassy and remained active in the Thai Chinese community. He attended functions at Chinese temples and invited Teochew opera troupes, which he loved, to perform in Chinatown. In November 1988, he passed away in Bangkok, mourned by Singaporean and Thai businessmen and officials alike (Owyang 1996). In his eulogy, Rajaratnam called Owyang "a model of the ideal Singaporean," who, despite having known nothing about how diplomacy works, had served Singapore well as a successful ambassador (Owyang 1996, 19).

FROM CHINESE SOJOURNERS TO SINGAPOREAN DIPLOMATS

Throughout much of the nineteenth and twentieth centuries, before the creation of nation-states in Southeast Asia, Chinese immigrants to Southeast Asia were mainly sojourners who looked to China as their homeland. In the first half of the twentieth century, Chinese-medium schools, which were attended by the three ambassadors discussed in this chapter, were modeled on the modern schools of Republican China, which emphasized ideas of citizenship and nationality (Teoh 2010). For Ho Rih Hwa, Singapore used to be merely a place where he could make a living. When he was an undergraduate at Lingnan University, he volunteered to visit and help boost the morale of Chinese frontline troops during the Japanese invasion of North China. As he recalled toward the end of his life, "Singapore in my student days was only an English colony . . . since I came from a Chinese-oriented family in Singapore, and since I was sent as a little boy to study in China where I had many fond memories, it was only natural that I regarded China as my country" (Ho 1990, 47, 255). While ensuring that his children enjoyed a sound foundation in English, Owyang discussed the teachings of ancient Chinese scholars and delighted in written exchanges in classical Chinese with his sons (Owyang 1996).

After the Second World War, the decolonization of the Malay archipelago and peninsula and the racial politics of the independence movements highlighted the differences between the Chinese and the native, majority populations. Although the citizenship laws initially proposed in Indonesia and Malaysia were favorable toward the Chinese—they had even allowed for dual citizenship—many indigenous political elites resisted them and advocated for a set of laws that both prohibited dual nationality and favored the indigenous population (Tan 2001). Singapore, on cue, also did not recognize dual citizenship, citing a potential threat to national solidarity by dividing loyalties; the Malaysians' assertion of Malay dominance was a major reason for the separation of Singapore in 1965 (Tan 2001). The Chinese in Singapore thus had to forge a new national identity for themselves, transforming from sojourners to citizens in the 1960s.

Tan Siak Kew, Ho Rih Hwa, and Chi Owyang identified themselves as Chinese, citing that they were born into Chinese families. Tan used to lament his lack of a Chinese education and chose to enroll in a school that offered traditional Chinese education; he would become a bilingual speaker of English and Mandarin and a skillful calligrapher (Tan 2014). As a child, Ho was "keen to see China for myself, and didn't feel the least bit of regret at leaving home and Singapore" (Ho 1990, 20). When he was old, he and his wife, who were fluent in the Chinese dialects and knowledgeable about Chinese legends, thought that they should learn to play mahjong, which ambassadors' wives in Bangkok called the "most Chinese of all Chinese games" (Ho 1990, 288). Owyang, before leaving Thailand for further education in China, "already" had "certain values . . . deeply rooted in him," which, according to his son, included the importance of self-reliance, the meaning of parental love, and the virtue of frugality (Owyang 1996, 28–30). Later in his life, he developed an interest in Teochew opera and "definitely derived tremendous pleasure" from watching it (Owyang 1996, 186–187). The self-racialization of Tan, Ho, and Owyang was not entirely the result of nation-building projects, as suggested by much of the existing scholarship. Rather, they had deployed ethnicity as a basis for self-identification while nurturing, in their official capacities as a businessman or as a diplomat, cultural attributes for the maintenance of ethnic-group boundaries.

In the ambassadors' autobiographies and biographies, so-called Chinese values helped to explain their successes in business and diplomacy. The ambassadors appeared comfortable with their place in and contribution to both Singapore and Thailand. If the production of texts about the Chinese in Thailand by Sino-Thai writers, as historian Thak Chaloemtiarana argues, indicates that "the Sino-Thai have shrugged off their cultural amnesia and have recovered their self-confidence to publish an endless string of books about their own history, their struggles, and their successes" (Thak 2014, 511), then the publication of autobiographies and biographies of Singapore's first ambassadors to Thailand confirmed their "fixed citizenship" as loyal diplomats who served only Singapore's interests.[6] The life stories of the ambassadors acknowledged their Chinese ancestry, filial piety, and patriarchal authority. They also served to emphasize how they achieved success through sheer grit, honesty, and industry, "values" that all self-professed Chinese would proudly claim. In positivist fashion, their stories illustrate the three key phases of Singapore's cultural discourse, conflating "rugged individualism," "Shared Values," and Lee Kuan Yew's evolving sense of "Asian Values" into their protagonists and hence emphasizing "the 'rights' of the state, the community, and the family ahead of the rights of the individual person" (Barr 2000b, 311). These were also "values" that the Thais seemed to appreciate, for they were portrayed as genuinely respecting the ambassadors. The perceived Chineseness of the ambassadors allowed the Thais to understand their actions, conduct, and accomplishments, even though such an understanding might appear to be essentialist, simplified, or problematic.

CONCLUSION

For decades during and shortly after the Cold War, state-centered binary approaches to studying the Cold War focused on diplomacy, foreign affairs, and military conflicts. In recent years, Cold War studies have experienced a cultural turn, which instead emphasizes emotions, gender, lifestyles, literature, memory, and visual media. As historian Cheng-Guan Ang finely summarizes, while the new Cold War historiography adds a more "human dimension" to the standard narratives, it merely offers a fuller picture of how geopolitics and national politics actually operated rather than challenges the basic assumptions underlying the preponderance of diplomacy and foreign relations during the Cold War (Ang 2018, 3–4). This chapter has suggested that biographies and autobiographies allow historians to move beyond official or state-narrated visions of interstate relations and study more subtle modes of interaction that played out during the Cold War. It has tried to combine the cultural or human aspects of change with diplomatic considerations and outcomes in its analysis of Singapore's selection of its first ambassadors to Thailand. That Singapore, a Chinese-majority nation, turned to prominent Chinese businessmen to serve as diplomats is perhaps unsurprising. But the concept of the migrant's corridor reveals that the Singaporean state and the ambassadors themselves considered a shared culture or value system and common commercial interests to be crucial determinants of appointment. Having traversed the migrant's corridor prior to their nation's independence, Singapore's first ambassadors to Thailand hoped to translate their experiences and resources into cordial relations between the two countries.

As elite capitalists (and, by implication, anti-Communists), the Singaporean ambassadors deployed their cultural and commercial ties to both their erstwhile homeland and Thailand to enhance corporate interests and bilateral relations. For the Thai elite, then, they were the "good Chinese," not the "bad Chinese" championing the Communist ideology that threatened to subvert the Thai monarchy and nation.

NOTES

1. A group joined Communist rebels in the northeastern forests to continue their resistance against the Thai state after the infamous Thammasat University massacre in 1976. See Winichakul (2020).

2. The migrant's corridor reconnected China in the 1980s, when reformers within the Chinese government initiated economic and market reforms to open up the country to foreign investments. On how it was reconnected between Singapore and China, see Kuah-Pearce (2011).

3. Although the aforementioned book is not written by Tan Siak Kew or his descendants, it is based on substantial sharing of memories by Tan's son Tan Puay Hiang.

4. Thai Wah's business was mainly manufacturing and exporting to Europe, Japan, and the United States; see Ho (1990, 257).

5. Hsuan Owyang was Chi Owyang's son, who served as the chairman of the Housing and Development Board in Singapore. Chi Owyang spent his childhood in Chinatown, "confined to Songwad Road"—hence the title for the biography (Owyang 1996, 30).

6. This is the opposite of the concept of "flexible citizenship," which anthropologist Aihwa Ong coined to describe the strategies of migration and settlement that people adopt when considering their economic options. See Ong (1999).

PART II

Contemporary Engagements

Chapter 4

Southeast Asian Studies in China

The Politics and Geopolitics of Knowledge Production

A crucial node in China's Belt and Road Initiative (BRI), Southeast Asia consists of rapidly developing economies that outperform the rest of the developing world and also lies between the contested regions of Northeast Asia and South Asia. Southeast Asia is home to transnational Chinese entrepreneurs and their privately owned enterprises, which have helped accelerate and sustain China's economic growth since the 1980s. For China, Southeast Asia, whether as a region or as a composite of nation-states, thus demands rigorous analysis of whole societies backed by humanistic thinking and quantitative data. The study of Southeast Asia, or the discipline that we may call Southeast Asian studies, is rendered even more imperative given the current scramble by great powers—China included—seeking to defend and expand their influence over the region's constituent nation-states in a global rivalry for consumer markets and diplomatic allies.[1]

However, as many scholars have suggested, the state of Southeast Asian studies in China remains subpar. From the perspective of those trained in the West, the situation has hardly improved over the past few decades. In the early 1980s, a delegation of Australian historians and social scientists, led by Wang Gungwu to evaluate Southeast Asian studies in China, noted that China at that time was "[not] interested in Southeast Asia . . . the level of Chinese scholarly concern with Southeast Asia is not what one would expect of a major world power, or even a regional power" (Hewitt 1982, 153). According to their report, Southeast Asian studies in China suffered from inadequate funding and training: "Career prospects are almost non-existent for graduates in Southeast Asian languages" (Hewitt 1982, 162). Two decades later, the Institute of Southeast Asian Studies (now renamed ISEAS-Yusof Ishak Institute) launched a project to summarize the field of Southeast Asian studies

65

in China. In the resultant book, *Southeast Asian Studies in China* (2006), one of its editors remarked that China continued to lag behind global centers of Southeast Asian studies, such as Japan, Singapore, and the United States, in terms of not only funding and training but also talent and language abilities. However, "a growing number of young Chinese are becoming more interested in Southeast Asia," he observed, "thanks to fast-developing bilateral relations between China and ASEAN" (Saw 2006, 6). True to his prediction, given China's professed foreign policy goal of becoming a responsible regional and global power, the Chinese government has channeled more resources into academic research on Southeast Asia in recent years. Kankan Xie, a Southeast Asianist at Peking University, confirmed that Chinese leaders and scholars have made noteworthy strides toward developing Southeast Asian studies in the country. Yet the development has been lopsided, assuming what he calls a "policy turn" over time. Southeast Asian studies in China is increasingly defined by policy-relevant research, dominated by economics, law, and political science, and characterized by the "rapid growth of language programs, absolute domination of short-term policy research [over long-term archival and ethnographical work], and further marginalization of humanistic subjects" (Xie 2021, 187). Xie's experience has been particularly revealing, considering that he is both an insider (a native Chinese) and an outsider (a scholar who was trained in the West) who has observed the state of Southeast Asian studies in China from the inside out. While scholars like Xie have raised provocative questions about how Southeast Asian studies can develop in China and have accurately pointed out that many, if not most, of China's Southeast Asianists have closely identified their research with serving state interests, they remain primarily interested in highlighting only the institutional and structural weaknesses of the discipline. Moreover, they tend to focus on the post-1949 period, after the Communist victory in mainland China, and describe the historical trajectory of Southeast Asian studies in China without acknowledging how specific nation-based studies can diverge from and reconnect with that trajectory in the country.

No matter how serious it is or where it is situated, that scholarship has never been divorced from politics may be a moot point. Still, the degree to which it is structured or influenced by political trends varies across time and space. Notwithstanding the well-studied limitations of Southeast Asian studies in China, this chapter suggests a silver lining to the politicization of scholarship in China. While state censorship and imperatives have constrained the development of Southeast Asian studies into a more accessible and more open discipline by Western standards, they have offered Southeast Asian studies unprecedented opportunities for becoming a niche discipline informed by international collaboration and supported by government funding. In addition to discussing how some Chinese institutes and universities capitalize on existing strengths or build on new faculty and resources to develop their Southeast Asian studies programs, the chapter emphasizes their agency, rather than the structure under which they operate, in helping advance the discipline of Southeast Asian studies in China. In arguing for the approach of biographical analysis to examine the state of China studies in Southeast Asia, political scientist Chih-yu Shih stresses the individualized and nuanced practices that are critical to the long-term evolution of intellectual history, of which Southeast Asian studies—or any discipline, for that matter—is a part (Shih 2019, 2). Such practices can be institutional in addition to being personal. This chapter highlights the agency of institutions more than individual scholars in meeting the Chinese state's demand for geopolitically relevant research on Southeast Asia, bringing to the fore the network of institutes, universities, government bureaus, and think tanks in creating and maintaining Southeast Asian studies in China.

This chapter comprises three key sections. The first section sketches the history of Southeast Asian studies in China. Although other scholars have undertaken this task in far greater detail, the section highlights the political and geopolitical aspects of change in scholarly trends, particularly the politicization of scholarship and historical methods from the Qing dynasty to the present day, for the uninitiated. Having set the context for further inquiry, the chapter proceeds with the second section, which explores how Southeast Asian studies has become a niche discipline in which universities and research institutes, both established and young, specialize as part of their vision for long-term growth and from which the state receives expert advice for policymaking and geopolitical outlook in the context of China's increasingly complex interactions with contemporary Southeast Asia. Aiming to historicize in a specific setting the emergence of Southeast Asian studies in China, which responded in part to the Western domination of Asian studies in general, the third section examines the case of Thai studies from its inception during the late nineteenth century to its current state as arguably the most thematically diverse and geopolitically relevant subfield of Southeast Asian studies in China, thanks to the popularity of Thai films and dramas among Chinese viewers and to Thailand's value as China's potential ally against American influence over the Asia-Pacific region.[2] A product of politics and geopolitics, Thai studies in China exemplify the historical trajectory of Southeast Asia-related studies in the country and the highly politicized nature of knowledge production for both domestic consumption and foreign reception. This chapter concludes with a brief discussion of the implications of producing knowledge about Southeast Asia for business and people-to-people cultural exchanges between China and Southeast Asia.

A BRIEF HISTORY OF SOUTHEAST ASIAN STUDIES IN CHINA: POLITICAL AND GEOPOLITICAL ASPECTS

Notwithstanding the vast corpus of Chinese historical records on what may be retrospectively called "Southeast Asia" (bearing in mind that the term did not come into widespread or conventional use until sometime around the Second World War), modern, systematic—read, institutional—or Western-style academic research on the region began during the late nineteenth and early twentieth centuries. This was the point at which Chinese intellectuals became exposed to Western humanities and social sciences, and their interest in the sea (and land) south of China (referred to as "Nanyang") developed in tandem with the reshaping of the Chinese worldview and sense of physical geography (Tang 1996). In 1906, Jinan University, which offered the first-ever courses on Chinese overseas and Southeast Asian history in China, was founded in Nanjing (it would relocate first to Shanghai and then to Guangzhou [Canton]) (Saw 2006, 2). Jinan University's earliest incarnation was Jinan Academy (暨南學堂), which was the first school in China for ethnic Chinese migrants and their offspring in Southeast Asia who wished to return for their studies (Seah 2017, 32). In particular, the Chinese in British Malaya and the Dutch East Indies lacked schools customized to their desire for cultural and language preservation. Most of Jinan's first students hailed from Batavia (modern-day Jakarta) and Singapore (Seah 2017, 37–38).

In 1927, Jinan University established the Nanyang Cultural and Educational Affairs Bureau (南洋文化教育事業部), the first of its kind in China (Ku 2006, 119). To disseminate studies on the Chinese overseas in Southeast Asia, the university published academic journals that featured the translation of Western writings (Park 2013, 48–49). One of the bureau's key contributions to Southeast Asian studies was the publication of its flagship journal *Nanyang Studies* (南洋研究), which focused on biographical accounts of prominent Southeast Asian Chinese, reports on Chinese schools in Southeast Asia, the contributions of Southeast Asian Chinese to the revolutionary cause in China, general histories of Southeast Asian Chinese, and the rubber industry in Malaya (Seah 2017, 43–44). Besides publishing academic writings on Southeast Asia, the bureau also collected a vast corpus of reference materials comprising maps and photographs, assisted organizations based in Southeast Asia in recruiting academic and administrative staff, and compiled teaching aids for Chinese schools in Southeast Asia. It launched the first major academic conferences on Southeast Asia in China, which were well attended by delegates from cities such as Batavia, Malacca, Penang, and Singapore. These delegates represented organizations such as clan associations, chambers of commerce, and newspaper presses. The conferences yielded results beyond the purely academic: the inaugural Conference on Nanyang Chinese Education, for example, yielded resolutions that the Nationalist government of China adopted to coordinate its policy toward Chinese education in Southeast Asia. The Nationalist state enjoyed limited success in controlling Chinese education in Southeast Asia, however, and many Chinese vernacular schools in Southeast Asia acted autonomously to educate Chinese children (Seah 2017, 45–50). Entrepreneurs and Western-educated intellectuals among the Chinese overseas funded these endeavors; one of their accomplishments was founding China's first private university, Xiamen (Amoy) University, in 1921, which became another key center for Southeast Asian studies in China (Park 2013, 48).

The contributions of Chinese overseas to the development of Southeast Asian studies in China extended beyond money. The pioneer generation of China's Southeast Asian studies comprised Chinese overseas intellectuals born in mainland China during the 1910s and 1920s and immigrated to Southeast Asia to escape the Japanese invasion during the 1930s. In 1940, a group of these intellectuals formed the China South Seas Society in Singapore, many of whom returned to China after the Second World War to train a new generation of Southeast Asian studies specialists at various universities (Park 2013, 49). The center of Southeast Asian studies, also known as Nanyang studies, thus shifted to Singapore, which sustained the discipline when China was embroiled in war and revolution.

In 1949, the Chinese Communists took over China from the Nationalists. The new Communist state adopted a revolutionary foreign policy toward Southeast Asia. Although it accepted national sovereignty as the fundamental principle of a new Cold War international order against colonialism and imperialist domination, the Chinese state supported Communist insurgencies in Burma, Indonesia, Malaysia, Thailand, and the Philippines to export revolution to Southeast Asia (Park 2013, 50). Therefore, although the Chinese state founded regional centers to study Southeast Asia—two institutes in Guangzhou and one each in Kunming and Xiamen—and several policy research units linked to the government and the Shanghai Academy of Social Sciences (Saw 2006, 2), Southeast Asian studies developed an insular outlook and was structured by Leninist, Marxist, and Maoist paradigms. Characterized by macro and superficial descriptions rather than micro and detailed analyses, Southeast Asian studies in the early Communist years were highly ideological and politicized. Common themes included class struggle, national liberation, and peasant uprising. Consequently, although Southeast Asian studies was established as a scholarly discipline during this period, the diversity and historical dynamism of Southeast Asia were deliberately concealed or overlooked (Park 2013, 50–51). For historian Park Sa-Myung, the first three decades of the so-called radical Communist period produced "almost little academic work of serious quality": "Even the studies of the history of the overseas Chinese in Southeast Asia were uninspiring (1950–66) and entirely closed (1967–78), as attested by the dearth of publications" (Park 2013, 51). Park's observations can perhaps explain the "dark age" or dire state of Southeast Asian studies as perceived by the Australian delegation in the early 1980s, which seemed a far cry from the transnational vibrancy and relative intellectual freedom that had marked the field during the Republican era.

That said, the freedom enjoyed by Republican-era Southeast Asian studies specialists should not be exaggerated. From a *longue durée* perspective, China's "century of humiliation," roughly from the late Qing period to the 1980s, conditioned the development of Nanyang or Southeast Asian studies into a politicized and sometimes ideologically laden discipline. At least until the so-called policy turn in recent years, historical studies had occupied a prominent place in China's Southeast Asian research institutes (Hewitt 1982, 157). Yet it was precisely the discipline of history that lent itself to political agendas during the Republican period. Although scientific historiography introduced from the West diminished the moral connotations of history as implied by Confucian historiography and Chinese classicist scholarship in general, history was used by both the Nationalist and the Communist regimes to justify their policies and furnish political legitimacy (Chan and Chen 2020, 4). The professionalization of the discipline of history and establishment or institutionalization of Southeast Asian studies as a scholarly field followed a similar trajectory in that they were both generated by political exigencies. The emerging group of new professional historians trained in the West and those exposed to Western historical methods or writings assigned a political mission to history and Southeast Asian studies as a whole, deploying these bodies of knowledge as a critical strategy for making loyal citizens and saving the Chinese nation during the late nineteenth and early twentieth centuries. Leading intellectuals such as Liang Qichao 梁啓超 (1873–1929) urged their contemporaries to turn their attention from dynastic chronicles to the history of the Chinese people. Their widely circulated writings also analyzed how colonized and semi-colonized societies, the perceived fellow victims of Western imperialism, had coped with their predicament, valorizing their struggles and seeking inspiration from them.[3] Chinese historians pegged history to national survival, stressing history's role as the repository of current society and future greatness. The so-called Chinese Enlightenment of delivering objective, rational, and scientific solutions to China's problems was thus at its inception riddled with contradictions, which remained unresolved in modern Chinese historiography and, more generally, Chinese humanities and social sciences.[4] Unlike history, however, Southeast Asian studies in twentieth-century China was not developed by scholars who were trained directly in the West by Western faculty, let alone by specialists who could embrace the advanced methodologies that would be used to examine Southeast Asia's culture, history, politics, and society after the 1980s. Overall, Southeast Asian studies in twentieth-century China suffered from a Sinocentric perspective and was more descriptive than analytical. Modeled after Western imperialism, Sinocentrism was translated into a thesis of Chinese colonization in Southeast Asia, precluding the possibility of an autonomous Southeast Asia. This thesis was well encapsulated in Liang Qichao's words: "As the people of more than 100 countries in the South Sea are mostly descendants of the Chinese, they are naturally Chinese colonies" (Park 2013, 48–49). The situation would improve slightly with less overtly racial overtones after the 1980s, even though Southeast Asian studies, as we will see, would become subtly ideological and yet deeply political as China developed into a regional and global power.

SOUTHEAST ASIAN STUDIES: A NICHE DISCIPLINE

Southeast Asian studies in China was paralyzed by the Cultural Revolution (1966–1976) when the ideologically driven and politically riven state viewed intellectual activities with suspicion. As a result of China's export of Communist revolution to Southeast Asia, China's relations with Southeast Asian nations were strained, and the diplomatic and informal exchanges were severed. During the reform era under Deng Xiaoping 鄧小平 (1904–1997), Southeast Asian studies was revived and became a vital objective of the Chinese state, which sought to improve its relations with neighboring countries and attract Chinese overseas investments to shore up its tattered economy. Chinese leaders also sought to learn from the historical transitions and overall developmental experience of Southeast Asian states, most notably that of Singapore, to chart and balance China's economic growth with political and social stability (Tang and Zhang 2006, 60). Thus, Chinese politics and scholarship shed their most radical tinge, and universities and research institutes resumed their teaching of Southeast Asian courses and languages. By the end of the 1980s, China's research institutes for Southeast Asia grew from four to twelve before the Cultural Revolution. Key centers included Jinan University, Peking University, Sun Yat-sen University, Xiamen University, and the academies for social sciences in Guangxi, Shanghai, and Yunnan. The Chinese government set up additional research units, such as the China Institute for Contemporary International Relations (under the Ministry of State Security), the China Institute of International Studies (under the Ministry of Foreign Affairs), the Shanghai Institute for International Studies, and the Institute for International Trade Studies (first under the Ministry of External Trade and then under the Ministry of External Trade and Economic Work). The state was thus heavily involved in recovering Southeast Asian studies in China, and policymakers frequently consulted scholars on Southeast Asian affairs (Saw 2006, 3).

Enjoying more significant opportunities for policy-related consultancy and research, Southeast Asian studies specialists prepared reports and policy papers for central and local governments. Their arguments and recommendations were referenced and generally accepted by state leaders and official study groups (Saw 2006, 3). Policy recommendations made by provincial institutes could influence how the central government conducts its foreign relations. Those in Guangxi and Yunnan, for instance, have had a significant impact on China's relations with Southeast Asia, especially with nations contiguous to the two provinces (Saw 2006, 4). For these institutes in Guangxi and Yunnan, Southeast Asian studies have become a niche discipline, allowing them to join the ranks of their counterparts at Jinan, Peking, Sun Yat-sen, and Xiamen Universities and become key centers of the field in their own right. Unlike those in Beijing and Shanghai, which developed expertise in regionwide issues, they have tended to focus on studying individual countries and subregional affairs. Saving "high" political issues such as national security, international relations, and macro economy for research centers in Beijing and Shanghai, the regional centers in Fujian, Guangdong, Guangxi, and Yunnan have researched "low" political issues such as culture, economics, ethnicity, history, religion, and Chinese overseas (Saw 2006, 4). The vastness of China's territories and the varied nature of China's Southeast Asian neighbors have resulted in this implicit division of labor along primarily geographical lines.

Using broad categorization, in the 1990s, when the Chinese economy took off and the positive aspects of impressive growth were felt by the increasingly affluent Chinese society, China's Southeast Asian studies focused on business and economic links between China and Southeast Asian nations, of which Indonesia and Singapore were the last to recognize China formally. In the 2000s, politics overtook economics as the primary focus, and scholars paid more attention to Southeast Asian history and society, including studying Chinese overseas (Saw 2006, 4–5). In recent years, the progress of "opened Southeast Asian studies" has been evident in terms of institutions, methods, and subjects. Institutions have become more competitive internally (i.e., among scholars) than hierarchical, which means scholars are now on a more even plane with one another. Methods have become more pluralistic than monistic. Most important, perhaps, subjects have been shifted from history to reality, from the superficial description of class struggle and national liberation to the concrete and less-ideologically motivated analysis of historical facts and current dynamics (Park 2013, 51–52). The well-established institutions such as Jinan University, Sun Yat-sen University, and Xiamen

University have continued to leverage their existing strong ties with the state and renewed links with Chinese overseas businessmen and scholars in expanding their Southeast Asian studies programs. Their prolific publication of bibliographical studies, fieldwork, and research articles has continued to serve as the powerhouse of Southeast Asian studies in China. They are frequently involved in policymaking and international conferences. These universities enjoyed a head start in that they were the home institutions of pioneers of Southeast Asian studies in China. Many of the pioneers were returned Chinese overseas (歸僑), and they based their research on Chinese sources rather than Western or Southeast Asian texts.[5] The policy turn of Southeast Asian studies in China had only exacerbated the situation, with Chinese scholars depending on only Chinese or English materials for research without acquiring Southeast Asian languages. Hope is in the air, however, as the popularity of Southeast Asian studies in recent years has offered foreign language universities such as Beijing Foreign Studies University unprecedented opportunities to establish new programs and help reinforce area studies with language teaching (Xie 2021, 184–185).

Unlike resource-rich research universities in Beijing and Shanghai and foreign language universities with well-established programs covering a wide variety of world regions, universities in the provinces are selective about the resources they can devote to area studies and have little intention of building all-inclusive programs. Developing Southeast Asian studies to their comparative advantage for universities in China's southern provinces has become a top priority. Jinan University, Sun Yat-sen University, and Xiamen University, which are renowned and well-endowed national universities, have researched Southeast Asia for decades. Of greater interest here, perhaps, are universities in Guangxi and Yunnan, which are historically less prominent but which have also started to prioritize Southeast Asian studies, especially studies of mainland Southeast Asia as geographical proximity and traditionally porous borders have facilitated constant exchanges in the borderlands (Xie 2021, 185–186). The division of labor in Southeast Asian studies is less a result of Beijing's centralized planning than a "vivid reflection of path dependency and fierce inter-provincial rivalry" (Xie 2021, 186). Since the 1990s, Guangxi and Yunnan have been competing with each other for the status of "Gateway to China-Southeast Asia interactions" (中國東南亞交流的門戶). Although Yunnan was initially successful in attracting six Southeast Asian countries to set up consulates in Kunming, Guangxi's capital city, Nanning, also managed to do the same. Nanning eventually gained the upper hand by becoming the permanent host site for the China-ASEAN Expo. The Guangxi and Yunnan provincial governments are also investing heavily in Southeast Asian studies, hoping to strengthen their gateway status. In this regard, Yunnan appears to lead, with more Southeast Asian studies centers and more prestigious journals on Southeast Asian studies. With its more diverse ethnic composition (twenty-six of China's fifty-six officially recognized ethnicities are based in the province) and supposedly closer historical links to Southeast Asia (Yang 2009), Yunnan seems well poised to serve as the academic bridge-head for China's exchanges with Southeast Asia (Xie 2021, 186). Together with Guangxi, Yunnan has not waited for directives from Beijing to push for cooperation with ASEAN economies on their own, and its attention to and investments in Southeast Asian studies should be understood in the context of greater agency on the part of provincial officials seeking broader cross-border engagements for economic growth and geopolitical relevance (Li 2020).

Yunnan's universities and research institutes are excellent examples of how Southeast Asian studies has been developed as a niche discipline within Chinese humanities and social sciences. Like the rest of China, Yunnan might have initiated its Southeast Asian studies during the Republican era, but systematic studies only began during the early 1950s when the Yunnan Institute of Southeast Asian Studies conducted research on Myanmar, following the independence of British Burma and the retreat of remnant Nationalist troops to the country. Since the establishment of the Yunnan Institute of Social and Historical Studies of Minority Nationalities in 1956, Chinese scholars have been studying the histories and nationalities of Cambodia, Laos, Myanmar, Thailand, and Vietnam. They have compiled historical records, conducted interviews and surveys on Chinese overseas and those who had returned to China, and translated foreign-language writings into Chinese.[6] After the Cultural Revolution, following which most research projects ground to a halt, Yunnan's Southeast Asian studies institutes quickly capitalized on China's development of a free trade zone with mainland Southeast Asian countries and established a considerable number of institutions, departments, and subdepartments to process and analyze the increasing volume of information produced by more intensive interactions with Southeast Asia. The Institute of Southeast Asian Studies at the Yunnan Academy of Social Sciences was perhaps the most comprehensive and successful among these institutions. With senior researchers who reported directly to the provincial government and reference materials procured with government funds, the institute was a special organ in Yunnan engaged in Southeast Asian studies under state auspices (Wang 2006, 106). Together with other major institutes of Southeast Asian studies in Yunnan, the institute developed specialties in international relations, which urged greater cooperation between China and Southeast Asia, and ethnological work, which toed the official line that the various races in the ancient Nanzhao and Dali kingdoms, leading to the contemporary Yunnan Province, constitute part of the Chinese nation. Yunnan's researchers argued against what they saw as an anachronistic theory that a Thai race had existed and founded the Nanzhao and Dali kingdoms in what is now modern-day China, which has resulted in heated discussions in China, Thailand, and elsewhere since the 1980s (Wang 2006, 108–110). Through academic exchanges and international conferences, Yunnan also received foreign dignitaries and visiting scholars from Southeast Asia. The "Southeast Asia boom" in the province promised to maintain official interest in furthering Southeast Asian studies there (Wang 2006, 116). In short, although Yunnan's universities and research institutes had not established themselves as key centers for Southeast Asian studies before the 1950s, as had Jinan University and Xiamen University, they astutely leveraged their geographical proximity to Southeast Asia and new opportunities presented by China's economic reforms to develop Southeast Asian studies as their niche discipline.

Another group of Chinese universities and research institutes did not enjoy a geographical advantage, let alone historical linkage, in developing Southeast Asian studies as a niche discipline. In 1981, the Department of History at Zhengzhou University, located in landlocked Henan Province, set up the first Institute of Vietnamese Studies in China.[7] Zhengzhou University's foray into Southeast Asian studies was somewhat fortuitous. It began when Dai Kelai 戴可來 (1935–2015), a history graduate of Peking University, had worked at the Central University for Nationalities (now Minzu University of China) from 1959 to 1976. He then transferred to Zhengzhou University, where he continued his studies of the China-Vietnam borderlands and the Spratly Islands, over which China and Vietnam have both claimed sovereignty.[8] Dai's interests thus became an institutional specialization, and his successors at the institute established the Collaborative Innovation Center for Territorial Sovereignty and Maritime Rights to strengthen China's claims over the Spratly Islands.[9] Another institute of interest here was the Institute for Thai Studies at Changzhou University, located in the coastal Jiangsu Province, which was more renowned for Chinese classical scholarship than for diasporic networks with Southeast Asia (Elman 1990). Again, the role of an individual scholar contributed to the development of a Southeast Asian studies institute. Li Renliang 李仁良, a scholar at the National Institute of Development Administration in Thailand, helped found the Institute for Thai Studies at Changzhou University in 2015. A native of Changzhou, Li used his personal contacts to forge links between Changzhou University and major academic institutions in Thailand, seeking long-term collaboration between Chinese and Thai scholars to promote the cause of the Belt and Road Initiative (BRI) for the Chinese state (*Kknews* 2017). Together with Zhengzhou University, Changzhou University was an example of how Southeast Asian studies had been developed as a niche discipline at universities and research institutes that had little to do with Southeast Asia in history.

THAI STUDIES IN CHINA: A CASE STUDY

A product of politics and geopolitics, Thai studies can illuminate the historical trajectory assumed by Southeast Asian studies in China, albeit with some differences and deviations. For decades, where studies of individual nations were concerned, Indonesia, for its population and territorial size, dominated Southeast Asian studies in China. However, in recent years, Thai studies has been increasingly pursued by Chinese scholars interested in history, international relations, and media studies. China's "Go West" strategy boosted its relations with Thailand by creating a regional environment in which China's economic expansion could be accommodated. The Chinese state aims to stimulate trade and tourism in western China and sees Thailand as a key player in realizing its objective (Busbarat 2016, 239). In addition, China has remained keen on constructing a canal across the Isthmus of Kra, located in southern Thailand, to expand its maritime influence and secure its access to imported gas and crude oil.[10] These factors may help explain why Thailand is where the Chinese state has had the greatest interest in setting up Confucius Institutes. A total of thirty-seven Confucius Institutes have been set up in Thailand since 2006, which constitutes 48 percent of the total number of Confucius Institutes in Southeast Asia. The Confucius Institutes in Thailand championed the slogan "Chinese and Thai are like one family" to promote Chinese culture and language and foster goodwill toward China among their Thai students (Li 2020, 70). No other Southeast Asian country has more Chinese overseas than Thailand does—as many as nine million or 14 percent of the total population, depending on the criteria used (Wade 2020, 179). The broad context of China's politics and geopolitics has thus created favorable conditions under which Thai studies can develop further in the country.

As one of only three sovereign nations—the other two were China and Japan—in colonial Asia during the late nineteenth and early twentieth centuries, Thailand, then known as Siam, captured the attention and imagination of Chinese intellectuals who sought both inspiration and lessons for the embattled Chinese nation against foreign imperialism. The Qing Empire's relationship with Siam was founded primarily on trade and tribute. Although court annals upheld the Qing emperor's superior status in the Sinocentric tributary order by describing the Siamese as "barbaric" (蠻夷 *manyi*), they indicated that Siam was the major power in Indochina (Viraphol 1977; Guo 2006). In Chinese-language newspapers at the time, King Chulalongkorn (r. 1868–1910), widely revered by the Siamese and regarded by the Thais as their great modernizer, was described as an "enlightened ruler" (明君 *mingjun*) who, by adopting Western ideas and institutions, transformed Siam into a modern state (Wang 1880, 177). *Xifa* 西法 (Western methods) became a political topos for changing China, as suggested by the newspaper reports that covered the Franco-Siamese War (1893). These reports urged defeated Siam to continue its self-strengthening movement through Western methods, as China did after failing to defend Vietnam's sovereignty during the Sino-French War (1884–1885). By using terms relating to Chinese experiences of defeat, loss, and modernization to describe Siam, late Qing dynasty writers encouraged Siam as much as they urged China not to lose hope in its dire situation.[11]

Qing-era commentaries and reports on Siam might be considered the archetype of Thai studies in China, focusing on Siamese history and politics. They tended to adopt Sinocentric perspectives and most sustained the trend of evaluating Siam through Chinese experiences, albeit with a twist. They included comparing Siam's resurgence after the Franco-Siamese War with China's Tongzhi Restoration (c. 1860–1875),[12] describing how King Chulalongkorn visited Europe and sent his children overseas for Western education and praising Siam for being able to persuade Britain to abrogate its extraterritorial rights (Liu 1903, 22–23; Xu 1908, 8). China's setbacks in the late 1890s and early 1900s—its defeat in the 1894–1895 Sino-Japanese War, the conservative elite's rejection of the Hundred Days' Reform (1898), and the foreign occupation of Beijing during the Boxer Rebellion (1900)—convinced many Chinese intellectuals that they had to help arrest China's decline. Sardonic editorials praised Siam for having the foresight to "reform" (維新), unlike China, which "would not change until death" (至死不變).[13] The Chinese practice of comparing their experiences with those of Siam mirrored what literary scholar V. Y. Mudimbe calls "epistemological ethnocentrism," that is, that nothing can be learned from "them" unless it is already "ours" or comes from "us."[14] The trend of Sinocentric or China-dominant scholarship on Southeast Asia, which implicitly denies the autonomous histories of Siam and other polities, thus has a long history stretching back beyond the late Qing period.

Late Qing Chinese intellectuals accepted Westernization as a universal value, or unit of positive change, by distinguishing it from the imagined West that had humiliated or oppressed China. For them, Siam was a valuable model for successfully negotiating its passage to modernity and resisting foreign domination.[15] However, most intellectuals continued to hold the impression that Siam was a backward and weak nation compared to China; they believed that Siam's lead over China in economic development and political reform was only temporary. Even after Siam experienced a bloodless coup that replaced the absolute monarchy with a constitutional government in 1932, Chinese intellectuals continued to belittle Siam as a lesser partner in China's anti-imperialism. In their writings, Siam was either grouped with formal possessions such as British Singapore as a weak nation and colony or characterized as a lethargic nation that miraculously survived British and French imperialism (Chan 2020, 519–520). Although Chinese intellectuals recognized that both China and Siam shared the dubious reputation of being half-colonies and fellow sufferers of foreign imperialism, their tone toward Siam ranged from didactic to backslapping (Chan 2020, 520). As discussed in chapter 3, in the Asian theater of the Second World War, when the Thai state promoted Pan-Thai nationalism, an aggressive, militant, and radical ideology that called for Siam (renamed Thailand in 1939) to reclaim its "lost territories" of the Malay sultanates of Kedah, Kelantan, Perak, and Terengganu, the Shan States in British Burma, the French protectorates of Cambodia and Laos, and, pertinent to this chapter, the parts of Guangxi, Guizhou, and Yunnan that were populated by the Tai (傣) race, which Siam claimed as a branch of the Thai nation, many Chinese intellectuals mobilized to counter the Thai state's discourse, determine the "nature" of Tai minorities, and clarify the Tai peoples' status within the Chinese nation. Pan-Thai nationalism thus played a crucial role in developing not only Thai or Thailand studies but also what might retrospectively be considered "frontier studies" (邊疆學 *bianjiang xue*) in wartime China (Chan 2019).

After the founding of the People's Republic of China in 1949, frontier studies developed into a conceptual, supposedly scientific, tool to classify and rule the nationalities within China (Mullaney 2010). Outside China, Communist influences intensified Thailand's fear of its domestic Chinese population as a major national threat. As an ally of the United States, Thailand pursued anti-Communist policies. At the same time, however, Thai elites did not want to alienate China entirely, fearing a shift of wind in favor of the Soviet bloc during the Cold War; the Thai state's balancing act between China and the United States, identified by political scientists as a flexible form of "bamboo diplomacy," has continued to the present (Busbarat 2016). After the Sino-US rapprochement in the 1970s, the Thai government highlighted the decades-old "China and Thai are brothers" discourse and normalized Sino-Thai relations. Thai leaders used the discourse to justify the shift in foreign policy publicly and officially ended their involvement in the Vietnam War in the name of brotherly love for China, which reciprocated by suspending its aid to the Communist Party of Thailand. While Thailand is not the only country for which China has used such rhetoric to describe its relationship with other countries, Thailand does not have territorial disputes or issues of historical interpretation—except during the wartime period—with China, which makes its brotherhood discourse with China particularly convincing and powerful (Tungkeunkunt and Phuphakdi 2018). By the 1980s, Thailand and China enjoyed a cordial relationship, with Thai leaders considering China a role model for Thailand's economic development and cheap source of military equipment (Hewison 2018). For both Chinese and Thai scholars, fieldwork and academic conferences became possible after relations were normalized. Those from China took the opportunity to revive Thai studies after the Cultural Revolution.

However, the more favorable conditions for scholarly research created opportunities for collaboration and, less frequently, divisions between the Chinese and the Thais. The debate on the identity of Tai nationalities in China resurfaced, albeit in a more benign or cordial manner. Thai ministers had visited Yunnan and somewhat insensitively reported that they felt close to the Tai people, causing a stern reaction from Chinese officials, who feared that the Tais might identify with Thailand instead of China (Eaksittipong 2021). Thai scholars believed that the Tai people in China retained pristine Thai culture; understanding them was an antidote to Western capitalism that diluted Thainess. Chinese scholars wanted to emphasize the homogeneity of their nation as per the official discourse and downplay the uniqueness of Tai peoples within China. Consequently, although Chinese and Thai scholars studied the Tai nationalities for their respective purposes, they arrived at a similar conclusion that the Tais are diverse, defined by cultural pluralism across rigidly demarcated borders. Together, they debunked the claim that Nanzhao had been a Tai kingdom and that the modern Thais had evolved from a southward exodus of Tai peoples from modern-day Yunnan Province. Thai scholars thus argued that the domain of Thainess was static, and Thais of Chinese descent could be considered part of the Thai nation because they shared more traits with the Thais than did the Tai peoples outside Thailand. However, Chinese scholars contended that China was a unitary multinational state, with the majority Han ethnicity as the core. Haunted by the specter of Pan-Thai nationalism during the wartime period, Chinese scholars launched a somewhat informal campaign outside China, speaking at Thai universities and research institutes to dispute the dual theory of Nanzhao as a Tai kingdom and the Tai southward exodus (Eaksittipong 2017).

In China, research related to how the Tai nationalities formed an inseparable group of the Chinese nation was disseminated through many channels. The Institute of Southeast Asian Studies at the Yunnan Academy of Social Sciences spearheaded the dissemination. Numerous research articles on the issue were published in its flagship journal. When referring to Nanzhao, Chinese scholars used terms such as "local power" (地方政權 *difang zhengquan*) and "local separatist regime" (地方割據政權 *difang geju zhengquan*) to signify that the kingdom had always been a part of China. According to these scholars, the conflicts between Nanzhao and the Chinese dynastic court were caused by a selfish Nanzhao ruling class that acted against the people's longing for national unity. The Mongol conquest of Nanzhao did not result in an en masse migration of people to the south. Instead, the ancestors of the modern Thai people hailed from the northern part of the Indochinese peninsula, these scholars argued, so Nanzhao was not a Tai kingdom, and the southward exodus never occurred (Eaksittipong 2017, 108–109). The Yunnan institute invited Thai scholars and politicians to visit cultural sites in the province and see how different the Tai people were from the Thais. It also translated Thai writings supporting the Chinese discourse into Chinese and published them in its journal. The Chinese campaign operated in tandem with the Thai intellectual movement to reorientate the Thai past and desacralize Thai history, which was dominated by the idea of a homogenous Thai race (Eaksittipong 2017, 109–110). In Thailand during the 1980s, the emergence of Marxist-inspired history, after the political upheavals and student movements of the previous decade, helped include the Thai Chinese in Thai history. This new history inadvertently portrayed the Thai kings, once viewed as benevolent and charismatic monarchs, as bourgeois capitalists who allied with Western imperialists to exploit the Thai people and stunt the Thai economy. In the revamped Thai studies within Thailand, scholars examined the somewhat more positive role of the Chinese in Thai economic history and, consequently, the history of Chinese overseas in Thailand, which linked them to their counterparts in China who were studying the Sino-Thai or Thai Chinese. In China, specialists in Southeast Asian research benefited from their interactions with Thai scholars, who reinforced their argument that China and Thailand are brothers more in discourse than in reality (Eaksittipong 2017, 110–112).

Western scholarship, specifically Anglophone scholarship, also influenced Thai studies in China. As early as 1962, anthropologist G. William Skinner's classic *Chinese Society in Thailand: An Analytical History* (1957) had been partly translated into Chinese and serialized in *Southeast Asian Studies: A Quarterly Journal of Translations* 南洋問題資料譯叢, a journal published by the Nanyang Institute of Xiamen University. During the Cold War, the Chinese Communist state hoped to reference the book in devising policies toward the Chinese in Thailand. During the late 1970s, after Sino-Thai diplomatic relations were established, Beijing ordered the Yunnan Institute of History to conduct a research project to help remove animosity between China and Thailand by deploying history as a tool. China's first ambassador to Thailand visited the institute in Yunnan. Chinese scholars dispatched to Thailand for fieldwork published learned articles intended for internal distribution among Chinese diplomats and experts in Southeast Asian affairs. Senior researchers from Sun Yat-sen University and Xiamen University also joined the project. The Chinese government elevated the project to become a state-level enterprise involving the major centers of Southeast Asian studies in China. Skinner's book was widely cited in the project's research writings, which accepted Skinner's assimilation paradigm and tended to highlight the

Sino-Thais' contributions to modern Thailand. This line of argument suited the Chinese state's aim to establish trust and cordial relations with Thailand.[16]

However, it was only in the 2010s that the first institutes of Thai studies were established in China. Unsurprisingly, the first such institute was founded in none other than Yunnan Province in 2010, in time for the thirty-fifth anniversary of the normalization of China-Thailand relations. Yunnan's Center of Thai Studies focuses on international relations and has an advisory board of diplomats, former ambassadors, and foreign scholars, working to promote the long-term relationship between China and Thailand (Center of Thai Studies 2022). Other institutes of Thai studies were subsequently set up at Sichuan University in 2013, Changzhou University in 2013, and Guiyang University in 2015 (Wang and Zhu 2020, 1). These universities and research institutes aim to carve out a niche in Thai studies, offering degree and language programs; many of their institutes of Thai studies developed from the latter. For instance, Sichuan University's Institute of Thai Studies came from an initial collaboration with Thailand's Chiang Mai University back in 2010, when Thai faculty helped establish a Thai cultural and language learning center in Sichuan (Wang and Zhu 2020, 1). China's institutes of Thai studies were visited by Thai dignitaries, including Princess Sirindhorn, who often served as their honorary patroness. Guiyang University founded its Research Center for Thai Studies to help integrate Guizhou Province in the BRI and strengthen cultural and social ties between China and Thailand.[17] In addition to the existing institutes of Thai studies, Sun Yat-sen University's Institute of Southeast Asian Studies fostered China's academic diplomacy and forged China-Thailand academic relations. With its forte in studies of Chinese overseas, the institute at Sun Yat-sen University invited Thai scholars and politicians, especially those of Chinese ancestry, to Guangdong Province and held academic discussions with its faculty. The Thai delegates were then taken to their ancestral hometowns in the province and King Taksin's cenotaph, which was loaded with cultural and historical meanings. Visiting their ancestral hometowns helped strengthen the bond between Thais of Chinese descent and China while visiting King Taksin's cenotaph conveyed China's goodwill to Thailand. To cater to rising interest in King Taksin among the Thais, the Chinese government repaired the cenotaph, which had been raided during the Cultural Revolution, and used it as a symbol of cordial China-Thailand relations (Eaksittipong 2021, 114–115).

Over a century, Thai studies in China had been transformed from a source of exotic imagination and political inspiration into a tool of academic diplomacy and informal exchanges. Thai studies in China resulted in changing perceptions of Thailand, ranging from a backward kingdom to a progressive nation, brotherly people, and friendly partner, and the constant reinforcement of historical narratives that denied the identity of the Nanzhao kingdom as Tai and emphasized the positive role of the Chinese in Thailand to the modern Thai nation helped sustain the cordial relations between China and Thailand. As China continues to weaken Thailand's alliance ties with the United States,[18] and as Thailand looks set to become one of China's most essential partners in mainland Southeast Asia (Ciorciari 2020, 311), the future of Thai studies in China appears promising, with the Chinese and Thai states sponsoring their scholars and setting up new institutes to cultivate the field. This is particularly important for China in seeking regional consensus that its high-speed rail project and plans for damming the Mekong River are beneficial to Thailand and other countries in mainland Southeast Asia. That said, a caveat is in order. As the state becomes the dominant patron of Thai studies, a little leeway is open to the autonomous histories of Thailand and the Tai people, the Nanzhao kingdom, and other subjects that are perceived as seditious.

CONCLUSION

This chapter has discussed how China's politics and geopolitical environment have conditioned the emergence of Southeast Asian studies as a scholarly discipline in the country. Since the late nineteenth century, Chinese intellectuals, exposed to Western methods of critical inquiry and perceiving the world through maps and dividing it into nation-states for analysis, have reconfigured their worldviews and viewed neighboring Southeast Asian polities, depending on their status, more as colonies or nations than as tributary states that had deferred to dynastic empires based in China. As some Chinese intellectuals evolved into specialists in area studies, they identified Siam (Thailand), the Dutch East Indies (Indonesia), the Philippines, Singapore, and others as their units of analysis and examined their culture, history, identity, and society. Over time, these experts realized that Southeast Asia was more than the sum of its parts. They set up institutes of Southeast Asian studies, mostly under state funding and patronage, at universities. Depending on their history and objectives, these universities and research institutes revived Southeast Asian studies as a niche discipline after the Cultural Revolution, which curtailed academic discussions within China and with the people of newly decolonized and independent Southeast Asian nations. After the 1980s, the political and geopolitical influences on Southeast Asian studies became more pronounced, and Southeast Asian studies developed further by fulfilling the Chinese government's desire to reengage and understand the region for strategic needs. The rise of ASEAN studies, a subset of Southeast Asian studies that focuses on the contemporary aspects of international relations and political economy in the regional bloc, may be regarded as a response to such needs, especially in the light of serving the BRI. The case of Thai studies illuminates the historical trajectory assumed by Southeast Asian studies, which has become a tool of academic diplomacy and a repertoire of resources for policymaking, domestic propaganda, and foreign relations.

But just as Southeast Asian studies has been understood to be more than a sum of its parts, the discipline encompasses meanings that stretch beyond politics and geopolitics, which might have necessitated its emergence but do not fully control its implications for non-state actors and the broader Chinese society. With China's knowledge production of Southeast Asia as a backdrop, the following chapters will discuss how the Chinese conducted business and people-to-people exchanges with their partners in Southeast Asia, informed by what they already knew in their country.

NOTES

1. The "Quad" of Australia, India, Japan, and the United States have announced the Free and Open Indo-Pacific (FOIP) initiative to balance China's influence. At work in the same vein, Taiwan's New Southbound Policy and South Korea's New Southern Policy have begun to make their presence felt in Southeast Asia. Britain, France, and Germany, which had colonized parts of (Southeast) Asia, are sending their navies into the South China Sea. See Qi (2019).

2. See Zawacki (2017).

3. A notable source of inspiration was the Philippines, whose people had lost their colonial wars against Spanish and American forces but had gained respect from Chinese intellectuals who bothered to look beyond Japan and the West in producing their nationalistic discourses. See Karl (2002).

4. See Schwarcz (1986).

5. See Suryadinata (2006, 34–37).

6. See Wang (2006, 103–104).

7. See Zhang (2006, 78).

8. The other claimants are Brunei, Malaysia, the Philippines, and Taiwan.

9. See Collaborative Innovation Center of Territorial Sovereignty and Maritime Rights, Zhengzhou University Branch, accessed February 11, 2022, http://www7.zzu .edu.cn/cictsmr_zzub/fzxgk1/fzxyg.htm.

10. See Lau (2015).

11. See Chan (2020, 518).

12. See Wang (1899, 18–21).

13. See Liu (1905, 3–4).

14. See Mudimbe (1988, 15).

15. For China's internalization of Western ideas and values, see Dirlik (1996).

16. For more on how *Chinese Society in Thailand* had been a project of Cold War ideologies and tensions, see Eaksittipong (2020).

17. See Research Center for Thai Studies, Guiyang University, accessed February 11, 2022, http://tgyjzx.gyu.cn/info/1073/1065.htm.

18. See Fingar (2020, 51).

Chapter 5

Responding to China's Soft Power

The Case of Indonesia

In its ascent to superpower, China has been actively engaging in cultural diplomacy and investing in the promotion of soft power by reaching out to the global audience through international communication (Chen et al. 2012). According to Nye (1990), soft power involves indirect or co-optive control to influence others through attraction rather than coercion. Besides providing aid, financial assistance, and exporting the "China model" of development, China's soft power strategy encompasses the global expansion of its premier state television channel, the CCTV, in English and other languages; establishment of Confucius Institutes around the world; funding international academic exchanges; and commissioning international outreach programs (Rawnsley 2012). The objectives for China to build its soft power are to help China rectify anti-China sentiment posed by the "discourse war" with the west (Shambaugh 2015) and to fend off the "China threat" argument for China to assure the world of its peaceful rise (Zhou and Luk 2016, 628).[1]

The global rise of the Chinese language and culture, also known as the "Mandarin Fever" (Hoon and Kuntjara 2019; Koh et al. 2021), is not a passive consequence of global development but a strategic part of China's proactive public diplomacy. The purpose is to help China build harmonious relations with neighboring countries and project a benign image on the world stage (Liu and Tsai 2014). China has been promoting Chinese culture and language by establishing the Office of Chinese Language Council International (漢辦 Hanban) in 1987, which set the path for Confucius Institutes to be exported worldwide. However, the geopolitical rivalry between the United States and China in recent years has seen the Confucius Institute vilified in the West as a part of the foreign mission and propaganda apparatus of the Chinese Communist Party, which led to its closure in many parts of the United States and Europe. As a result of these controversies, Hanban was rebranded as the Centre for Language Education and Cooperation in June

2020, and a non-governmental charitable organization named the Chinese International Education Foundation was formed to take over the responsibility of developing the Confucius Institute and its financial resources.[2] With now 40 Confucius Institutes spanning ASEAN countries, Chheang (2021) argues that "while Confucius Institutes have lost momentum in the West over concerns about foreign influence, censorship, and academic freedom, they have enjoyed more traction in Southeast Asia."

China has also carefully calibrated international higher education as a state-craft to serve its foreign policy and diplomacy. Before the 1978 Reform and Opening-Up Policy, international students in China mainly originated from Eastern Europe, Vietnam, and the Soviet Union. They shared a similar political ideology to the Chinese Communist Party. After 1978, the foreign student population comprised students from countries where China shared proximity and economic interests (Theo 2018, 23–24). After the Cold War and with the rise of China, international education was further utilized as a soft power instrument to target diasporic Chinese and international students for them to serve, or at least be sympathetic to, China's broader interests (Suryadinata 2017). As Shambaugh (2021, 159) asserts, Chinese bureaucrats are hoping to produce international graduates who "know China and are friendly to China" (知華友華) so that they can become "ambassadors" to convey a positive image of China upon return to their home countries. Although Cai (2020) calls this an "illusion" of the Chinese government, the strategy is in line with the current state campaign of "telling China's story well" (講好中國故事). This political discourse first appeared in a speech by President Xi Jinping at the National Propaganda and Ideology Work Conference in August 2013 during the first year of his administration.

The launch of the "Outline of China's National Plan for Medium and Long-term Education Reform and Development (2010–20)" and the "Study in China" plan by the Chinese Ministry of Education in 2010 was a clear signal of the government's commitment to the further opening up of China's education system (Theo 2018, 25; Cai 2020). The national plan aimed to introduce quality education resources abroad and promote and upgrade international exchanges and cooperation. It also set a target of 500,000 international students in higher education institutions, elementary and secondary schools, and 150,000 in degree programs by 2020. This target was almost met in 2018 when the total number of international students in Chinese higher education reached 492,185, overtaking the United Kingdom as the world's second-largest host to international students after the United States (Cai 2020). In 2019, the Chinese State Council published the China's Education Modernization 2035 plan, which would see the continuation of the Study in China plan but with a shift in focus from quantity to quality (Cai 2020). This is seemingly a move in the right direction, as Rawnsley (2012, 123) reminds us that soft power is an intangible long-term process, and quantifiable measures of outputs reveal little about the impact.

How do Southeast Asian countries respond to China's education campaign? Students from Southeast Asia in China gradually emerged almost a decade after the normalization of China-ASEAN diplomatic relations in 1990 (see table 5.1). In August 2010, the "Double 100,000 Plan" was declared in a meeting between China and ASEAN Ministers of Education in Guiyang. The ambitious plan aimed to exchange 100,000 Chinese and ASEAN students to each other's campuses by 2020 (Welch 2014, 115). The number of Southeast Asian students in China rose further after President Xi Jinping announced the Belt and Road Initiative (BRI) in 2013 (Gong and Wu 2020). One of the five primary goals of the BRI is to promote "people-to-people (P2P) ties" (民心相通), which entails the deepening of mutual understanding between the people of the countries involved in the BRI. Education exchanges play a significant role in fostering P2P ties, as outlined in the "Education Action Plan for the Belt and Road Initiative" released by the Chinese Ministry of Education in 2016 (MoE 2018b). To promote P2P exchanges, the Chinese government, provincial government, and individual universities have offered generous scholarships for international students to study in China. The most relevant to ASEAN students are the China-AUN (ASEAN University Network) Scholarship, Guangxi Government Scholarship for ASEAN Students, and the Silk Road Scholarship that supports up to 10,000 students from BRI countries each year.[3] In 2018, 20 percent of international students in China came from Southeast Asia (MoE 2018a). As shown in table 5.1, the most significant number came from Thailand, followed by Indonesia, Laos, Vietnam, Malaysia, Myanmar, Singapore, Cambodia, the Philippines, and Brunei Darussalam. From the perspective of China, providing scholarships to Southeast Asian students is a strategic investment in "cultivating China-friendly talents" (培養友華人才) who can help to promote the BRI and become a bridge for bilateral relations (Gong and Wu 2020, 237).

Table 5.1 shows that in two decades from 1999 to 2018, the number of Southeast Asian students in China had increased by 20 times.[4] Such dramatic increase was driven by the economic impetus related to the rise of China, given the promising job prospects at home for graduates who are Mandarin literate and "China-ready" (Hoon and Kuntjara 2019). To understand the dynamics of Southeast Asian students in China and the effectiveness of China's soft power through higher education, this chapter will focus on the case of Indonesia. Being the largest and most populous country in Southeast Asia, Indonesia has had a troubled and tumultuous relationship with its Chinese minority and China throughout Indonesian history. Indonesia was one of the first countries to establish diplomatic relations with the People's Republic of China in 1950 and had enjoyed close ties with Beijing under

Table 5.1. Number of Southeast Asian Students in China from 1999 to 2018

Year	Philippines	Cambodia	Laos	Malaysia	Myanmar	Thailand	Brunei	Singapore	Indonesia	Vietnam	Total
1999	185	115	278	454	49	512	0	466	2411	471	4941
2000	217	121	298	490	123	667	27	854	1947	647	5391
2001	456	89	312	632	149	860	4	344	1697	1170	5713
2002	638	151	333	840	232	1737	4	583	2583	2336	9437
2003	602	139	403	841	232	1554	4	551	2563	3487	10376
2004	1375	180	509	1241	397	2371	6	929	3750	4382	15140
2005	2176	188	569	1589	494	3594	7	1322	4616	5842	20397
2006	1512	221	833	1743	538	5522	10	1392	5652	7310	24733
2007	1335	225	943	1908	645	7306	13	1480	6590	9702	30147
2008	2362	330	116[1]	2114	652	8476	36	2155	7084	10396	34766
2009	2273	406	1557	2792	1026	11379	22	3198	7926	12247	42826
2010	2989	502	1859	3885	972	13177	31	3608	9539	13018	49580
2011	2662	775	2395	4259	1529	14145	36	4483	10957	13549	54790
2012	2642	1336	2773	6045	1872	16675	44	4250	13144	13038	61819
2013	2917	1390	3999	6126	2299	20106	29	5290	13492	12799	68447
2014	2829	1446	5040	6645	2317	21296	10	5031	13689	10658	68961
2015	3343	1829	6918	6650	4733	19976	8	4865	12694	10031	71047
2016	3061	2250	9907	6880	5662	23044	55	4983	14714	10639	81195
2017	4442	3016	14222	7948	6233	27884	121	5259	14573	11311	95009
2018	2786	4047	14645	9479	8573	28608	112	4718	15050	11299	99317

Sources: Data from 1999 to 2013 were adapted from Fang (2013, 80), and data from 2014–2018 reports on "Concise Statistics on International Students in China," published by Department of International Cooperation and Exchanges, Ministry of Education, The People's Republic of China (MoE 2014, 2015, 2016, 2017 and 2018a). We thank Kaili Zhao for helping us gather the data.

President Sukarno. However, the relationship was frozen by the succeeding president, Suharto, in the aftermath of the alleged Communist coup in 1965 (Anwar 2019). While the Indonesia-China relations were normalized in 1990, it was only after the fall of President Suharto in 1998 that the bilateral ties began to strengthen. Although the post-Suharto democratization and *Reformasi* processes brought cultural liberalization for Chinese Indonesians, anti-Chinese sentiment remained a sensitive issue easily stirred at times of political unrest. The increasing presence of Chinese FDI in Indonesia has led to the "Mandarin Fever" manifest in a sharp rise of Mandarin learners and the pursuit of higher education in China among Indonesians. In light of this situation, the present chapter examines how P2P exchanges in higher education have contributed to public diplomacy and how non-state actors such as students can bridge the cultural gulf between Indonesia and China.

INDONESIA, CHINA, AND CHINESE INDONESIANS

Indonesia was one of the earliest countries in ASEAN to establish diplomatic relation with China in 1950, under Sukarno, Indonesia's first president. However, the relationship lasted less than twenty years when President Suharto suspended it in 1967. For more than three decades under Suharto's New Order regime (1966 to 1998), the Indonesian government negatively perceived China for Beijing's alleged role in the abortive Communist coup of September 30, 1965 (Zhou 2019). The "Communist" coup attempt provided the legitimacy for a military offensive against the Indonesian Communist Party and the ethnic Chinese. After the coup, a surge of anti-Communist and anti-Chinese sentiment swept through the country as Indonesia witnessed one of the "worst bloodbaths in modern Asian history" (Williams 1991, 149). The "China threat" discourse widely held by the political elites was actively transmitted to the Indonesian public during the New Order. Such discourse was characterized by the suspicion that the ethnic Chinese in Indonesia might potentially be a "fifth column" of China that could help the Communists make a political comeback (Herlijanto 2017b). The climate of suspicion resulted in distrust of the ethnic Chinese by the Indonesian state and society, which justified their discrimination and cultural oppression (Sukma 1999, 143–145). The perception of the "China threat" did not wane even with the fall of President Suharto in 1998. Indonesian scholars argue that anti-Communism discourse is still a powerful tool for political mobilization to create a "common enemy," especially during the elections. However, such a threat has become less relevant to the younger generation (Rohman et al. 2020, 46). Despite the improvement of Indonesia-China relations after 1998, Indonesia's engagement with China remains cautious, fearing potential backlash from domestic forces that still view China with suspicion (Herlijanto 2017a).

Perceptions of China in Post-Suharto Indonesia

Herlijanto (2013) argues that the perception of China within contemporary Indonesian society is mainly positive. His study shows that China has been successful in disseminating the discourse of its economic transformation to Indonesians. This is reflected in the Indonesian public discourse of "learn from China," which suggests Indonesia emulate China's development model, especially when juxtaposed against the failing condition of their own country (Herlijanto 2013, 208). More recent surveys reported the similar favorable sentiment of Indonesians toward China, albeit with some reservations about conflicting economic interests and security issues. For example, the findings from the 2017 Indonesia National Survey Project conducted by ISEAS-Yusof Ishak Institute in Singapore found that 76.7 percent of Indonesian respondents reported to "admire" China. However, this figure was ranked the lowest when compared with respondents who admired Singapore (85.6 percent), Malaysia (85.3 percent), Thailand (82.8 percent), Australia (79.5 percent), and the United States (79.3 percent). Similarly, although 77.3 percent of the respondents viewed China as "important" to Indonesia, this figure stood the lowest compared to their perception of the relative importance of the other countries. When asked whether they think the rise of China will bring positive or negative impact to Indonesia, 41 percent of the respondents answered "positive," and slightly more than 39 percent responded "negative." Furthermore, most respondents (62.4 percent) think that close economic ties with China will only bring a slight benefit to Indonesia (Fossati et al. 2017, 40–46).

According to Weatherbee (2017), the post-Suharto engagement with China began with President Abdurrahman Wahid, who restored many of the citizenship rights of the ethnic Chinese and articulated a "look to Asia" policy in his brief term from 1999 to 2001. His successor, President Megawati Sukarnoputri, further warmed the ties with China using her cachet as Sukarno's daughter. The seeds planted by Wahid and Megawati led to the historic declaration of "Indonesia-China strategic partnership" in 2005 under President Susilo Bambang Yudhoyono. This was upgraded to a "comprehensive strategic partnership" in 2013 that saw further expansion of trade, investment, and soft credit (Weatherbee 2017). The present era of President Joko Widodo (popularly known as Jokowi) marks another period of significant improvement in bilateral relations between Indonesia and China. For instance, China was the first country that Jokowi visited after he won the 2014 election. He has visited China four times in the seven years of his presidency as of 2021, more than any other former Indonesian president (Wattimena 2021, 44).

Under Jokowi's administration, bilateral ties between the two countries continued to strengthen across different spheres: political (Goh 2018), economic (Aisyah 2018), and military (Parameswaran 2018), even though historically, the armed forces were very hostile toward China. Tjhin (2012) argues that such development signifies the waning of Indonesia's perception of China as an ideological threat. As Indonesia's largest trading partner, China's BRI and FDI in Indonesia play a complementary role with Jokowi's ambitious vision of developing Indonesia into a global maritime fulcrum. Indonesia's economy had improved during the first term of President Jokowi (2014–2019) and is expected to further progress in his second term from 2019 to 2024 (Negara 2019). Kishore Mahbubani (2021) described such improvement as "the genius of Jokowi." The economic cooperation between Indonesia and China reached a new height with various Chinese infrastructure projects in Indonesia under the BRI, the Jakarta-Bandung high-speed rail construction, and China's planned involvement in building the smart city technology for the future new capital of Indonesia in Kalimantan, Borneo.

Notwithstanding the much-improved relations between Indonesia and China, scholars argue that Indonesian elites' perception of China is still divided. Some of them are notably worried about Indonesia's growing reliance on Chinese loans, the influx of Chinese workers, and the South China Sea security threats (Herlijanto 2017a). In his study of the perception of 50 Indonesian diplomats on the BRI, Yeremia (2020, 43) found the responses of his informants to represent "a high level of perceptual sophistication": that is, while their responses are somewhat favorable, "the presence of some negative perceptions of China's intentions does not prevent these diplomats from seeing positive aspects of this grand initiative." His findings suggest that Indonesia should engage cautiously with the BRI (Yeremia 2020, 44). However, the level of distrust of China among the Indonesian grassroots has also increased. According to the "State of Southeast Asia 2021" survey conducted by the ISEAS-Yusof Ishak Institute, 60.5 percent of Indonesian respondents do not trust China, and a majority of them think that China's economic and military power could be used to threaten Indonesia's interest and sovereignty (Seah et al. 2021, 42–43). The close economic relations between Jokowi's administration and China have prompted widespread conspiracy theory that Jokowi was China's puppet to sell out Indonesia for China's economic gains (Rakhmat and Aryanshah 2020). Cognizant of the domestic forces of nationalism and Islamism that used China's growing economic presence in Indonesia to undermine Jokowi's legitimacy, the administration's policy on China endeavored to strike a balance between economic development involving China and exhibiting nationalism and religiosity to appease local pressure groups (Yeremia 2021). The trust deficit of Indonesians toward China shows that China's soft power and cultural diplomacy have yet to succeed in promoting mutual understanding on the P2P level in Indonesia.

The Legacy of Anti-Chinese Sentiment

Scholars have observed that the ties between Indonesia and China have always been entangled with Indonesian domestic politics, particularly about its ethnic Chinese minority (Anwar 2019; Hiebert 2020, 437). Such intertwinement is characterized by how anti-China sentiments are conflated with views against Indonesians of Chinese descent. Representing 1.2 percent of Indonesia's population of approximately 270 million, the Chinese minority was described by Wang (1976) as "unique" because of their problematic identity as Indonesia's perennial outsiders (Sai and Hoon 2013). This minority suffered a long history of persecution since the first ethnic cleansing carried out by the Dutch in Java in 1740. They were rendered convenient targets of social hostility at different historical periods, culminating in the violence of May 1998 (Hoon 2008, 45). Even though the Chinese have lived in the archipelago for many generations, especially some of the *peranakan* who have lineages extending back to the 1600s (Pan 1990), many *pribumi* (lit. "persons of the soil," "native" or "indigenous" Indonesians) continue to treat them as outsiders or foreigners. It can be argued that the racial hierarchy used in colonial divide and rule policy had artificially created a Chinese minority in the Dutch East Indies. The Dutch policies implanted the historical seeds of prejudice that occasionally flourished into the tension between the ethnic Chinese and the *pribumi*, at the same time producing Chineseness. This constructed Chineseness later became a political tool manipulated by postcolonial Indonesian regimes for political gains.

The ethnic Chinese were repeatedly targeted as scapegoats during times of national crisis, such as the 1965 abortive coup and the 1998 Asian financial crisis. The birth and death of President Suharto's regime were marked by anti-Chinese violence. The difficult position of the ethnic Chinese as a pariah is described in 1960 by the late writer Pramoedya Ananta Toer (1998, 54) as "foreigners who are not foreign." These words were published in response to the Presidential Instruction 10/1959 (known as the PP-10)—a discriminatory policy implemented by President Sukarno to prohibit the Chinese from trading in rural areas. This policy caused more than 100,000 ethnic Chinese to leave Indonesia for China (Mandal 1998). Together with Chinese Indonesian students who pursued higher education in China in the 1950s and 1960s, and those who fled Indonesia to escape the terror of the anti-Communist purge between 1966 and 1967, there were at least 164,000 Chinese Indonesians "returnees" (歸僑 *guiqiao*) living in China by the end of the 1960s (Zhou

2019, 191). Most of them lived on the overseas Chinese farms located in the Southern provinces of Fujian, Guangdong, and Hainan. They were treated as outsiders by the Chinese nationals, as they were by the *pribumi* when they were in Indonesia. They were distrusted in China because of "overseas connections"; they were attacked as "imperialists," "spies," "mongrels," and "foreign devils"; and their patriotism and "Chineseness" were called into question (Godley and Coppel 1990, 180). Nonetheless, the *guiqiao* eventually became an essential force for China to attract overseas Chinese investment after the state implemented Deng Xiaoping's Reform and Opening-Up Policy in the late 1970s (Zhou 2019, 210).

However, in Suharto's Indonesia, Chineseness was subject to state suppression and was considered a security threat associated with Communism. According to Allen (2003, 387), the ethnic Chinese—their culture, their religion, their role in the nation's economy, and their very existence—were labeled *Masalah Cina* (the Chinese Problem). To manage this "problematic" minority, the state implemented a military-backed assimilation policy to prohibit all expressions of Chineseness in the public sphere, including Chinese names, schools, organizations, media, and cultural practices. The fact that printed matter in Chinese characters fell under prohibited imports like narcotics, pornography, and explosives when entering Indonesia is a testament to the gravity of the regime's treatment of Chineseness as a menace to the nation (Heryanto 1999). Even though this paranoia faded after Sino-Indonesian relations were normalized in 1990, anti-Chinese sentiment did not. An article written by a New Order military officer, Letjen TNI (Purn) Sayidiman Suryohadiprojo (1997), calling for Chinese Indonesians to assimilate through compulsory military conscription, shows that the regime, especially the military, was still suspicious that Communist China might use the Chinese overseas for its agenda.

While the ethnic Chinese were given the privilege to expand the nation's economy and their wealth, they were paradoxically marginalized and discriminated against in all social spheres (Hoon 2008). This continuous and intentional discrimination placed them in a vulnerable position of ethnic and class hostility. In 1998, when Indonesia was devastated by the financial crisis sweeping through East and Southeast Asia, there were mounting pressures from the public calling for President Suharto to resign. The government, however, made the ethnic Chinese scapegoats and held them responsible for the economic turmoil (Budiman 2001, 279–280). Massive anti-Chinese riots broke out in May 1998, giving vent to the surfacing of anti-Chinese sentiment. Property of the ethnic Chinese was ransacked, looted, and burned down, and there were physical attacks on the Chinese and rapes of Chinese women. The reaction of the Chinese government toward the atrocities in Indonesia was noticeably restrained. The riots happened when China was emerging from the Cold War and had just restored bilateral relations with Indonesia in 1990, which it did not want to damage (Weatherbee 2017). Moreover, as the ethnic Chinese were Indonesian citizens, it was not in China's interest to interfere in Indonesia's domestic affairs (Suryadinata 2017, 62).

The 2017 Indonesia National Survey Project shows a worrying trend of re-emerging anti-Chinese sentiment in Indonesia (Fossati et al. 2017, 24–26). The survey confirmed the longstanding stereotypes of Chinese Indonesians as wealthy and having questionable loyalty to Indonesia. It also highlighted various negative prejudices against the influence of Chinese Indonesians in national politics and the economy. As Setijadi (2017, 11) notes, "[t]he results of the survey are alarming because they show that, despite the reforms of the past two decades, old stereotypes of ethnic Chinese still persist and are perhaps stronger than before" (cf. Kuntjara and Hoon 2020). More recently, Rakhmat and Aryanshah (2020) observed another wave of anti-Chinese sentiment in Indonesia, which they claimed to be a domestic reaction toward China's "inhumane policy towards the Uighurs." The Uighurs issue is only a smokescreen to the causes of the renewed hatred toward the Chinese, which are more precisely related to the Islamic "conservative turn," religious nationalism and the ongoing issue of economic inequality.

Scholars argue that 2004 was the watershed moment for the "conservative turn" in Indonesia, for radical Islamic forces began to aggressively dominate the public sphere (van Bruinessen 2013). The most vivid example of the latent intolerance toward the Chinese minority after the 1998 riots was the mass rallies of radical Islamists against the ethnic Chinese Christian candidate, Basuki Tjahaja Purnama (popularly known as Ahok), before the 2017 Jakarta gubernatorial election. After losing the election in April 2017, Ahok was sentenced to two years in prison for defaming the Holy Quran in a speech he gave during his election campaign, which was construed as blasphemous and insulting. On November 4 and December 2, 2016, between 100,000 and 500,000 people participated in anti-Ahok rallies in Jakarta demanding his arrest and prosecution. Strangio (2020, 239) contends that from the start, Ahok's blasphemy campaign was marked by anti-China and anti-Chinese rhetoric, which was seen in the banners held by demonstrators that read, "Crush the Chinese" (*Ganjang Cina*).

Ahok's opponents had linked him to China-sponsored megaprojects in Jakarta that they claimed would bring millions of Chinese nationals to Indonesia, which raised local anxieties that Communist China might control Indonesia (Yeremia 2021, 336). The large-scale anti-Ahok rallies reawakened the fear and trauma of the ethnic Chinese, reminding them of the anti-Chinese riots of 1998 (*BBC News* 2017). During the election, Ahok's rival candidate, Anies Baswedan, opportunistically exploited racial and religious fault lines during the election in his repeated appeal for voters to choose a

Muslim *pribumi* as their leader. In his inauguration speech on October 16, 2017, at the Presidential Palace in Jakarta, Baswedan emphasized that indigenous Indonesians should be the masters of their own home: "In the past, we *pribumi* were oppressed and defeated. Now we have independence, now is the time to be the host in our own home" (Simanjuntak 2017). The discourse of "indigenism" (Chen 2022) articulated by the governor once again evoked the marginal position of the ethnic Chinese in Indonesia as the internal outsiders.

THE MANDARIN FEVER AND THE STUDY IN CHINA WAVE

The collapse of the Suharto regime in 1998 marked the end of the authoritarian New Order era and the beginning of a new democratic era of reformation (*Reformasi*) in Indonesia. The post-Suharto era is characterized by substantial legal reforms, including revocation of discriminatory citizenship laws and religious and cultural expressions concerning the ethnic Chinese (Hoon 2008). From being a stigmatized and suppressed identity, Chineseness has become a celebrated ethno-commodity in Indonesia (Sai and Hoon 2013). The unprecedented proliferation of Indonesians who take up the Chinese language after *Reformasi* has been referred to by scholars as the "Mandarin Fever" (Hoon and Kuntjara 2019). After the government lifted the prohibition to teach Chinese in 1999, Chinese studies departments in universities, private Chinese language learning centers, and trilingual schools that use Indonesian, English, and Chinese as their medium of instruction mushroomed across Indonesia (Hoon 2008).

Since 2007, seven Confucius Institutes have been established in Indonesia to promote Chinese language and culture among Indonesians and ethnic Chinese who have lost the language and cultural familiarity. Besides Confucius Institutes, China has also invested in the U2U (university to university), a track two diplomacy scheme, to promote P2P exchange with Indonesia through student exchange, scholar exchange, and long-term cooperation (Wattimena 2021, 68). However, the "Mandarin Fever" phenomenon in Indonesia must be read closely with the rise of China because learning Mandarin is instrumentally driven by pragmatic economic factors such as to increase career opportunities and competitiveness rather than by cultural affinity such as to identify with China and its culture. The same economic reason is observed among *pribumi* Indonesians who learn Chinese. Mandarin proficiency has become very attractive in the Indonesian market as it fetches a higher salary with the growing commercial demands in areas like education, business, translation, and tourism (Hoon and Kuntjara 2019).

The soaring demands for Mandarin proficiency in Indonesia have also driven a proliferation of Indonesian students to study in China. Table 5.1 shows that Indonesian students in China rose from 2,411 in 1999 to more than 15,000 in 2018, making Indonesians the seventh-largest foreign student population in China (MoE 2018a). It was also reported that in 2017, Beijing announced 197 undergraduate and graduate scholarships for Indonesians, a sharp rise from merely 15 of such scholarships in 2015 (Llewellyn 2018a). On top of that, the Chinese government has offered 600 technical education scholarships and 1,500 scholarships for short courses to Indonesian nationals (RICH 2020, 30). Due to the closure of Chinese schools for more than three decades, there has been a severe shortage of Chinese teachers to cater to the post-Suharto Chinese language boom in Indonesia. Among the majors, Chinese language and teaching Chinese as a foreign language are the first choice for most Indonesian students in China (Gunawan 2018).

While the new opportunities offered by getting an education in China have attracted Indonesians from different ethnicity, religion, and social class, Chinese Indonesians still dominate the population of Indonesian students in China. Scholars have noted that Chinese Indonesian parents who were deprived of a Chinese education have encouraged their children to study in China, hoping that they can reidentify with their cultural heritage (Gunawan 2018; Theo 2018). However, like some of their "returnee" predecessors in the 1950s and 1960s, many Chinese Indonesian students felt foreign in China and preferred to acquaint themselves with the Indonesian community there (Wattimena 2021). Theo (2018, 106) observes that some Chinese Indonesian students had acquired their "Indonesianness" or expressed Indonesian nationalism in China through participating in the cultural activities organized by the Indonesian Students' Association. Ironically, such identification was not present in Indonesia, where they were Othered as outsiders. While the motive for these millennial Chinese Indonesians is more pragmatic than cultural, Theo (2018, 62) argues that all three aspects of cultural, political, and economic factors must be considered to have a comprehensive understanding of the phenomenon of Indonesian student mobility to China. As she explains,

> It is an economically driven mobility amidst the current logic of economic globalization. It is also a politically driven mobility, due to both countries' political reforms and freshening bilateral cooperation. It is a culturally driven mobility that resulted from a long cultural silencing and identity politics.

"Seek Knowledge as Far as China": The Experience of Indonesian Muslims in China

The discourse of "learning from China" in Indonesia has been promulgated among the Muslims through the oft-cited hadith (teachings of Prophet Muhammad) that urges them to "seek knowledge as far as China" (Theo 2018, 59). This is partly behind China's success in recruiting Muslim Indonesian students, especially the *santri* (devout Muslim students who attend Islamic boarding schools) affiliated with Nahdlatul Ulama (NU), the most prominent Islamic organization in Indonesia. NU plays a vital role in Indonesian politics by holding a "traditionalist" and moderate religious view. This is demonstrated in the appointment of the current vice president of Indonesia, Maaruf Amin, who was NU's former chairman. Since 1998, various Chinese Indonesian Muslim organizations have been socializing the knowledge about Islam in China to their fellow Indonesians. Their objective is to trace Indonesian Islam to a Chinese origin to legitimize Chinese Muslims in Indonesia as authentically Indonesians. The claims that early propagation of Islam in the archipelago was carried out by the Ming dynasty admiral Cheng Ho and that some of the saints (*walisanga*) of Indonesian Islam have Chinese ancestry were among such authentication strategies. They have also built Chinese-style mosques (known as the Masjid Cheng Ho) in various cities in Indonesia and organized study trips for Indonesian Muslim leaders from NU and Muhammadiyah to visit Muslim organizations and observe Muslim life in China (Hew 2014). These efforts have helped to contribute to the positive reception of China by NU and other moderate Muslims amid the climate of growing religious conservatism and nationalism in Indonesia.

To showcase the spiritual outlook of the Chinese people to the international community, the Chinese government in recent years has recognized that faith diplomacy can be an essential component of its public diplomacy for China's advocation of a "harmonious world" (Xu 2015, 20). China is aware of the critical role of that moderate Muslims can play in the promotion of China-Indonesia relations and in dispelling the "China threat" that radical Islamic groups have weaponized. Since 2016, the Chinese ambassador in Indonesia has participated in the breaking of fast with the Muslims at Nahdlatul Ulama's Islamic boarding schools during the holy month of Ramadan, during which he would also present donations to the organization and extend invitations for Indonesian Muslims to visit China to witness the religious freedom enjoyed by Chinese Muslims (Embassy of People's Republic of China in Republic of Indonesia 2016). China has also developed a special friendship with NU and its *santri* by providing them with special scholarships and allowing them to register a NU branch in China (Wattimena 2021, 127).

The *santri* who study in China are a fitting example of how the four objectives of public diplomacy—introducing, appreciating, engaging, and influencing—can be achieved through P2P exchange (Rohman et al. 2020, 19).[5] Dubbed *"Diplomasi Santri"* or "Santri Diplomacy," the Indonesian *santri* studying in China are important agents that play the role of bottom-up diplomacy bridging China and Indonesia (Wattimena 2021, 127). Addressing the *santri* studying in China in a webinar, Indonesian media tycoon Dahlan Iskan, who was also the former minister of state-owned enterprises, advocated for these students to contribute as agents of change in giving a positive impression of Muslims to the Chinese nationals with their good conduct, and to change the attitude of Indonesians toward China upon their return to Indonesia (*Republika* 2020). Besides actively promoting education in China by sharing their positive experience living in China to the Indonesian public, the *santri* have actively defended China on issues related to the Uighurs in Xinjiang. For example, in January 2021, a few *santri* who graduated from China set up a website called *aseng.id*[6] and social media accounts on Facebook, YouTube, Twitter, and Instagram to promote a critical understanding of China and Chinese Indonesians. The website aims to provide a space for "gleeful discussions on China/Chinese" (*riang gembira berbincang Cina*), "without suspicions" (*tanpa syak wasangka*). It publishes short essays on Chinese Indonesians, China-Indonesia relations, and the external relations and the internal dynamics of China, such as China's relations with the Muslim world, the Uighur issues, and the governance of Chinese Communist Party (CCP). Cyberspace became a site for *santri* diplomacy as they published counter-narratives to the coverage on China in religious-nationalist newspapers.

According to *Antara News* (2021), the issue of Xinjiang remains one of the largest "stumbling blocks" in the constellation of Indonesia-China relations. After returning from a tour to Xinjiang organized by Beijing in early 2019, the NU leadership dismissed allegations of CCP human rights violations in Xinjiang. In his visit to Indonesia in October 2020, U.S. Secretary of State Mike Pompeo urged Indonesian Muslims to challenge China's Xinjiang policies for "destroying Muslim cemetery," "taking children away from their parents," and "forcing Uighur Muslims to eat pork during Ramadan" under the banner of counterterrorism. In response, the secretary general of the NU Supreme Council alluded to the possible bias in Pompeo's speech, noting the context of the US-China rivalry, and demanded more evidence before NU could reach a final position on the issue (Nurbaiti and Septiari 2020). Wattimena (2021, 128) observes that the NU branch in China had also launched "counter attacks" each time the Indonesian media reported "bad news or fake news" about Muslim repression in Xinjiang.

While China has gained approval by the top leadership of NU, other Muslim elites' sentiments on China have been mixed. This situation is reflected in the "Final Report on Islam, Indonesia and China: Analysis on the potential of elevating people to people connectivity between China and Indonesia from the perspective of Indonesian Muslim elites," a joint study conducted by Indonesia's Ministry of Foreign Affairs and the State Islamic University Sunan Ampel in Surabaya.[7] Nonetheless, most of the informants in the report expressed their agreement on promoting P2P exchange between the two countries. They also suggested to further strengthen the following: (1) education cooperation: academics and student exchange, joint research on religious and social cultural studies, short-term "live in" programs for students and representatives from civil society, and Chinese language teaching in Madrasah and Islamic higher educational institutions; (2) socio-cultural cooperation: celebrations of cultural festivals, dialogue to find the meeting points between Confucianism and Islam, establishment of social institutions of collaboration, and tracing Islamic civilizations in both countries; and (3) religious cooperation: missionary exchange to introduce Indonesian Islam to China, Quranic recitation contests, and discussions of publications by Islamic scholars of both countries.

The Role of Diasporic Indonesian Student Organizations in P2P Exchange

Student organizations have played an important role in Indonesian political history. Youth and student movements have been at the forefront of effecting change in Indonesia. They contributed to the shaping of national consciousness in 1908, the struggle for independence in 1945, and the building and subsequently toppling of the New Order (Arditya 2020). Established after the First Youth Congress in 1926, *Perhimpoenan Peladjar-Peladjar Indonesia* (PPPI or Indonesian Students Association) was one of the earliest student organizations in Indonesia. As a nationalist youth organization that included young intellectuals from all over Indonesia, PPPI was instrumental in initiating the Second Youth Congress in 1928, which birthed the historic Youth Oath (*Sumpah Pemuda*) that gave rise to Indonesian nationalism with the pledge of "one nation, one homeland, one language" (Foulcher 2000). This legacy of political activism has characterized student organizations of subsequent generations in Indonesia.

Diasporic student organizations are usually established as a support network that provides familiarity and comfort of "home away from home" to transnational students. They also function as a site for networking to promote national, religious, or ethnic solidarity. Other than the NU branch in China mentioned above, there are other religious organizations established and managed by Indonesian students and community in China, such as the Lingkar Pengajian (Circle for Quranic Recitation) for Muslims, Keluarga Katolik Indonesia (Indonesian Catholic Family), Persekutuan Reform Injil Indonesia (Indonesia Reformed Evangelical Fellowship), and Organisasi Buddhist Manggala (Manggala Buddhist Organization) (Theo 2018, 105).

The largest and most active Indonesian student organization in China is the Indonesian Students' Association in the PRC (PPIT or *Perkumpulan Pelajar Indonesia Tiongkok* 在華印尼學生協會), which was founded in 2012 under the auspices of the Indonesian embassy in Beijing. Aiming to play the role of a "bridge" that strengthens diplomacy between Indonesia and China, PPIT has set up branches spanning 29 Chinese cities where Indonesians study.[8] After receiving a decree from the Ministry of Law and Human Rights of Indonesia in 2019, PPIT officially became a legal entity (Wattimena 2021). Theo (2018, 105) contends that the current PPIT is the heir of the Indonesian student organization that Indonesian leftist students in China first established. A contingent of between 60 and 100 students was sent by Sukarno's government to study in socialist countries in the 1960s before the succeeding government severed ties with China. Unsurprisingly, PPIT has never linked itself to its predecessor for the apparent Communist stigma it carried.

As a student organization for Indonesians in China, PPIT plays a dual role in representing Indonesia in China and representing China in Indonesia. Due to the legal restrictions circumscribed by the Chinese government on political activities and mass gatherings, PPIT's primary function in China leans toward socio-cultural rather than political. PPIT regularly organizes social and cultural events in China, such as food carnivals, fun walks, education and career expos, and cultural festivals. As most of these activities were sponsored by the Indonesian embassy, they highlight Indonesian nationalism in the spirit of its dictum, unity-in-diversity (Theo 2018, 110). Under the accoladed ambassador, Djauhari Oratmangun (周浩黎), who was appointed on August 20, 2018, the Indonesian embassy in China has been very active in promoting economic and cultural diplomacy with the involvement of Indonesian corporations and students in China. Since 2019, the embassy started a quarterly magazine called "RICH" that features activities of the embassy and Indonesians in China, such as diplomatic engagements and hosting of business forums, expos, and national events commemorations.

One of the stories featured in RICH stood out with interest to P2P connection. At the celebration of Indonesian National Day on August 17, 2019, a group of elderly Indonesian "returnees" (*guiqiao*) participated in performing Indonesian provincial dances and instruments (the *Angklung*) at the Embassy (RICH 2019, 25). The Indonesian *guiqiao* who "returned" to China in the 1950s and 1960s formed a tight-knit diasporic community that spoke Indonesian or a regional language and married within their circle (Godley and Coppel 1990, 193). Now above eighty years of age, these *guiqiao* have become Chinese nationals. Their annual participation in the flag-raising ceremony and cultural performance to commemorate Indonesian Independence Day at the Indonesian Embassy is a testament to their entangled identity with Indonesia.

Cultural events are the main bridging activities of Indonesian students during their mobility in China. These events resonate well with the state's P2P narrative. Since PPIT is dominated by young, self-funded, middle-class Chinese-Indonesians, who are "self-censored, cautious, ignorant or sceptical" (Theo 2018, 110) about politics, cultural activities are more popular than critical discussions on political and social issues among PPIT members. However, with more *pribumi* students joining PPIT, the organization has become a site for intercultural and interreligious exchanges. While Theo (2018, 110–111) noted that Indonesian students in China take "calculated actions" in response to socio-political structure and narratives, she believes that the student organization is "capable of gradually empowering students to take a political stance." This view is demonstrated in the PPIT website (www .ppitiongkok.org) and its online tabloid, *Yinnihao*. These online sites publish socio-cultural content about students' experiences and places of interest in China and actively promote Indonesian political and nationalist discourses such as the Youth Oath and the national ideology of Pancasila. The content published by PPIT are in Indonesian, indicating its intended audience. None of its discussion is related to the socio-political situation of China.

At home in Indonesia, PPIT has played an important role in influencing the public perception of China by offering counter-narratives to negative news on China. For example, during the Jakarta gubernatorial election in 2017, hoax news about millions of Chinese laborers inundating Indonesia had caused widespread anxiety and aroused anti-Chinese and anti-China sentiment. In response, PPIT and the Association of Chinese Alumni in Indonesia (PERHATI) rectified the fake news with facts on interviews with BBC Indonesia and Metro TV (Theo 2018, 110). A year later, Indonesia's leading Islamic newspaper, *Republika*, published an article claiming that Indonesian students were subject to Communist indoctrination in China, which triggered a controversy in Indonesia (Llewellyn 2018b). Given the decades of Communist phobia, such news could cause repercussions among Indonesian students in China, graduates or alumni from China, and the ethnic Chinese in Indonesia. PPIT, together with PERHATI and the NU Youth Special Branch, immediately issued public statements to strongly object to the news article and to clarify that Indonesian students in China never undertook Communist education (Wattimena 2021, 126). These incidents demonstrate the outcomes of P2P exchange through education, whereby knowledge of and experience living in China have effectively turned students and alumni into cultural ambassadors for China in Indonesia.

CONCLUSION

Along with the rise of China, the Chinese state has multiplied its soft power investment, including promoting higher education and Chinese language and culture as part of its proactive public diplomacy strategy. Under the BRI framework, education exchanges form an essential part of the promotion of P2P ties, one of the key elements of the BRI. The government has been offering numerous scholarships to attract international students to study in China. International students in China from Southeast Asia began to gain momentum almost a decade after the normalization of China-ASEAN diplomatic relations in 1990. This number increased dramatically over the past two decades, driven by economic impetus and promising job prospects for Chinese-literate graduates. The case of Indonesia discussed in this chapter attests to the soaring demands for Mandarin proficiency, which propelled a proliferation of Indonesian students to study in China.

Granted, as a result of the historical animosity of Indonesia toward China during the New Order era and the three decades of suspended relations, the "China threat" discourse is still held by some political elites and the Indonesian public until this day. The ethnic Chinese in Indonesia have borne the brunt of such discourse as their loyalty to the Indonesian republic was questioned. They were rendered scapegoats each time Indonesia experienced social and political unrest. However, China's economic transformation has prompted the "learning from China" fever as it becomes an object of emulation for many Indonesians. With the Islamic maxim "seek knowledge as far as China," higher education in China has become a popular option for Chinese Indonesians and Indonesian Muslims, particularly the moderate *santri* from NU. Cognizant of the radical force that tends to weaponize the anti-Chinese rhetoric, China—through its embassy in Jakarta—actively engages the moderate Muslims to dispel theories about the "China threat" and the alleged oppression of the Uighur minority.

Recent polls have shown that there is still generally a trust deficit among Indonesians toward China, especially in light of the growing reliance on Chinese loans, influx of Chinese workers, and security threats associated with the South China Sea conflicts. However, the discussions on the Indonesian students and their organizations in China highlighted some success of P2P exchanges in achieving the objectives of public diplomacy: introducing, appreciating, engaging, and influencing. The transnational mobility experience of Indonesian students in China has placed them in an ambassadorial position to bridge the knowledge gap between the two countries and influence China's public perception in Indonesia by offering counter-narratives to negative media representations. Their experience can offer insights on the importance of soft power and track two diplomacy to China-ASEAN relations through P2P exchanges in higher education.

NOTES

1. For a comprehensive discussion of the origin and development of "China threat" discourse, see Pradt (2016).

2. See Confucius Institute U.S. Center (n.d.).

3. According to Shambaugh (2021, 6), the China Scholarship Council has committed to providing more than 20,000 government scholarships for ASEAN students between 2018 and 2021.

4. Despite such increase, according to the ISEAS-Yusof Ishak Institute survey report on "The State of Southeast Asia 2021," only 3.3 percent of the respondents chose China for the question "Which country would be your first choice if you (or your child) were offered a scholarship to a university?" (Seah et al. 2021, 53). This result shows that there is still long way for China to build and brand its international education to be a destination of preference for Southeast Asian students.

5. The objectives of public diplomacy of introducing, appreciating, engaging, and influencing (Rohman et al. 2020) was adapted from Leonard et al. (2002, 8–9) that can be elaborated as follows: increasing people's familiarity with one's country through introduction, increasing people's appreciation of one's country, and engaging people with one's country by strengthening ties and influencing public perception.

6. The use of the term *Aseng* is a deliberate play on words. It rhymes with the Indonesian word *asing* (foreign) and has been used by the Indonesian public and media as nomenclature for "Chinese" (both local and foreign) and China. In the past few years, there has been an "anti-*aseng*" and "anti-*asing*" movement, which aimed to reject the influx of Chinese workers and capital to Indonesia. As the Chinese Indonesians have long been Othered as *asing* (foreigners) by the native Indonesians, they sometimes bore the brunt of the locals' anger toward the new Chinese migrants to Indonesia.

7. See Rohman et al. (2020).

8. See PPIT website at http://www.ppitiongkok.org.

Chapter 6

Southeast Asian Capital in China

The Role of the State and the Chinese Diaspora

Since the first decade of the twentieth century, the world has witnessed a transformation in global and regional power structures as China's economy has rapidly risen. With its continuing high GDP growth, China is predicted to overtake the United States as the largest economy in the world before 2030 (Colvin 2017). The Chinese overseas in Greater China, Southeast Asia, and elsewhere played an instrumental role in the early stages of China's journey of economic growth. They brought in as much as two-thirds of foreign direct investment (FDI) flows when China implemented the Reform and Opening-Up Policy in the late 1970s and gave China a resource unavailable to any other rising power (Lee 2016). Occupying a leading role in the private sector of many Southeast Asian countries, the ethnic Chinese are referred to by Chua (2004) as a "market-dominant minority." In the early period of the Opening-Up Policy, Southeast Asian Chinese conglomerates invested primarily in China's Special Economic Zones (SEZs) out of patrimonial and speculative reasons (Chia 2008; Cheong et al. 2017). These investments laid the foundations for their China operations and helped build a local network with Chinese authorities and businesses.

Southeast Asian Chinese capitalists earned their trust from the Chinese state for being the pioneers to establish holdings and production during China's transition into a socialist market economy when the country required transmission of resources and knowledge from capitalist economies (Samphantharak 2011, 67). Their understanding of cultural norms and personal networks has helped them mitigate some of the inherent risks non-Chinese foreign investors face. China's Nationality Law promulgated by the National People's Congress on September 10, 1980, that rejected dual citizenship for any Chinese nationals had further become an enabler for China to attract more direct investments from Chinese overseas in Southeast Asia as the law had reduced the anxieties of Southeast Asian governments over the loyalty of their ethnic Chinese population (Wong 1999).

Dubbed the "Bamboo Network," the family or clan-based network (關係 *guanxi*) and the "Confucian" ethic that characterized overseas Chinese capitalism had captured the Orientalist imagination of many Western scholars in the 1990s.[1] This phenomenon continues to dominate the literature on the Chinese diaspora's business practices and political economy (Lasserre and Ching 1995; Haley et al. 2009; Menkhoff 2014; Santasombat 2017; Luo 2020). The social and cultural network possessed by the overseas Chinese capitalists gave them the advantage in trade and access to capital. Early ventures into business gave these migrant entrepreneurs a comparative advantage for their enterprises to grow progressively into giant business entities in their host society (Yen 2003). Moreover, the success of these Southeast Asia Chinese conglomerates was also attributed to their involvement in the "elite coalition" (Suryadinata 2007) or patron-client relationship with indigenous power elites, who provided license and protection in return for material gains. Besides their role in bringing FDI into China, in recent years, the Chinese overseas have played a reverse role in facilitating China's outward investment into their host countries (Huang 2014). Hence, the new maritime Silk Route and the Belt and Road Initiative (BRI) announced by President Xi Jinping in 2013 provided an opportunity for Beijing to build on the role strategically played by the Chinese diaspora in Southeast Asia and vice versa as these entrepreneurs turn their cultural capital into fiscal capital (Hoon and Chan 2021, 321). Furthermore, as Liu et al. (2016) argue, overseas Chinese organizations can deploy their social capital and knowledge of the Southeast Asian market and become conduits in promoting the BRI in the region.

Recognizing the importance of its diaspora, China has intensified its engagement with this community in recent decades through soft power and public diplomacy (Ding 2014). To try to woo FDI from Chinese overseas in the late 1970s, the Chinese state launched a new discourse to glorify the primordial and enduring ties of the overseas Chinese (華僑華人 *huaqiao huaren*) to their ancestral village (Peterson 2012, 173). Furthermore, in 1995 when Xi Jinping was the party secretary of Fuzhou, he advocated for "big overseas Chinese work" (大僑務 *da qiaowu*). After ascending to the presidency, the Overseas Chinese Affairs (僑務 *qiaowu*) remains an integral part of Xi's "Chinese Dream" discourse of economic modernization, scientific and technological innovation, and cultural revival (Liu and van Dongen 2016, 805). To this end, the Chinese government tends to coalesce the categories of ethnic Chinese of foreign citizenship (華人 *huaren*) and Chinese nationals who reside overseas (華僑 *huaqiao*) into a homogenous "Chinese compatriots overseas" (僑胞 *qiaobao*) category and hail them indiscriminately as "members of the Chinese family" (Strangio 2020, 185). Furthermore, at a conference of Overseas Chinese Associations in 2014, Xi Jinping gave a speech in which he declared that "the rejuvenation of the Chinese nation is the common dream" of the "sons and daughters of China within and outside China" (Hiebert 2020, 89). Suryadinata (2017, 6) argues that the nationality of Chinese overseas is strategically blurred when the Chinese leaders feel it is in the interest of China.

Jacques (2008) conjectures that with the proliferating global interests in rising China, "the Chinese diaspora is likely to expand greatly; enjoy growing prestige as a result of China's rising status; and feel an even closer affinity with China." However, Wang (2015) argues that China endeavors to create an environment where it is not feared as a great power but respected for its wealth and creativity, which are necessary conditions for modern civilization—one that its diaspora can share its pride. With a proliferating international trade, especially after the ASEAN–China Free Trade Agreement (ACFTA) in 2010, China became ASEAN's largest trading partner. Therefore, Wang (2015) further asserts that there is no alternative for ASEAN apart from seeking a sustainable balance in its relationship with the newly emerged superpower. In its engagement with ASEAN, China has learned to respect ASEAN centrality and the "ASEAN Way," which points to the system of non-confrontational consultation to reach consensus (Acharya 1998).

As China continues to dominate the global economy, the BRI is expected to play an essential role in driving the economy of Southeast Asia. However, Hiebert (2020, 5) contends that Southeast Asian countries view China with mixed emotions of "expectation and fear, aspiration and frustration." Beijing's generous aid and infrastructure investments have incited strong concerns from the recipient countries in Southeast Asia. Some of the fears include the mounting debt, trade deficit, unilateral dominance, and militarization of the South China Sea in relation to China's increasing economic involvement in the region (Seah et al. 2021). Hiebert (2020, 7–9) delineated three non-watertight clusters of Southeast Asian nations by each of their responses and orientations toward China's economic incentives: Myanmar, Laos, and Cambodia belong to the first cluster for their Chinese-dependent economy and geographic proximity with China. With no interests in the South China Sea disputes, these countries appeal to China's economic support in terms of aid, infrastructure development, and favorable trade policies and are more likely to align themselves with Beijing's initiatives. The second group, consisting of Thailand and Vietnam, has been seeking to achieve a balance in collaborating with China and the United States, commonly referred to as "hedging strategy" (Lim and Cooper 2016). Both countries react sensitively to policies from either side of the two superpowers. In contrast to the two previous clusters, the third grouping consists of the Philippines, Indonesia,

Malaysia, Singapore, and Brunei Darussalam, which are in China's maritime periphery. Although the distance made them less vulnerable to China's direct influence, these countries also hedge carefully between the two superpowers based on their economic and strategic interests (Kuik 2008; Suzuki and Lee 2017; Chen 2019).

The discussion on China's economic role in Southeast Asia has been adequately examined in scholarly books in the past two decades (Ho and Ku 2005; Ho 2009; Kim 2016; Blanchard 2019; Hiebert 2020; Strangio 2020; Emmerson 2021). Departing from this, the present chapter explores the role of Southeast Asian capital in China, with a focus on the role of ethnic Chinese conglomerates. It also examines how the Chinese state has responded to the presence of these investments over time. As active players caught between their host nation and China, any changes in political and economic ties between the two sides will invariably affect the behavior of these business conglomerates. Hence, the dynamic geopolitical contexts of China and Southeast Asia relations will be critically considered. Following the typology by Hiebert (2020) above, the chapter will draw cases from all three groups, specifically Myanmar, Singapore, Indonesia, Malaysia, and Thailand. These countries were chosen for the significant role the ethnic Chinese play in their domestic economy, as well as the ways in which these ethnic minority capitalists responded to Deng Xiaoping's invitation to invest in post-Mao China. We will begin with a discussion of Southeast Asian capital in China since the Reform and Opening-Up Policy in 1978 before proceeding to case studies of individual ASEAN countries.

SOUTHEAST ASIAN CAPITAL IN CHINA SINCE 1978

Deng Xiaoping's Reform and Opening-Up Policy in 1978 paved the way for China to reintegrate itself into international capitalism and gradually opened China to foreign direct investment (FDI) (Wang 2008, 25). The post-1978 Chinese state can be described as development-oriented and outward-looking as it yearned to reestablish ties with other nations. To this end, China introduced a series of incentives to drive inward FDI and carried out diplomatic visits to establish relations. Deng Xiaoping's visit to three member states of ASEAN—Thailand, Malaysia, and Singapore—in late 1978 shows the importance of the regional bloc in the foreign policy of post-Mao China (Lee 1981). These diplomatic actions ensured that China would not be seen as a threat as it moved toward a socialist market economy. At the same time, China decided to cease its support of insurgencies in Southeast Asia, which significantly reduced political violence in the region and improved relations between China and Southeast Asia (Wade 2020, 173).

Most of the large-scale FDI in the early period of the reform policy in China came from Hong Kong, the United States, and Japan, which exported technology and expertise to China for it to start its manufacturing industry (Gambe 1996, 95; Wang and Lin 2008, 147; Samphantharak 2011, 67). The FDI from different Southeast Asian nations arrived in China at other times due to their varying reactions to China's reform and diplomatic missions.[2] For instance, the Cold War, the alleged Communist coup, and anti-Chinese sentiment had left adverse reactions toward China in Indonesia. However, decades of Western arms embargo on Myanmar had boosted its relations with China, on which the military regime depends for trade and weapon supplies (Stuart-Fox 2003, 213). Thailand, Singapore, and Malaysia were more neutral in their diplomacy with China, as they continued to take a pragmatic approach by hedging the United States while engaging China's potentially lucrative market (Wong 1999).

Anxious at first, Southeast Asia investors—primarily ethnic Chinese conglomerates and prominent capitalists—began to invest in the Special Economic Zones (SEZs) or their ancestral homeland located in the coastal provinces of southern China (Manarungsan 2009, 301; Samphantharak 2011, 74; Bolesta 2018, 26; Zeng 2019, 164). Most of these investments served the Chinese domestic market during the initial phase of China's opening up (Samphantharak 2011, 70). Many conglomerates focused initially on agribusinesses before expansion into vertical industries, including retail, motor vehicles, petrochemicals, wholesale, banking, finance, and hospitality. Although these early investments in China rarely earned satisfactory financial returns, the success lies in their contribution in lifting the standards of living in the SEZs by providing stable employment to local people, thereby earning trust and social capital from their mainland Chinese counterparts (Wong 1999, 7; Wang and Lin 2008, 147). Nonetheless, accounting for 1.7 percent of total FDI in China, the scale of investment from Southeast Asia remained insignificant before 1992 (Sheng 2008, 258).[3] Many Southeast Asian states were generally still speculative and cautious toward China's reform. This situation was compounded by the fact that China's investment environment, bureaucracy, and legal structure were still not conducive at that time (Wang 1994, 13; Riady 2017, 190–191).

Investments from Southeast Asian Chinese capitalists surged after the normalization of diplomatic relations between China and various Southeast Asian countries at the end of the Cold War (Wong 1999, 14; Sheng 2008, 261; Tong and Lim 2017, 166). Furthermore, Deng Xiaoping's southern tour in 1992, widely known as "Nanxun" (南巡), was the real watershed for China's Opening-Up Policy (Samphantharak 2011, 67; Tong and Lim 2017, 166). The tour encompassed the southern Chinese cities of Shenzhen, Zhuhai, Guangzhou, and Shanghai and reinforced the commitment to economic reforms and opening up in China. Following Deng's tour, more regions in interior China were opened up to FDI, and selected coastal cities and industrial sectors previously closed to FDI, such as foreign markets, domestic trade, insurance, finance, aviation, and infrastructure projects, were now permitted (Wong 1999, 5). Positive developments in international relations between China and Southeast Asia as well as domestic reforms in China were the main impetuses that attracted capital from Southeast Asia.

The Asian Financial Crisis that swept through the region in 1997 also became a catalyst for Southeast Asian conglomerates to invest in China at a larger scale and frequency. The crisis affected China much less than Southeast Asia due to the large reserves maintained by the Chinese state. In turn, China played a supportive role in stabilizing the region's economy by not devaluing the Renminbi (Tisdell 2008, 16). After the crisis, with Singapore as an example, Southeast Asian governments became more aware of the risk in focusing FDI only in the already slow-growing Southeast Asian region (Siddiqui 2016, 181). Hence, they encouraged local businesses to go further to diversify their investments, where China appeared to be the closer and more viable option (Samphantharak 2011, 67). From a business perspective, the crisis had exposed the uncertainty in investing in Southeast Asia.

In contrast, China's economic and political stability became attractive to Southeast Asian capitalists (Wong 1999, 24). Furthermore, the persistent anti-Chinese sentiment in countries such as Indonesia had prompted conglomerates, particularly those owned by ethnic Chinese, to shift their capital abroad (Chua 2008, 88). The investments by Southeast Asian capitalists in China will be discussed based on case studies of individual countries in the following subsections.

Myanmar

After achieving independence in 1948, the nonaligned government of Burma (the official name was changed to Myanmar in 1989) maintained good ties with China (Hiebert 2020, 101–110). Burma was the first non-Communist country to recognize the Chinese Communist regime and the People's Republic of China in 1949 (Bolesta 2018, 24). The historical intimate bilateral relations between the countries are often described as "sibling-like," known as *paukphaw* (Kivimaki 2016, 138). However, Steinberg (2021, 354–355) called the sibling relations a "myth and illusion" as he unveiled the lack of fraternal equality between the two countries. According to him, China has always assumed the position of an "elder brother," to whom the younger Burmese sibling should defer. Burma-China relations soured after the military coup in 1962 carried out by General Ne Win. After the coup, nationalizing policies were imposed on the ethnic Chinese businesses in Myanmar. The

Chinese state's support for the Communist Party of Burma (CPB) during the Cultural Revolution further deteriorated the bilateral relations. It contributed to riots against the ethnic Chinese in Yangon in 1967. The bilateral relations only normalized during Deng Xiaoping's reform era when China reduced support for the CPB (Hiebert 2020, 102–103).

In 1988, Ne Win's Burma Socialist Programme Party was replaced by the military junta—known as State Law and Order Restoration Council (SLORC)—after a bloody coup following a violent suppression of the People Power Uprising. After the incident, the West imposed sanctions and boycotts, and Myanmar was removed from the larger international order. Consequently, Myanmar's economy became reliant on China for aid, trade, investments, infrastructure development, and arms sales for the next two decades. With the increase in China's economic role in Myanmar and the revocation of restrictions on the Chinese language, culture, and institutions after 1988, the number of Chinese immigrants grew rapidly in Myanmar. Many new Chinese immigrants (新移民 *xin yimin*) settled down in the northern Burmese city of Mandalay, located 450 kilometers from Yunnan (Strangio 2020, 157). Chinese migrants, including copious illegal immigrants, are currently estimated to make up almost half of the city's population of 1.4 million, with Chinese-owned enterprises holding 60 percent of Mandalay's economy (Hiebert 2020, 108). The rising value of real estate in Mandalay driven by ethnic Chinese developers forced many locals to relocate to the city's outskirts. This gave rise to local anxieties, fearing that the Chinese may take over their city, and by extension, their country (Strangio 2020, 156–157). As Steinberg (2021, 358) notes, "China's ethno-economic presence has fueled feelings of insecurity and vulnerability and a concomitant increase in ethnic nationalism among the Burman majority."

Bolesta (2018, 24) observes that from 1988 to 2011, Myanmar developed a high trade deficit and unfavorable terms of trade with China. Sino-Burmese tycoons who acted as bridges between the junta and Chinese patrons accumulated their wealth. Crony capitalism between SLORC generals and Chinese entrepreneurs gave rise to Sino-Burmese plutocrats like Lo Hsing Han, an infamous drug kingpin turned tycoon (Chua 2004). Widespread resentment toward China and the ethnic Chinese was found among the average Burmese. They felt that Chinese FDI only benefited a small group of elite officials and their cronies (Bolesta 2018, 26). Two ethnic Chinese business conglomerates with close connections to the military regime and Chinese investors are Asia World and Serge Pun and Associates (Min and Kudo 2014). Established in 1992 by Lo Hsing Han, Asia World is one of the largest and most prominent conglomerates in Myanmar. Its activities in the Burmese economy encompass hotels, construction, logistics, supermarket chains, contractors, garments, paper mills, palm oil, and infrastructure projects. It became a leading business partner of the junta and a conduit for China and Southeast Asian ethnic Chinese investments in Myanmar (Strangio 2020, 154). A case in point was the joint ventures between Lo Hsing Han and Chinese Malaysian tycoon Robert Kuok that "turned Mandalay and Rangoon into booming hubs for mainland Chinese and Southeast Asian Chinese business networks" (Chua 2004, 28). Another ethnic Chinese Burmese tycoon who played an intermediary role is Serge Pun, who was born in Myanmar but fled to China after the 1962 coup. He founded the Serge Pun and Associates Group, operating in the real estate industry in Hong Kong in the late 1980s. After returning to Myanmar in the early 1990s, Pun expanded his company's operation to Myanmar. He started First Myanmar Investment, a subsidiary of Serge Pun and Associates Group and a publicly listed company that ventured across industries including real estate, automobile, banking, manufacturing, and healthcare (Min and Kudo 2014). Although overland economic activities between Myanmar and China across the border, including illegal trade, reach billions of dollars every year (Strangio 2020, 154), little information is available on Burmese investments in China. Much of the literature has focused on the Chinese economic presence in Myanmar.

China is the largest investor and trading partner of Myanmar (Mizuno 2016). In addition to Myanmar's geopolitical importance to China, economic interests characterized the Sino-Myanmar bilateral relations. Myanmar has significant deposits of energy and other natural resources that China can use to fuel its growth. More important, Myanmar occupies a strategic geopolitical position as an alternative route to the Malacca Straits to transport energy and natural resources from Africa and the Middle East to China and for China to export goods to Europe, the Middle East, and Africa (Bolesta 2018, 25). However, the advantage that China previously had over Myanmar is now in the past. President Thein Sien's political reform in 2011 marked Myanmar's early stage in breaking away from its China-dependent legacy as the country sought to improve ties with the US and European nations. The quasi-civilian government suspended several large Chinese investment projects in September 2011 following protests over environmental concerns, including the US$3.6 billion Myitsone Dam on the Irrawaddy River and the Letpadaung copper mine. This was followed by the cancelation of the proposed US$20 billion railway project in 2014, which was planned to connect Yunnan with Myanmar's Rakhine western coast (Malik 2019, 134). After the US and Europe abolished previously imposed sanctions and began to engage with Myanmar in 2011, China was put in equal competition with Myanmar's new international partners (Kivimaki 2016, 137). This pivotal turn gave Myanmar leverage to negotiate terms with China on its infrastructure investments, as seen in the agreement on the China-Myanmar Economic Corridor—a BRI project—in 2018, which provided Myanmar with unprecedented concessions from China (Heibert 2020, 82). China's assurance of non-interference in Myanmar's Rohingya crisis had once again brought Aung San Suu Kyi's National League for Democracy (NLD) government into closer ties; the Lady had long recognized the need to "be careful" with China (Strangio 2020, 163–164).

Singapore

The tiny size of Singapore and the lack of natural resources force the country to rely on international trade for economic survival. Singapore is open to establishing ties and trade with any country as long as its sovereignty and security are not threatened. To increase its global competitiveness, Singapore sought to become a regional hub in providing specialized services, including complex industries such as telecommunications, electronics, pharmaceuticals, and all levels of manufacturing activities (Siddiqui 2016, 181). While Singapore has maintained good relations with its neighbors in the Malay world, its majority ethnic Chinese population continues to incite ASEAN members' suspicion of its relationship with China. For instance, Indonesia and Malaysia feared that China would use Singapore as a Chinese client state in the region (Hiebert 2020, 402). Singapore treaded carefully by being one of the last ASEAN member states to establish formal ties with China in 1990, even though relations between the two nations date back to the 1970s when Lee Kuan Yew met with Mao Zedong in Beijing in 1976 and with Deng Xiaoping in Singapore in 1978 (Strangio 2020, 189). Deng's visit to Singapore opened his eyes to the success of the market system in driving the economy. Since then, the Chinese state has imported and tinkered with the "Singapore Model" selectively, which even brought about the "Singapore Fever" in China (Lim and Horesh 2016). It was noted that both Deng Xiaoping and Xi Jinping looked to Singapore's approach to governance as a model for China to emulate (Tan 2021, 197). As Deng famously remarked during his southern tour in 1992, "there is good social order in Singapore. They govern the place with discipline. We should draw from their experience and do even better than them" (*China News* 2009).

Since 2013, China has been Singapore's largest trading partner, and Singapore has been China's largest foreign investor (*The Straits Times* 2021). In 2009, the China-Singapore Free Trade Agreement was signed, which was upgraded in 2018 to allow Singapore companies in China to have increased market access to services and greater investment protection (Hiebert 2020, 405). Over the years, the target industries of Singaporean investors in the Chinese market have diversified from real estate, food processing, and manufacturing to the service and hospitality market, finance, insurance, logistics, communications, and the digital industry, as well as involvement in large-scale infrastructure projects in collaboration with government-linked corporations (GLCs) from China and other countries. After the signing of Avoidance of Double Taxation Treaties between Singapore and China in 1985, Singaporean investments in China proliferated. Most of these investments landed in the southern coastal provinces of China, especially Guangdong and Fujian (Chan and Tong 2014, 119). Since 1994, Singaporean investments had begun to encroach beyond the southern area to the northern provinces such as Jiangsu, Liaoning, and Shandong and, in the past two decades, to areas such as Yunnan and Sichuan, as older SEZs have become less lucrative to the investors.

The launch of the US$20 billion Suzhou Industrial Park (SIP) project by the governments of China and Singapore in 1994 led the way for more Singaporean GLCs to enter China. GLCs such as Sembawang Corporation, Keppel Corporation, and CapitaLand focused on investing in real estate and infrastructure projects such as developing industrial and business parks. For instance, Ascendas, a subsidiary to the Jurong Town Corporation (JTC), followed the Suzhou Industrial Park model in providing a "one-stop concept" of infrastructure contracting and expert services to build and manage business complexes in Shanghai, Suzhou, Beijing, Shenzhen, Hangzhou, and Shenyang (Kumar et al. 2005). Another GLC, National Parks Board, also followed the model set forward by JTC-Ascendas in creating its subsidiary, Singapore Garden City, to enter the civil planning, land development, and horticulture market in China. Led by the experience of these GLCs, the Singaporean government continued to promote collaboration between GLCs and private enterprises in diversifying Singaporean investments in China.

Besides SIP, Singapore invested in two other major joint-venture sustainable development projects. The first is the Sino-Singapore Tianjin Eco-City, which features a smart city and green transportation and encompasses industrial parks, residential areas, community centers, schools, and a hospital. A more recent BRI investment is the China-Singapore Chongqing Connectivity Initiative, which includes the New International Land-Sea Trade Corridor (western corridor) that links Chongqing and western China to Southeast Asia. To spur economic growth in less developed western China, the initiative will allow Singapore companies to participate in China's BRI, tap opportunities in the Chengdu-Chongqing Economic Circle, and expand overseas hinterlands for Singapore companies (Yu 2020).

Being a Chinese-majority state can be a blessing and a curse for Singapore in its trade and international relations. The insecurity of being surrounded by dominant Malay neighbors puts Singapore in a perennial siege mentality. However, Siddiqui (2016, 157) contends that Singapore's Chinese dominance gives it an advantage in structuring business networks with other ethnic Chinese across Southeast Asia and with counterparts in China. Ethnic Chinese business associations in Singapore function as key nonstate actors in promoting Singapore-China ties, including "collecting business information, protecting commercial credit, organizing relevant trade activities, providing collective bargaining ability and reducing transaction costs" (Liu et al. 2021, 222–223). However, China has occasionally expected Singapore to "comply to its wishes" due to its Chinese heritage, particularly on issues such as the South China Sea dispute (Hiebert 2020, 391). Nonetheless, like many of its ASEAN neighbors, Singapore continues to hedge against China and the United States by harnessing the economic opportunities presented by China's rise to grow its economy while maintaining a strong partnership with the United States, which it sees as the "top Pacific power and main strategic guarantor" (Tan 2021, 199).

Indonesia

As discussed in the previous chapter, Indonesia had a turbulent relationship with China despite being one of the first ASEAN countries to recognize and establish bilateral ties with the PRC in 1950. Sukarno's ideological confrontation against Western imperialism gained Indonesia's friendship with China, which led to the formation of the "Beijing-Jakarta Axis." The Bandung Conference in 1955 witnessed the signing of the dual citizenship agreement between China and Indonesia, which forced the ethnic Chinese in Indonesia to pick either side of citizenship and undermined the CCP's alliance with overseas Chinese (Koning and Susanto 2008, 163). However, the alleged Communist coup of September 30, 1965, put the two countries' good relations into a void. The bilateral ties frozen by Suharto's New Order government, which controlled Indonesia with an iron fist from 1966 to 1998, were only thawed in 1990. However, real improvements in Indonesia-China relations did not take place until after the fall of Suharto in 1998. Under the leadership of President Susilo Bambang Yudhoyono, an "Indonesia-China strategic partnership" was announced in 2005 and was upgraded to a comprehensive strategic partnership in 2013, which expanded the capacity of trade, investment, and soft credit (Weatherbee 2017). However, like many other countries in Southeast Asia, Indonesia is experiencing an increasing deficit in its trade with China, which has been an ongoing source of domestic concern (*Reuters* 2021). Notwithstanding the intimate ties with China under the current Jokowi administration, the legacy of the Communist threat continues to fuel the distrust toward China among Indonesian elites and the public.

The ethnic Chinese in Indonesia have often been portrayed as economic creatures and wealthy businesspeople because a large proportion of Indonesia's private economy pre-1998 was dominated by a handful of Chinese conglomerates (Hoon 2014). The New Order did not follow in the footsteps of Sukarno's policy in indigenizing the economy of Indonesia.

Instead, the development-oriented Suharto government utilized ethnic Chinese business skills to recover the sinking economy after the 1965 abortive coup. Departing from Sukarno's disastrous "Guided Economy" that drove Indonesia into hyperinflation, the New Order introduced the Indonesian economy to market forces where deregulation of policies and competition were encouraged. These fundamental changes facilitated the formation of the sectors in the property market, construction, real estate, retail industry, banking, and finance. They presented unprecedented economic opportunities for ethnic Chinese conglomerates to emerge (Chua 2008). The government's embarkation on a market-oriented economic strategy only succeeded due to the Chinese's contribution because they alone had the commercial experience and ready access to foreign capital. However, the lack of acknowledgment of the economic and other contributions of the Chinese to Indonesia prompted Jusuf Wanandi (2012, 127)—a prominent Chinese Indonesian who had worked closely with the New Order regime—to lament, "We [Chinese Indonesians] were treated as minor wives, enjoyed but not recognized."

Privileges and opportunities provided by the New Order bolstered the positions of Chinese Indonesian businesses, contributing to the rapid growth of their economic power. A small group of Chinese Indonesians, referred to as the *cukong* (lit. 主公 masters), accumulated wealth through cooperation with Indonesian power elites—usually military and political leaders. Such crony capitalism, known as the *cukong* system, had a reciprocal function: the *cukong* provided skills and capital in running the business, while the *pribumi* partner gave protection and patronage to the *cukong*. These personal ties protected the Chinese from potential harassment as an ethnic minority with commercial monopoly power (Lim and Gosling 1997). One of such *cukong* was Liem Sioe Liong (also known as Sudono Salim), founder of the Salim Group and the most prominent tycoon in Suharto's Indonesia. Liem supported the Suharto regime financially for unrestricted access to develop his business empire (Dieleman and Sachs 2006).

The Salim Group started from Liem Sioe Liong's early venture in provisioning soldiers of the new republic, including Suharto's military unit, after the end of the Japanese occupation in 1945 (Borsuk and Chng 2014, 3). The patron-client relationship established between Suharto and Liem allowed the Salim Group to enjoy monopolies and preferential treatment during the New Order. The conglomerate grew massively and was diversified across different industries in both local and foreign markets between 1960 and 1990. Domestically, the Salim Group dominated three primary industries: food, cement, and banking (Mackie 2003). Episodes of anti-Chinese riots in Indonesia reminded the Chinese Indonesians of their vulnerability and prompted them to put "their eggs in baskets elsewhere" (Borsuk and Chng 2014, 262). The conglomerate started its investment overseas in the banking industry in Hong Kong with prominent Chinese Indonesian banker Mochtar Riady in 1975 (Yeung 1999, 115). It incorporated the First Pacific Group in Hong Kong in 1981, which later managed most of the Salim Group's operations and holdings outside Indonesia. After the Asian Financial Crisis, the First Pacific Group expanded its scale to increase its investment in China and reduce its activities in Indonesia (Dieleman and Sachs 2006, 530).

As a first-generation migrant from Fuqing county in Fujian, China, Liem had deep sentimental ties with his native town. Affectionally addressed by the locals as *laoban* (老闆 the boss), Liem was regarded as a demigod and an outstanding example of someone who "loves his country and village" (愛國愛鄉) (Borsuk and Chng 2014, 491). He was instrumental in transforming the provincial backwater into a modern city by contributing financially to develop its infrastructure, including "the roads, bridges, shopping malls, hospitals, schools, industrial areas and even a port" (Borsuk and Chng 2014, 490). Dieleman (2007) argues that the "僑鄉 *qiaoxiang* sentiment" (Chinese overseas' affection for the hometown) motivated Liem to maintain his business operations in Fuqing for the benefit of the local people despite them being unprofitable. Liem had been an old friend of Xi Jinping since Xi held various party positions in Fujian in the 1990s. Xi visited Liem in his office in Jakarta in 1991 during his visit to Indonesia, and the two of them met again in Singapore in 2010 after Xi had risen to the rank of Vice President (Borsuk and Chng 2014, 473). However, Liem's youngest son and successor, Anthoni Salim, did not share his father's emotional ties with the *qiaoxiang* and was pragmatic in handling the company's investments in China. This is demonstrated in the subsequent expansion of the Salim Group's operations in China beyond Fujian to Shanghai in the mid-1990s, which helped the conglomerate to reap the lucrative Chinese market.

Mochtar Riady, the founder and chairman of the Indonesian multinational conglomerate Lippo Group, is another prime example of a prominent Chinese Indonesian businessman who invested heavily in the Chinese market. Riady was born of a Chinese Fujianese migrant in the city of Malang in East Java in 1929. He received his higher education in philosophy at Nanjing University in China after the Dutch authorities exiled him for participating in anti-colonial activities. Dubbed the "Magic Man of Bank Marketing," he was known for his outstanding skills and experience in revitalizing ailing banks. This reputation earned him a position as Liem's right-hand man in Salim Group's Bank Central Asia, which he managed to develop from having IDR 12.8 billion worth of assets when he joined in 1975 to IDR 5 trillion when he left in 1990 (Hoon 2012). Successes in the Lippo Bank, the core business of the Lippo Group founded by Riady, propelled the conglomerate to diversify in the stock brokerage, retail, insurance, and real estate industries after 1989 (Chua 2008, 100). The Lippo Group has become a multinational group of companies spanning the Pacific basin with interests in financial investment, property and infrastructure development, retail, education, and media.

Like Liem, Riady shares a strong *qiaoxiang* sentiment with his ancestral home in Putian, Fujian. He followed Liem's footsteps in investing in the Fujian Province in the 1990s, including building the Meizhou Bay power plant in Putian, and financially supported the establishment of Putian University. Riady had played a role in improving the trade relations between China and Indonesia before the normalization of their bilateral relations in 1990. For instance, in 1986, as the managing director of Bank Central Asia, he was involved in the official negotiation on a bank remittance agreement between Indonesia and China. He signed the "Correspondent Bank Agreement" with the Bank of China in Beijing (Ren 2020). Like the Salim Group, the Lippo Group did not stop in Fujian. After witnessing the success of Shenzhen as an experimental ground for Deng's reform policy, Riady became convinced of the potential of the Chinese market. Lippo began its foray into China by increasing its investments in Hong Kong in preparation for the transfer of sovereignty in 1997 (Riady 2017, 176–177). Specializing in real estate development, the Lippo Group now has a conspicuous presence, owning shopping malls, hotels, and office and residential buildings across major cities in China.

Malaysia

Malaysia established formal diplomatic ties with China after the historic visit to China by Prime Minister Tun Abdul Razak in 1974. However, there were no significant improvements in bilateral trade because the Communist Party of China was still providing aid and support to the Communist Party of Malaya, which had staged various insurgencies (Cheong et al. 2017). Suspicions of the Malaysian federal government toward the CPC led to Malaysian investors' reluctance to invest directly in China. Hence, Hong Kong became a proxy for Malaysians like Robert Kuok to enter the Chinese market in the 1970s (Chia 2008, 62). The Malaysian government under Prime Minister Dr. Mahathir Mohamad in the 1980s openly called for stronger economic ties with China (Hiebert 2020, 372). Bilateral trade in the 1980s began with Malaysia exporting mainly rubber and palm oil to China. Over the next two decades, these expanded to electronics, chemical products, and mineral oil (Lee 2013, 246). The Asian Financial Crisis in 1997 and China's membership in the World Trade Organization (WTO) in 2001 caused a pivotal increase in Malaysian investment in China, when Malaysian GLCs such as Sime Darby, the owner of the world's largest palm oil plantation, and Khazanah Nasional, Malaysia's sovereign wealth fund, also began to invest in China (Lean and Smyth 2016; Hiebert 2020, 362). By 2017, Malaysian cumulative FDI in

China had reached \$7.5 billion, which ranked second highest in Southeast Asia, just behind Singapore (Hiebert 2020, 362).

Malaysian investments in China, especially in the early period of China's reform, were primarily carried out by the ethnic Chinese. Their business activities began in southern coastal cities and were expanded to eastern regions of China, focusing on the retail industry, primary product manufacturing, hospitality, and real estate development. However, except for the pioneers like the Kuok Brothers and the Lion Group, most of these companies do not have significant operations in China (Cheong et al. 2017). The New Economic Policy (NEP) was introduced in Malaysia in 1971, which aimed to restructure wealth distribution through an affirmative action that gave privileges to the majority Malays and other indigenous groups (or *Bumiputera*) at the expense of ethnic Chinese companies. As the new regulatory measures had made Malaysia less conducive for the ethnic Chinese capitalists to conduct business and accumulate capital, international markets like China became a viable option to mitigate risk (Wong and Tan 2017, 88). Under the NEP, Chinese-owned businesses could only expand and succeed with *Bumiputera* partners and personal connections with local political elites (Mackie 2003, 113). For instance, William Cheng of the Lion Group ventured into the Chinese market in the 1990s with senior Malaysian politicians, which marked the beginning of increased Malay participation in Malaysian investments in China (Chia 2008, 62). According to Cheong et al. (2017), the current largest Malaysian investors in China are engaged in property development (Kerry, Guoco, Lion), hotels (Shangri-la, YTL), commodities (Wilmar, IOI), and retail (Parkson).

The earliest and most prominent Chinese Malaysian business magnate who ventured into China driven by "patrimonial" motivation and profit was Robert Kuok (Cheong et al. 2017). Popularly known as the "Sugar King," Kuok incorporated the Kuok Brothers company with his brother in 1949. His family's close relation to the Sultan of Johor landed his company an exclusive license to operate the sugar and rice industry. He eventually expanded his operations beyond Malaysia across Southeast Asia, Japan, and China. The Kuok Brothers began diversification into other industries such as shipping, food and beverages, and a luxury hotel chain in the early 1990s (Gambe 1996). Like the Salim Group, crony capitalism and government patronage were prominent features of Kuok's business, as he was strategic in utilizing his networks with Malaysian political elites (Wong and Tan 2017, 98). Kuok started to frequent mainland China during the Cultural Revolution in the mid-1960s and revealed his disappointment with the red tape and suspicions of the Communist state toward foreigners, which were not conducive to foreign investment. His confidence in the Chinese economy was restored only after Deng Xiaoping introduced the Reform and Opening-Up Policy. He began to use Hong Kong as a gateway to enter the Chinese market (Kuok and Tanzer 2017). Wong and Tan (2017, 99) hailed Kuok as "one of the pioneering Chinese overseas businessmen who started investing in China at a time when many were still inhibited by the ideological and legal constraints imposed by a newly opened China trying to find its way in international business."

Thailand

Thailand established diplomatic relations with China in 1974, a year after the collapse of its military regime that was hostile toward China. Prime Minister Kukrit Pramoj visited China in 1975 and accorded deference to China as a younger brother would do to his older brother, which Mao Zedong found pleasing and reciprocated with gracious hospitality (Stuart-Fox 2003, 197). The family metaphors of "brothers" or "blood-bonded relatives" have since been customarily used by Thai and Chinese officials when describing the relations of the two countries (Strangio 2020, 128). After the normalization of bilateral ties, Thailand resumed trade with China in 1975. In the same year, both countries founded the Thailand-China Joint Committee on Economic Cooperation, which led to the signing of the Thailand-China Joint Trade Committee agreement in 1978. Trade between Thailand and China increased considerably after 1991, and the volume multiplied sharply after China joined the WTO in 2001. Before the financial crisis in 1997, Thailand exported mainly rubber and rice to China. This was diversified into industrial and basic commodity-based goods such as computer components, petrochemical products, crude and finished oil, and rubber products after 1997 (Manarungsan 2009).

Thailand-China relations deepened during the administration of Prime Minister Thaksin Shinawatra, a descendant of Hakka immigrants from the southern province of Guangdong in China. Referring to Thailand as the "closest" and "most sincere" friend of China, Thaksin expanded economic, political, and security ties with China (Strangio 2020, 126). The Thai military junta that seized power from the caretaker government of Thaksin's younger sister, Prime Minister Yingluck Shinawatra, in 2014 further strengthened ties with China because Western nations reacted to the coup with trade sanctions (Parameswaran 2014). As China has become Thailand's most significant and only viable trade partner, economic exchanges with China multiplied under the military regime and the BRI. However, average Thai citizens were concerned with the increasing economic dependency on China, fearing that Thailand might drift into a "vassal state" relationship with China like Laos and Cambodia (Raymond 2019, 349). The bilateral relations grew increasingly intimate until 2017, when Trump's administration renewed US engagement with Thailand. The Thai state decided to hedge toward the United States to rebalance its international standing and reduce its dependency on China (Hiebert 2020, 282). Even Sino-Thai SME traders resented the influx of cheap products from China.

Like many other Southeast Asian nations, the ethnic Chinese own a considerable proportion of businesses in the domestic economy of Thailand. State-owned enterprises and ethnic Chinese businesses emerged as the main industrialists post–World War II. Before the war, ethnic Chinese business activities focused on rice milling and exporting; they later expanded to complementary areas such as banking, insurance, and shipping to reap higher profits from the lucrative rice exporting industry (Gambe 1996, 95). Many ethnic Chinese chose to abandon their Chinese identity under the assimilationist and nationalist forces of the Phibun administration during the postwar period. While economic nationalism was pursued by the state, the government also understood the indispensable role of the Chinese capitalists in the Thai economy, which explained the formation of the alliance between Chinese business leaders and Thai political elites (Burusratanaphand 2001, 76). Big business groups owned by ethnic Chinese began to emerge in Thailand in the 1950s; they continue to play an influential role in the Thai economy (Mackie 2003, 119). After the geopolitical realignment following the normalization of Thai relations with China and the opening up of China in the 1970s, Thai nationals with Chinese lineage were able to visit their ancestral homeland, which allowed them to rediscover their Chineseness. The Charoen Pokphand, or CP Group, headed by Dhanin Chearavanont (or Chia Kok Min 謝國民), was the first foreign firm and the first Thai business group to invest in China in 1979. The Group held the first foreign investment permit, coded 0001, to operate in Shenzhen and Shantou (Handley 2003, 159). Other major Sino-Thai investors, such as Saha-Union Group, moved into China only in the early 1990s (Liu and Jayanthakumaran 2016, 78). Reynolds argues that "the commodification of Chinese identity signifies the triumph of the Sino-Thai bourgeoisie as *the* national bourgeoisie" (1996, 137).

With more than 200 business subsidiaries across mainland China, the CP Group (known in China as 正大集團 *Zhengda Jituan*) is arguably more heavily invested in China than in Thailand (Reynolds 1996, 137). It started with agribusiness and agro-industries before gradually diversifying and expanding into automotive and industrial production, petrochemicals, retail distribution, entertainment, and other manufacturing ventures with Chinese state enterprises and other partners (Manarungsan 2009). The conglomerate has built a reciprocal relationship with the Chinese state by bringing new technologies, foreign investments, and capital to China, in return for the permission to diversify and expand its operations into new industries and provinces that were formerly not opened for marketization. This situation also allows CP to build its influence as an intermediary between the Chinese state and foreign investors (Pananond 2001, 61). Despite such diversity, returns from its core feed mill business continued to top the list in the conglomerate's turnover (Hiebert 2020, 301). Like many other big businesses in Southeast Asia, CP has also maintained a close association with Thai political elites, particularly the military. Its loyal support to China's economic reform over the decades has also earned Dhanin and his family close personal ties with the Chinese Communist Party. As an economic ally of Beijing and the Thai government, the CP Group has become the main conduit for Chinese investments in Thailand's "Eastern Economic Corridor"—a key component of the "Thailand 4.0" economic policy announced by the Thai military junta in 2016 (Schmidt and Chuwiruch 2019).

CONCLUSION

During the era of Deng's Reform and Opening-Up Policy, when China desperately needed FDI to develop its economy, ethnic Chinese capitalists in Southeast Asia and globally took a leap of faith to invest in the transitioning economy of post-socialist China. The chapter has demonstrated that Chinese identity was both a currency and motivation for them to contribute to the Chinese economy. As Sawada (1998, 140) argues, besides China's low labor costs as an ideal production base during the 1990s, the shared cultural background between the Chinese overseas investors and local Chinese was able to help them foster trust and develop relationships with key figures and other major investors. While the investment of older-generation Chinese migrant entrepreneurs such as Liem Sioe Liong, Mochtar Riady, Robert Kuok, and Dhanin Chearavanont were initially motivated by the primacy of patrimony, especially to their ancestral provinces, their subsequent generations who have little emotional attachments with China were primarily driven by profit (Cheong et al. 2017). In making business decisions and dealing with their mainland Chinese counterparts, the current generation of diasporic Chinese entrepreneurs continues to exercise their agentic power—arguably based on pragmatic economic calculation rather than emotive cultural affinity—in turning their cultural capital into fiscal capital (Hoon and Chan 2021, 322). This development can be seen in the shift in their investment location over the past two decades from southeast provinces of China that are associated with their ancestral heritage to other regions with the greatest economic opportunities and most conducive infrastructure.

As state capitalism has become a feature of the Chinese economic structure, the party-state's institutional encroachment in the realms of economic activity is increasingly common (Pearson et al. 2021). Since the 1980s, the Chinese state had been deeply impressed with the Southeast Asian Chinese conglomerates for their capital, technologies, and local networks and had offered them various investment opportunities (Ren and Liu 2021). In the case of the CP Group, the Chinese state had encouraged the conglomerate to expand investments to other industries and locations beyond the SEZs (Handley 2013, 169). It had also invited Southeast Asian capitalists to engage in joint-venture with the Chinese state-owned enterprises in various industrial and development projects. The Suzhou Industrial Park project with Singapore and the building of the World Trade Center Tower with the Kuok Brothers were prime examples of such collaboration. This shows that while the ethnic identity of diasporic Chinese entrepreneurs had provided them the impetus and facilitated their entry into the Chinese market, many other factors had led them to opportunities for expansion in China under the Chinese state's supervision (Liu and Jayanthakumaran 2016, 79). This situation also signifies that ethnic identity has gradually become less relevant in doing business in China as the Chinese economy matures and emphasizes competitiveness rather than interpersonal relationships (Kumar et al. 2005, 30).

Domestically, except Singapore, crony capitalism—manifested in the client-patron relationship between Chinese capitalists and politico-bureaucrats in the oligarchy—appears to be a common feature in the Southeast Asian Chinese conglomerates discussed in the chapter. While navigating the treacherous waters of anti-Chinese policies and sentiments in their host society, ethnic Chinese capitalists in Myanmar, Indonesia, Malaysia, and Thailand managed to establish patronage with the indigenous ruling class (the military, political elites, and royal families). They do this not only for survival but also, and more important, for market domination. As they built their business empires and personal wealth, these Chinese entrepreneurs became targets of extortion, but, paradoxically, they also actively perpetuated and reproduced a predatory political-business system (Chong 2018). The political environment in these countries can be described as volatile, often characterized by coups and the constant change of governments. Nevertheless, ethnic Chinese capitalists had been resourceful and flexible in their engagement with local political parties, which normally meant not putting all their eggs in one basket. Their networks with local political parties place them in an excellent position to be a conduit to help China navigate local politics in Southeast Asia for its BRI projects.

In 2013, the Development Research Centre of the State Council of the People's Republic of China, through its journal *Management World* (管理世界), published a 500-page volume titled *Chinese philanthropists: The charitable acts and contributions of 50 Chinese leaders to China and the world* (華人慈善家—50 位華人領袖的中國及世界慈善行動與貢獻). The volume featured profiles of "exemplary" global Chinese entrepreneurs and societal leaders, including a handful from China, who had contributed financially to philanthropic work in China to build schools, hospitals, and orphanages and donated to catastrophic events like the Wenchuan earthquake. Thirteen out of the fifty featured philanthropists were ethnic Chinese capitalists from Southeast Asia (seven from Indonesia, three from Singapore, two from Malaysia, one from Thailand, and one from the Philippines). While the editorial preface stated that the selected individuals were "role model" figures of their society, ironically at least two of them (Henry J. Gunawan 吳俊亮 and Tansri Chandra 陳明宗)—both from Indonesia—were convicted of illegal activities in their home country in 2020. It appears that the judgment of character had come from the hegemonic lens of the Chinese state, which seemed to be narrowly defined by one's emotional connection and financial contribution to the ancestral land, rather than by the integrity of one's personal and business practices.

A new wave of nationalism based on the old Middle Kingdom mentality is evident in the logic of the rising Chinese state and its leaders as they continue to incorporate the Chinese overseas in their strategy to re-center China (Chan and Hoon 2021, 8). A case in point was the inaugural "World Overseas Chinese Entrepreneurs Conference" (世界華僑華人工商大會) organized by the Chinese government's Overseas Chinese Affairs Office (僑辦) in July 2015, which invited over 300 prominent entrepreneurs of Chinese descent from all around the world. Suryadinata (2017, 162) observes that in the speeches of top Chinese leaders at the conference, 華商 *huashang* (diasporic Chinese entrepreneurs) were referred to as 僑商 *qiaoshang* (compatriot entrepreneurs overseas). The former normally refers to Chinese descent of foreign citizenship, while the latter refers to Chinese nationals. The conflation of the two has been a witting strategy used by the Overseas Chinese Affairs Office since its establishment in 1978 to homologize global Chineseness to a China-centric Chineseness (Chan and Hoon 2021, 16). At the same conference, Chinese Premier Li Keqiang urged these Chinese entrepreneurs to serve the interests of China first and stated three expectations he had for them: to foster the economic transformation and development of China, to build a bridge between China and foreign countries for BRI economic cooperation, and to build a positive image of Chinese entrepreneurs globally (Suryadinata 2017, 156–157).

The Chinese overseas are an essential resource for China's rising political ambitions and economic globalization agenda, including the "Going Out" or "Go Globally" strategy and outward FDI under the framework of the BRI (Ren and Liu 2021). In the past few decades, ethnic Chinese entrepreneurs in Southeast Asia had expanded into the transnational domains and developed "multiple situated embeddedness" with their host country and China (Santosombat and Lee 2017, 28). However, Ren and Liu (2021) cautioned us that such economic transnationalism might reinforce perceived cultural affinity to China, which might amplify the contested racial politics, especially in Southeast Asian countries where the ethnic Chinese are a pariah minority. The case of the World Overseas Chinese Entrepreneurs Conference described above shows precisely how an increasingly assertive China regards its diaspora and its presumed role in serving the interests of the "ancestral land." With the rising resentment of the Southeast Asian indigenous population toward mainland Chinese capital and economic encroachment, China's indiscriminate conflation of the overseas Chinese entrepreneurs with its nationals can rekindle the deep-seated suspicion of the ethnic Chinese as a fifth column of China. The challenge for Southeast Asian Chinese capitalists to negotiate and balance their national and political identity with their cultural and ethnic identity has never been more urgent.

NOTES

1. See, for example, Redding (1990), Drucker (1994), Seagrave (1996), and Weidenbaum and Hughes (1996). Aihwa Ong (1997) argues that Orientalist imaginations on Chinese capitalism were also deployed by Asian leaders who, through self-Orientalizing representations, attempted to reify Western concepts of Chineseness, *guanxi* networks, and neo-Confucianism to explain cultural differences between Asia and the West, in order to demonstrate that the former is not inferior to the latter.

2. For example, Southeast Asian/ASEAN countries established diplomatic relations with the People's Republic of China at different times: Vietnam, Myanmar, and Indonesia in 1950, though Indonesia suspended its relations with China in 1967 and only resumed them in 1990; Cambodia in 1958; Laos in 1961; Malaysia and Thailand in 1974; the Philippines in 1975; Singapore in 1990; and Brunei Darussalam in 1991.

3. However, Wong (1999, 14) notes that prior to 1992, "a lot of Southeast Asian capital flowing into China has been routed via Hong Kong and Macau. It is well known that many large investment projects in China by Southeast Asian ethnic Chinese are first incorporated in Hong Kong and then treated by China as officially 'Hong Kong investment.'"

Glossary

ACFTA	ASEAN–China Free Trade Agreement
ASEAN	Association of Southeast Asian Nations
AUN	ASEAN University Network
bianbao (邊胞)	frontier compatriots
Bianjiang xingzheng sheji weiyuanhui (邊疆行政設計委員會)	Frontier Administration Design Committee
bianjiang xue (邊疆學)	frontier studies in Nationalist China
Bianjiang zhoukan (邊疆周刊)	*Frontier weekly*
BRI	Belt and Road Initiative by China
Bumiputera	Malays and other indigenous groups
CCP	Chinese Communist Party
chouzhen (籌賑)	relief funds
CPB	Communist Party of Burma
cukong (主公)	masters
da qiaowu (大僑務)	big overseas Chinese work
da Taizu zhuyi (大泰族主義)	Pan-Thaiism
dahoufang (大後方)	Great Rear
Daluo (打洛)	a border town of Yunnan
difang geju zhengquan (地方割據政權)	local separatist regime
difang zhengquan (地方政權)	local power
diguo zhuyi guojia (帝國主義國家)	imperialistic nations
fan faxisi (反法西斯)	anti-fascist
FDI	foreign direct investment
Ganjang Cina	Crush the Chinese
GLC	government-linked corporation
gong (工)	laborers

Glossary

guanxi (關係)	family or clan-based network
guiguo nanqiao (歸國難僑)	refugee-returnees
guiqiao (歸僑)	returned overseas Chinese
guiqiao	returnees
Guoli xi'nan lianhe daxue (國立西南聯合大學)	National Southwest Associated University
haiwai shiyezhe (海外失業者)	jobless people from abroad
Hanban (漢辦)	Office of Chinese Language Council International, currently known as Centre for Language Education and Cooperation
Hanhua (漢化)	Sinicized
huaqiao (華僑)	Chinese nationals who reside overseas
huaren (華人)	ethnic Chinese of foreign citizenship
huashang (華商)	diasporic Chinese entrepreneurs
hukou (戶口)	registered residency status
Jinan xuetang (暨南學堂)	Jinan Academy
jishu rencai (技術人才)	technical talents
JTC	Jurong Town Corporation
kangzhan de jingji zhongxin (抗戰的經濟中心)	economic center for the war of resistance
Keluarga Katolik Indonesia	Indonesian Catholic Family
Kuomintang	Chinese Nationalist
laoban (老闆)	boss
Lingkar Pengajian	Circle for Quranic Recitation
manyi (蠻夷)	barbaric
Masalah Cina	Chinese Problem
mingjun (明君)	enlightened ruler
minxin xiangtong (民心相通)	promotion of people-to-people ties
minzu da tuanjie de hexin (民族大團結的核心)	core of minzu unity
MPI	magnetic particle inspection
nanmin (難民)	war refugees
Nanxun (南巡)	Deng Xiaoping's southern tour in 1992
Nanyang huaqiao chouzhen zuguo nanmin zonghui (南洋華僑籌賑祖國難民總會)	Nanyang China Relief Fund
Nanyang xuehui (南洋學會)	South Seas Society in Nanyang

Nanyang wenhua jiaoyu shiyebu (南洋文化教育事業部)	Nanyang Cultural and Educational Affairs Bureau
Nanyang yanjiu (南洋研究)	Nanyang Studies journal
NCRF	Nanyang China Relief Fund
neiyou (内憂)	domestic concern
NEP	New Economic Policy
NLD	National League for Democracy government of Myanmar
nong (農)	farmers
NU	Nahdlatul Ulama
OCAC	Committee of Overseas Chinese Affairs (subsequently Overseas Chinese Affairs Commission of the People's Republic of China)
Organisasi Buddhist Manggala	Manggala Buddhist Organization
P2P	people-to-people
paukphaw	"sibling-like," refers to historical intimate bilateral relations between countries
Persekutuan Reform Injil Indonesia	Indonesia Reformed Evangelical Fellowship
PP-10	Presidential Instruction 10/1959 in Indonesia
PPIT	*Perkumpulan Pelajar Indonesia Tiongkok* or Indonesian Students' Association in the People's Republic of China
PPPI	*Perhimpoenan Peladjar-Peladjar Indonesia* or Indonesian Students Association
pribumi	persons of the soil, native or indigenous
qiaobao (僑胞)	Chinese compatriots overseas
qiaojuan (僑眷)	dependents of returned overseas Chinese
qiaoshang (僑商)	compatriot entrepreneurs overseas
qiaowu (僑務)	Overseas Chinese Affairs
qiaoxiang	hometown
qiaoxiang (僑鄉)	Chinese overseas' affection for their hometown

quanpan xihua (全盤西化)　　　total Westernization (of China)
Reformasi　　　　　　　　　　Reformation
renzhong (人種)　　　　　　　race
santri　　　　　　　　　　　　devout Muslim students who attend
　　　　　　　　　　　　　　　　Islamic boarding schools
SCCCI　　　　　　　　　　　　Singapore Chinese Chamber of Com-
　　　　　　　　　　　　　　　　merce and Industry
SEATO　　　　　　　　　　　　Southeast Asia Treaty Organization
SEZs　　　　　　　　　　　　　Special Economic Zones
Shan (撣)　　　　　　　　　　other reference for the Tai
shang (商)　　　　　　　　　merchants
shi (士)　　　　　　　　　　scholars
SIP　　　　　　　　　　　　　Suzhou Industrial Park
SLORC　　　　　　　　　　　　State Law and Order Restoration
　　　　　　　　　　　　　　　　Council
SME　　　　　　　　　　　　　small and medium-scale enterprise
Sumpah Pemuda　　　　　　　Youth Oath
Tai (傣) Dai　　　　　　　　　a branch of the Thai race
tianxia (天下)　　　　　　　under heaven
tusi (土司)　　　　　　　　nuptials of chieftains
waihuan (外患)　　　　　　foreign threat
walisanga　　　　　　　　　saints
weixin (維新)　　　　　　　reform
WTO　　　　　　　　　　　　　World Trade Organization
Xi'nan minzu (西南民族)　　　southwestern races at Lianda
Xifa (西法)　　　　　　　　Western methods
xin yimin (新移民)　　　　　new Chinese immigrants
Xinan yunshu chu (西南運輸處)　Southwest Transport Agency
xuetong (血統)　　　　　　　blood
Yan Huang de xueye (炎黃的血液)　Thai elite, including the royal family,
　　　　　　　　　　　　　　　　who had Chinese blood
Yishi bao (益世報)　　　　　benefiting the world
Yunnan sheng dang'an guan (雲南　Yunnan Provincial Archives
省檔案館)

zaihua yinni xuesheng xiehui (在華　*Perkumpulan Pelajar Indonesia*
印尼學生協會)　　　　　　　*Tiongkok* or Indonesian Students' As-
　　　　　　　　　　　　　　　　sociation in the People's Republic of
　　　　　　　　　　　　　　　　China
Zhongguo benbu (中國本部)　China proper
Zhongguoren (中國人)　　　skin color of Chinese

Zhonghua minzu (中華民族)	the Chinese nation, Chinese race, or various races of China
Zhonghua quanguo guiguo huaqiao lianhehui (中國全國歸國華僑聯合會)	All-China Federation of Returned Overseas Chinese
Zhongyuan Hanzu (中原漢族)	Han race of the Central Plain
zongzhi (宗支)	clan branches of the Zhonghua minzu
Zhongguo dongnanya jiaoliu menhu (中國東南亞交流的門戶)	Gateway to China-Southeast Asia interactions
Zhongshan wenhua jiaoyu guan (中山文化教育館)	Sun Yat-sen Institute for Culture and Education
Zhonghua minguo qiaowu weiyuan-hui (中華民國僑務委員會)	Republic of China Overseas Chinese Affairs Commission

Bibliography

Acharya, Amitav. 1998. "Culture, Security, Multilateralism: The 'ASEAN Way' and Regional Order." *Contemporary Security Policy* 19, no. 1: 55–84.

Aisyah, Rachmadea. 2018. "Chinese investments trending in Indonesia." *Jakarta Post*, May 2. http://www.thejakartapost.com/news/2018/05/02/chinese-investments-trending-in-indonesia.html.

Akashi, Yoji. 1970. *The Nanyang Chinese Salvation Movement, 1937–1941*. Lawrence, KS: Center for East Asian Studies, University of Kansas.

Alitto, Guy. 1979. *The Last Confucian: Liang Shu-ming and the Chinese Dilemma of Modernity.* Berkeley: University of California Press.

Allen, Pamela. 2003. "Literature and the Media Contemporary Literature from the Chinese 'Diaspora' in Indonesia." *Asian Ethnicity* 4, no. 3: 383–400.

Ang, Cheng-Guan. 2009. *Southeast Asia and the Vietnam War*. London: Routledge.

Ang, Cheng-Guan. 2013a. *Lee Kuan Yew's Strategic Thought*. New York: Routledge.

Ang, Cheng-Guan. 2013b. *Singapore, ASEAN, and the Cambodian Conflict, 1978–1991*. Singapore: NUS Press.

Ang, Cheng-Guan. 2018. *Southeast Asia's Cold War: An Interpretive History*. Honolulu: University of Hawai'i Press.

Antara News. 2021. "Xinjiang (Masih) Jadi Batu Sandungan Indonesia-China" [Xinjiang Remains as a Stumbling Block for Indonesia-China Relations]. January 23. https://www.antaranews.com/berita/1964444/xinjiang-masih-jadi-batu-sandungan-indonesia-china.

Anwar, Dewi Fortuna. 2019. "Indonesia-China Relations: To Be Handled with Care." *ISEAS Perspective*, no. 19: 1–7.

Arditya, Andre. 2020. "Throughout History, Youth Movements Hold a Generational Consciousness of a Better Indonesia." *The Conversation*, August 12. https://theconversation.com/throughout-history-youth-movements-hold-a-generational-consciousness-of-a-better-indonesia-144211.

Arkush, David. 1981. *Fei Xiaotong and Sociology in Revolutionary China.* Cambridge, MA: Council on East Asian Studies, Harvard University.

Babones, Salvatore. 2020. "From *Tianxia* to Tianxia: The Generalization of a Concept." *Chinese Political Science Review* 5: 131–147.

Baker, Chris, and Pasuk Phongpaichit. 2009. *A History of Thailand.* New York: Cambridge University Press.

Barme, Scot. 1993. *Luang Wichit Wathakan and the Creation of a Thai Identity.* Singapore: ISEAS.

Barr, Michael D. 2000a. *Lee Kuan Yew: The Beliefs Behind the Man.* Washington, DC: Georgetown University Press.

Barr, Michael D. 2000b. "Lee Kuan Yew and the 'Asian Values' Debate." *Asian Studies Review* 24, no. 3: 309–334.

Barr, Michael D. 2014. *The Ruling Elite of Singapore: Networks of Power and Influence.* London: I.B. Tauris.

BBC News. 2017. "Ahok Trial: The Blasphemy Case Testing Indonesian Identity." February 14. https://www.bbc.com/news/world-asia-38902960.

Blackburn, Kevin, and Karl Hack. 2012. *War Memory and the Making of Modern Malaysia and Singapore.* Singapore: NUS Press.

Blanchard, Jean-Marc F. 2019. *China's Maritime Silk Road Initiative and Southeast Asia: Dilemmas, Doubts, and Determination.* Singapore: Palgrave Macmillan.

Bolesta, Andrzej. 2018. "Myanmar-China Peculiar Relationship: Trade, Investment and the Model of Development." *Journal of International Studies* 11, no. 2: 23–36.

Borsuk, Richard, and Nancy Chng. 2014. *Liem Sioe Liong's Salim Group: The Business Pillar of Suharto's Indonesia.* Singapore: ISEAS.

Brah, Avtar. 1996. *Cartographies of Diaspora: Contesting Identities.* London: Routledge.

Budiman, Arief. 2001. "Rethinking Ethnicity and Nationalism: Anti-Chinese and Anti-Australian Sentiment in Indonesia." In *Indonesia: The Uncertain Transition*, edited by Damien Kingsbury and Arief Budiman, 264–291. Adelaide: Crawford House Publishing.

Burusratanaphand, Walwipha. 2001. "Chinese Identity in Thailand." In *Alternate Identities: The Chinese of Contemporary Thailand*, edited by Chee-Kiong Tong and Chan Kwok Bun, 67–84. Singapore: Times Academic Press.

Busbarat, Pongphisoot. 2016. "'Bamboo Swirling in the Wind': Thailand's Foreign Policy Imbalance between China and the United States." *Contemporary Southeast Asia* 38, no. 2: 233–257.

Cai, Yuzhuo. 2020. "China's 2020 Target: Reshaping Global Mobility Flows." European Association for International Education Blog. https://www.eaie.org/blog/china-2020-target-reshaping-global-mobility-flows.html.

Cen, Jiawu [岑家梧]. 1992a. "Guizhou Minzu Yanjiu Shulue" 貴州民族研究述略 [Brief Account of Guizhou Ethnological Research]. In *Cen Jiawu Minzu Yanjiu Wenji* 岑家梧民族研究文集 [Ethnological Writings of Cen Jiawu]. Beijing: Renmin chubanshe.

Cen, Jiawu [岑家梧]. 1992b. "Xi'nan Minzu Yanjiu De Huigu Yu Qianzhan" 西南民族研究的回顧與前瞻 [Review and Outlook of Research on *Xi'nan Minzu*]. In *Cen Jiawu Minzu Yanjiu Wenji* 岑家梧民族研究文集 [Ethnological Writings of Cen Jiawu]. Beijing: Renmin chubanshe.

Center of Thai Studies, Yunnan University. Accessed February 11, 2022. http://www.ctsynu.com/Introduction.php.

Chan, Chow Wah. 2009. *Light on the Lotus Hill: Shuang Lin Monastery and the Burma Road*. Singapore: Khoon Chee Vihara.

Chan, Kwok Bun, and Chee-Kiong Tong. 2014. "Singaporean Chinese Doing Business in China." In *Chinese Business: Rethinking Guanxi and Trust in Chinese Business Networks*, edited by Chee-Kiong Tong, 119–130. Singapore: Springer.

Chan, Ying-kit. 2019. "Ethnicity and Frontier Studies in Southwest China: Pan-Thai Nationalism and the Wartime Debate on National Identity, 1932–1945." *Twentieth-Century China* 44, no. 3: 324–344.

Chan, Ying-kit. 2020. "'Don't Belittle Our Southern Neighbor': Chen Xujing's View of Thailand." *Tsing Hua Journal of Chinese Studies* 50, no. 3: 511–550.

Chan, Ying-kit, and Chang-Yau Hoon. 2021. "Introduction: The Historicity of Nation and Contingency of Ethnicity." In *Contesting Chineseness: Ethnicity, Identity and Nation in China and Southeast Asia*, edited by Chang-Yau Hoon and Ying-kit Chan, 1–24. Singapore: Springer.

Chan, Ying-kit, and Fei Chen. 2020. "Introduction: Politicized Histories in Modern China." In *Alternative Representations of the Past: The Politics of History in Modern China*, edited by Ying-kit Chan and Fei Chen, 1–22. Berlin: De Gruyter.

Chen, Bisheng [陳碧笙]. 1938. *Dian Bian Jingying Lun* 滇邊經營論 [About Managing the Yunnan Frontier]. Hankou.

Chen, Chwen Chwen, Cinzia Colapindo, and Qing Luo. 2012. "The 2008 Beijing Olympics Opening Ceremony: Visual Insights into China's Soft Power." *Visual Culture* 27, no. 2: 188–195.

Chen, Daya [陳達婭], ed. 2010. *Nanyang 1939* 南洋 1939. Beijing: Zhongguo huaqiao chubanshe.

Chen, Gongcun [陳共存], ed. 2006. *Nanqiao Hun: Chen Jiageng Yu Nanyang Huaqiao Jigong Huiguo Kangri Fuwu Jishi* 南僑魂: 陳嘉庚與南洋華僑機工回國抗日服務紀實 [The Soul of Nanyang: Chen Jiageng and Nanyang Volunteers]. Kunming: Yunnan meishu chubanshe.

Chen, Jonathan. 2022. "Representing Chinese Indonesians: Pribumi Discourse and Regional Elections in Post-Reform Indonesia." *Journal of Current Southeast Asian Affairs* (forthcoming).

Chen, Qijin [陳其津]. 1999. *Wo De Fuqin Chen Xujing* 我的父親陳序經 [My Father Chen Xujing]. Guangzhou: Guangdong renmin chubanshe.

Chen, Shaofeng. 2019. "Are Southeast Asian Countries Willing to Join the Chorus of China's Maritime Silk Road Initiative?" In *China's Maritime Silk Road Initiative and Southeast Asia: Dilemmas, Doubts, and Determination*, edited by Jean-Marc F. Blanchard, 35–64. Singapore: Palgrave Macmillan.

Chen, Su-Ching [Chen Xujing]. 1929. *Recent Theories of Sovereignty*. Canton: Lingnan University Bookstore.

Chen, Su-Ching [Chen Xujing]. 1944. *China and Southeastern Asia*. Chongqing: China Institute of Pacific Relations.

Chen, Wen, and Liao Shaolian. 2005. *China-ASEAN Trade Relations: A Discussion on Complementarity and Competition*. Singapore: Institute of Southeast Asian Studies.

Chen, Xujing 陳序經. 1941. *Xianluo Yu Zhongguo* 暹羅與中國 [Siam and China]. Chongqing: Shangwu yinshuguan.

Cheong, Kee Cheok, Poh Ping Lee, and Kam Hing Lee. 2017. "From Patrimonialism to Profit: The Changing Flow of Funds from the Chinese in Malaysia to China." *Journal of Contemporary Asia* 47, no. 5: 687–703.

Chheang, Vannarith. 2021. "Cambodia Embraces China's Controversial Confucius Institutes." *Fulcrum: Analysis on Southeast Asia*. ISEAS-Yusof Ishak Institute. https://fulcrum.sg/cambodia-embraces-chinas-controversial-confucius-institutes/.

Chia, Jack Meng-Tat. 2008. "Buddhism in Singapore-China Relations: Venerable Hong Choon and His Visits, 1982–1990." *China Quarterly* 196: 864–883.

Chia, Oai Peng. 2008. "Malaysian Investments in China: Market Forces or Political Needs?" In *China in the World: Contemporary Issues and Perspectives*, edited by Emile Kok Kheng Yeoh and Joanne Hoi Lee Loh, 61–69. Kuala Lumpur: Institute of China Studies.

Chiang, Kai-Shek [蔣介石]. 1943. *Zhongguo Zhi Mingyun* 中國之命運 [China's Destiny]. Chongqing: Zhengzhong shuju.

Chiang, Yung-Chen. 2001. *Social Engineering and the Social Sciences in China, 1919–1949*. New York: Cambridge University Press.

China News. 2009. "鄧小平30年前說借鑒新加坡是客套話嗎?" [Was It Mere Courtesy When Deng Xiaping Said He Wanted to Emulate Singapore Thirty Years Ago?] https://www.chinanews.com.cn/hb/news/2009/03-30/1624231.shtml.

Chinese Philanthropists: The Charitable Acts and Contributions of 50 Chinese Leaders to China and the World [華人慈善家—50 位華人領袖的中國及世界慈善行動與貢獻]. 2013. 國務院發展研究中心《管理世界》雜志.

Chinvanno, Anuson. 1992. *Thailand's Policies towards China, 1949–54*. Oxford: St. Anthony's College.

Chong, Wu-Ling. 2018. *Chinese Indonesians in Post-Suharto Indonesia: Democratisation and Ethnic Minorities*. Hong Kong: Hong Kong University Press.

Chua, Amy. 2004. *World on Fire: How Exporting Market Democracy Breeds Hatred and Global Instability*. New York: Anchor Books.

Chua, Christine. 2008. *Chinese Big Business in Indonesia: The State of Capital*. New York: Routledge.

Chua, Daniel Wei Boon. 2017. *US-Singapore Relations, 1965–1975: Strategic Non-Alignment in the Cold War*. Singapore: NUS Press.

Chun, Allen. 2017. *Forget Chineseness: On the Geopolitics of Cultural Identification*. Albany, NY: State University of New York Press.

Ciorciari, John D. 2020. "Distance and Dominance: China, America, and Southeast Asia's Northern Tier." In *The Deer and the Dragon: Southeast Asia and China in the 21st Century*, edited by Donald K. Emmerson, 299–328. Stanford: Stanford University Press.

Cohen, Paul A. 1997. *History in Three Keys: The Boxers as Event, Experience, and Myth*. New York: Columbia University Press.

Cohen, Paul A. 2009. *Speaking to History: The Story of King Goujian in Twentieth-Century China*. Berkeley: University of California Press.

Cohen, Paul A. 2017. *History and Popular Memory: The Power of Story in Moments of Crisis.* New York: Columbia University Press.

Cole, James H. 1979–1980. "'Total Westernization' in Kuomintang China: The Case of Ch'en Hsu-Ching." *Monumenta Serica* 34: 77–143.

Collaborative Innovation Center of Territorial Sovereignty and Maritime Rights, Zhengzhou University Branch. Accessed February 11, 2022. http://www7.zzu.edu .cn/cictsmr_zzub/fzxgk1/fzxyg.htm.

Colvin, Geoff. 2017. "Study: China Will Overtake the U.S. as World's Largest Economy Before 2030." *Fortune*, February 9. http://fortune.com/2017/02/09/study -china-will-overtake-the-u-s-as-worlds-largest-economy-before-2030/.

Confucius Institute U.S. Center. "Clarity Around Name Change." https://www .ciuscenter.org/clarity-around-name-change/.

Conroy-Krutz, Emily. 2015. *Christian Imperialism: Converting the World in the Early American Republic.* Ithaca, NY: Cornell University Press.

Davies, Henry Rodolph. 1909. *Yün-nan: The Link Between India and the Yangtze.* Cambridge: Cambridge University Press.

Diamant, Neil J. 2011. "Conspicuous Silence: Veterans and the Depoliticization of War Memory in China." *Modern Asian Studies* 45, no. 2: 431–461.

Diaz-Barriga, Miguel, and Margaret E. Dorsey. 2019. *Fencing in Democracy: Border Walls, Necrocitizenship, and the Security State.* Durham, NC: Duke University Press.

Dieleman, Marleen, and Wladimir Sachs. 2006. "Oscillating Between a Relationship-Based and a Market-Based Model: The Salim Group." *Asia Pacific Journal of Management* 23: 521–536.

Dieleman, Marleen. 2007. *The Rhythm of Strategy: A Corporate Biography of the Salim Group of Indonesia.* Amsterdam: Amsterdam University Press.

Ding, Sheng. 2014. *Chinese Soft Power and Public Diplomacy: An Analysis of China's New Diaspora Engagement Policies in the Xi Era.* Working Paper. Seoul: The East Asian Institute.

Diokno, Maria Serena, Hsin-Huang Michael Hsiao, and Alan H. Yang, eds. 2019. *China's Footprints in Southeast Asia.* Singapore: National University of Singapore Press.

Dirlik, Arif. 1996. "Chinese History and the Question of Orientalism." *History and Theory* 35, no. 4: 96–118.

Drucker, Peter. 1994. "The New Superpower: The Overseas Chinese." *Asian Wall Street Journal*, December 21.

Eaksittipong, Sittithep. 2017. "From Chinese 'in' to Chinese 'of' Thailand: The Politics of Knowledge Production During the Cold War." *Rian Thai: International Journal of Thai Studies* 10, no. 1: 99–116.

Eaksittipong, Sittithep. 2020. "The Social and Political Lives of G. William Skinner and *Chinese Society in Thailand.*" In *Alternative Representations of the Past: The Politics of History in Modern China*, edited by Ying-kit Chan and Fei Chen, 85–118. Berlin: De Gruyter.

Eaksittipong, Sittithep. 2021. "The Chinese of Thailand: Academic Diplomacy and the Convergence of Sino-Thai Intellectual Nationalisms." In *Contesting*

Chineseness: Ethnicity, Identity, and Nation in China and Southeast Asia, edited by Chang-Yau Hoon and Ying-kit Chan, 101–122. Singapore: Springer.

Eastman, Lloyd E. 1972. "Fascism in Kuomintang China: The Blue Shirts." *China Quarterly* 49: 1–31.

Eastman, Lloyd E. 1974. *The Abortive Revolution: China under Nationalist Rule.* Cambridge, MA: Harvard University Press.

Edwards, Louise. 2016. *Women Warriors and Wartime Spies of China.* New York: Cambridge University Press.

Elman, Benjamin A. 1990. *Classicism, Politics, and Kinship: The Ch'ang-chou School of New Text Confucianism in Late Imperial China.* Berkeley: University of California Press.

Embassy of People's Republic of China in Republic of Indonesia. 2016. "Chinese Embassy in Indonesia and NU Host Fast-breaking and Donation Ceremony." June 22. https://www.mfa.gov.cn/ce/ceindo/eng/sgdt/t1375559.htm.

Emmerson, Donald K., ed. 2021. *The Deer and the Dragon: Southeast Asia and China in the 21st Century.* Singapore: ISEAS.

Esherick, Joseph. 2006. "How the Qing Became China." In *Empire to Nation: Historical Perspectives on the Making of the Modern World*, edited by Joseph Esherick, Hasan Kayali, and Eric Van Young, 229–259. Lanham, MD: Rowman & Littlefield.

Evans, Grant, Christopher Hutton, and Kuah Khun Eng, eds. 2000. *Where China Meets Southeast Asia: Social and Cultural Change in the Border Regions.* Singapore: ISEAS.

Fang, Bao. 2015. "On Changing Trends of China's Education of ASEAN Students in the Past 15 Years: An Analysis of the Related Statistical Data of 1999–2013" [近十五年東盟國家來華留學生教育的變化趨勢研究：基於 1999–2013 年相關統計數據的分析]. *Comparative Education Review* [比較教育研究], no. 11: 77–86.

Fang, Guoyu [方國瑜]. 2001. "Zixu: Lueshu Zixue Jingli" 自序：略述自學經理 [Autobiography: A Brief Description of My Learning Experience]. In *Fang Guoyu Wenji* 方國瑜文集 [Collected Writings of Fang Guoyu], Vol. 1, edited by Lin Chaomin 林超民. Kunming: Yunnan jiaoyu chubanshe.

Feng, Laiyi [馮來儀]. 1992. "Zuozhe Zhuanlue" 作者傳略 [Biography of the Author]. In *Cen Jiawu Minzu Yanjiu Wenji* 岑家梧民族研究文集 [Ethnological writings of Cen Jiawu]. Beijing: Renmin chubanshe.

Fingar, Thomas. 2020. "China's Changing Priorities in Southeast Asia: Security and Development in Historical Context." In *The Deer and the Dragon: Southeast Asia and China in the 21st Century*, edited by Donald K. Emmerson, 41–64. Stanford: Stanford University Press.

Fossati, Diego, Hui Yew-Foong, and Siwage Dharma Negara. 2017. *The Indonesia National Survey Project: Economy, Society and Politics, Trends in Southeast Asia No. 10.* Singapore: ISEAS.

Foulcher, Keith. 2000. "Sumpah Pemuda: The Making and Meaning of a Symbol of Indonesian Nationhood." *Asian Studies Review* 24, no. 3: 377–410.

Fu, Sinian [傅斯年]. 2003. "Zhi Gu Jiegang" 致顧頡剛 [To Gu Jiegang]. In *Fu Sinian Quanji* 傅斯年全集 [The Collected Writings of Fu Sinian], Vol. 7, edited by Ouyang Zhesheng 歐陽哲生. Changsha: Hunan jiaoyu chubanshe.

G.E.T. 1942. "Wings for the Burma Road." *Far Eastern Survey* 11, no. 5: 59–60.

Gambe, Annabelle. 1996. *Overseas Chinese Entrepreneurship in Southeast Asia* (Forschungsberichte aus dem Seminar für Politikwissenschaft und Soziologie Nr. 14). TU Braunschweig.

Gao, Weinong [高偉濃], and Kou Haiyang [寇海洋]. 2011. "Erzhanhou Xin Ma Huaqiao Fanhui Yuan Qiaojudi Wenti Chutan" 二戰後新馬華僑返回原僑居地問題初探 [An Exploration of Overseas Chinese Repatriation to Singapore and Malaya after the Second World War]. *Dongnanya Nanya Yanjiu* 東南亞南亞研究, no. 3: 77–94.

Gerstle, Gary. 2017. *American Crucible: Race and Nation in the Twentieth Century*. Princeton, NJ: Princeton University Press.

Giersch, Patterson C. 2006. *Asian Borderlands: The Transformation of Qing China's Yunnan Frontier*. Cambridge, MA: Harvard University Press.

Godley, Michael R., and Charles A. Coppel. 1990. "The Pied Piper and the Prodigal Children. A Report on the Indonesian-Chinese Students Who Went to Mao's China." *Archipel*, no. 39: 179–198.

Goh, Chor Boon. 2013. *Technology and Entrepot Colonialism in Singapore, 1819–1940*. Singapore: ISEAS.

Goh, Evelyn, and Sheldon W. Simon. 2008. *China, the United States, and Southeast Asia: Contending Perspectives on Politics, Security, and Economics*. New York and London: Routledge.

Goh, Sui Nui. 2018. "China Wants Closer Ties with Indonesia, Says Premier Li Keqiang." *Straits Times*, February 9. https://www.straitstimes.com/asia/se-asia/china-wants-closer-ties-with-indonesia-says-li.

Gong, Yiwen, and Jianwen Wu. 2020. "A Cross-cultural Perspective on the Identification of Southeast Asian Studies with China's Reform and Opening" [跨文化視域下東南亞留學生對中國改革開放的認同研究]. *International Public Relations Journal* [國際公關], no. 2: 237–240.

Gu, Jiegang [顧頡剛]. 1939a. "'Zhongguo Benbu' Yi Ming Ji Ying Feiqi" "中國本部" 一名亟應廢棄 ["China Proper" Should Quickly Be Discarded]. *Qianxian* [Frontline] 2, no. 2: 21–24.

Gu, Jiegang [顧頡剛]. 1939b. "Zhonghua Minzu Shi Yi Ge" 中華民族是一個 [The *Zhonghua Minzu* is One]. *Bianjiang Zhoukan, Yishi Bao* 9, February.

Gu, Jiegang [顧頡剛]. 2007. *Gu Jiegang Riji* 顧頡剛日記 [Diary of Gu Jiegang], Vol. 4. Taipei: Lianjing.

Gunawan, Elizabeth Susanti. 2018. "The Growing Interest of Indonesian Students Studying in China Post Suharto Era." *Journal of Chinese Overseas* 14, no. 1: 115–132.

Guo, Yanfang [郭艷芳]. 2006. "Qingdai Zhongguoren De Xianluo Guan" 清代中國人的暹羅觀 [Chinese Views of Siam during the Qing Dynasty]. MA diss., Shandong University.

Guy, Kent R. 2010. *Qing Governors and Their Provinces: The Evolution of Territorial Administration in China, 1644–1796.* Seattle: University of Washington Press.

Haley, George T., Usha C. V. Haley, and Chin Tiong Tan. 2009. *New Asian Emperors: The Business Strategies of the Overseas Chinese.* Singapore: Wiley.

Han, Xiaorong. 2013. "The Demise of China's Overseas Chinese State Farms." *Journal of Chinese Overseas* 9, no. 1: 33–58.

Handley, Paul. 2003. "De-mythologizing Charoen Pokphand: An Interpretive Picture of the CP Group's Growth and Diversification." In *Ethnic Business Chinese Capitalism in Southeast Asia*, edited by Jomo K. S. and Brian C. Folk, 155–182. New York: Routledge Curzon.

Harper, Tim. 2021. *Underground Asia: Global Revolutionaries and the Assault on Empire.* Cambridge, MA: Harvard University Press.

Herlijanto, Johanes. 2013. "Emulating China: Representation of China and the Contemporary Critique of Indonesia." PhD diss., Vrije Universiteit, Amsterdam, and Macquarie University, Sydney.

Herlijanto, Johanes. 2017a. "How the Indonesian Elite Regards Relations with China." *ISEAS Perspective*, no. 8.

Herlijanto, Johanes. 2017b. "How the Indonesian Elite Regards Relations with China." *ISEAS Perspective*, no. 89.

Heryanto, Ariel. 1999. "Rape, Race and Reporting." In *Reformasi: Crisis and Change in Indonesia*, edited by Arief Budiman, Barbara Hatley, and Damien Kingsbury, 299–334. Clayton: Monash Asia Institute, Monash University.

Hew, Wai-Weng. 2014. "Beyond 'Chinese Diaspora' and 'Islamic Ummah': Various Transnational Connections and Local Negotiations of Chinese Muslim Identities in Indonesia." *Sojourn: Journal of Social Issues in Southeast Asia* 29, no. 3: 627–656.

Hewison, Kevin. 2018. "Thailand: An Old Relationship Renewed." *Pacific Review* 31, no. 1: 119.

Hewitt, Pamela. 1982. "Southeast Asian Studies in China." *Australian Journal of Chinese Affairs*, no. 7: 151–162.

Hiebert, Murray. 2020. *Under Beijing's Shadow: Southeast Asia's China Challenge.* Lanham, MD: Rowman & Littlefield.

Ho, Elaine Lynn-Ee. 2015. "Transnational Identities, Multiculturalism, or Assimilation? China's 'Refugee-Returnees' and Generational Transitions." *Modern Asian Studies* 49, no. 2: 525–545.

Ho, Elaine Lynn-Ee. 2018. *Citizens in Motion: Emigration, Immigration, and Re-Migration Across China's Borders.* Stanford: Stanford University Press.

Ho, Khai Leong, and Samuel C. Y. Ku, eds. 2005. *China and Southeast Asia: Global Changes and Regional Challenges.* Singapore: ISEAS.

Ho, Khai Leong, ed. 2009. *Connecting and Distancing: Southeast Asia and China.* Singapore: ISEAS.

Ho, Rih Hwa. 1990. *Eating Salt: An Autobiography.* Singapore: Times Books International.

Hong, Lysa. 1984. *Thailand in the Nineteenth Century: Evolution of the Economy and Society.* Singapore: ISEAS.

Hoon, Chang-Yau. 2006. "Assimilation, Multiculturalism, Hybridity: The Dilemmas of the Ethnic Chinese in Post-Suharto Indonesia." *Asian Ethnicity* 7, no. 2: 149–166.

Hoon, Chang-Yau. 2008. *Chinese Identity in Post-Suharto Indonesia*. Brighton, UK: Sussex Academic Press.

Hoon, Chang-Yau. 2012. "Mochtar Riady." In *Southeast Asian Personalities of Chinese Descent: A Biographical Dictionary*, edited by Leo Suryadinata, 926–928. Singapore: Chinese Heritage Centre.

Hoon, Chang-Yau. 2014. "Evolving Chineseness, Ethnicity and Business: The Making of the Ethnic Chinese as a 'Market-Dominant Minority' in Indonesia." In *Catalysts of Change: Chinese Business in Asia*, edited by Thomas Menkhoff, Chay Yue Wah, Hans-Dieter Evers, and Chang-Yau Hoon, 107–128. Singapore: World Scientific.

Hoon, Chang-Yau, and Esther Kuntjara. 2019. "The Politics of 'Mandarin Fever' in Contemporary Indonesia: Resinicization, Economic Impetus, and China's Soft Power." *Asian Survey* 59, no. 3: 573–594.

Hoon, Chang-Yau, and Ying-kit Chan. 2021. "Conclusion: Chineseness, Quo Vadis?" In *Contesting Chineseness: Ethnicity, Identity and Nation in China and Southeast Asia*, edited by Chang-Yau Hoon and Ying-kit Chan, 319–324. Singapore: Springer.

Hoon, Chang-Yau, and Ying-kit Chan, eds. 2021. *Contesting Chineseness: Ethnicity, Identity, and Nation in China and Southeast Asia*. Singapore: Springer.

Hostetler, Laura. 2001. *Qing Colonial Enterprise: Ethnography and Cartography in Early Modern China*. Chicago: University of Chicago Press.

Hsu, Madeline Y. 2000. *Dreaming of Gold, Dreaming of Home: Transnationalism and Migration Between the United States and South China, 1882–1943*. Stanford: Stanford University Press.

Huang, Jianli, and Lysa Hong. 2004. "History and the Imaginaries of 'Big Singapore': Positioning the Sun Yat Sen Nanyang Memorial Hall." *Journal of Southeast Asian Studies* 35, no. 1: 65–89.

Huang, Xiaojian [黃小堅], Zhao Hongying [趙紅英], and Cong Yuefen [叢月芬]. 1995. *Haiwai Huaqiao Yu Kang Ri Zhanzheng* 海外華僑與抗日戰爭 [Chinese Overseas and China's War of Resistance with Japan]. Beijing: Beijing chubanshe.

Huang, Xingtao [黃興濤]. 2018. *Chongsu Zhonghua: Jindai Zhongguo "Zhonghua minzu" Guannian Yanjiu* 重塑中華: 近代中國 "中華民族" 觀念研究 [Remolding Chinese: A Study of the Concept of *Zhonghua Minzu* in Modern China]. Beijing: Beijing shifan daxue chubanshe.

Huang, Yukon. 2014. "Can a Chinese 'Maritime Silk Route' Cool Tensions in Asia?" *East Asia Forum*, May 5. http://www.eastasiaforum.org/2014/05/05/can-a-chinese-maritime-silk-route-cool-tensions-in-asia/.

Israel, John. 1998. *Lianda: A Chinese University in War and Revolution*. Stanford, CA: Stanford University Press.

Jacobs, Justin M. 2017. *Xinjiang and the Modern Chinese State*. Seattle: University of Washington Press.

Jacques, Martin. 2008. "As China's Power Grows, the Diaspora Starts to Flex Its Worldwide Muscle." *The Guardian*, June 11. https://www.theguardian.com/commentisfree/2008/jun/11/china.comment.

Jiang, Xiaolin. 2005. *Jiang Yingliang Zhuan* [Biography of Jiang Yingliang]. Guilin: Guangxi shifan daxue chubanshe.

Jiang, Yingliang [江應梁]. 1938a. *Kangzhan Zhong De Xi'nan Minzu Wenti* 抗戰中的西南民族問題 [The Question of *Xi'nan Minzu* in Wartime]. Chongqing: Zhongshan wenhua jiaoyu guan.

Jiang, Yingliang [江應梁]. 1938b. "Yunnan Xibu Bo Yi Minzu Zhi Jingji Shehui" 雲南西部伯夷民族之經濟社會 [Economy and Society of the Bo and Yi in Western Yunnan]. *Xi'nan Bianjiang* 1, no. 1: 63–82.

Jiang, Yingliang 江應梁. 1948. "Qing Queding Xi'nan Bianjiang Zhengce" 請確定西南邊疆政策 [Petition to Devise a Policy for the Southwestern Frontier]. *Bianzheng Gonglun* [Frontier Affairs] 7, no. 1: 1–3.

Kaisan, Tejapan. 1992. "Pigtail: A Pre-History of Chineseness in Siam." *Sojourn* 7, no. 1: 95–122.

Kapp, Robert A. 1973. *Szechuan and the Chinese Republic: Provincial Militarism and Central Power, 1911–1938.* New Haven, CT: Yale University Press.

Karl, Rebecca E. 2002. *Staging the World: Chinese Nationalism at the Turn of the Twentieth Century.* Durham, NC: Duke University Press.

Kim, Young-Chan, ed. 2016. *Chinese Global Production Network in ASEAN.* Cham: Springer.

Kinzley, Judd C. 2012. "Crisis and the Development of China's Southwestern Periphery: The Transformation of Panzhihua, 1936–1969." *Modern China* 38, no. 5: 559–584.

Kinzley, Judd C. 2018. *Natural Resources and the New Frontier: Constructing Modern China's Borderlands.* Chicago: University of Chicago Press.

Kirby, William C. 1984. *Germany and Republican China.* Stanford, CA: Stanford University Press.

Kivimäki, Timo. 2016. "Politics of Economic Relations Between China and Myanmar." In *Chinese Global Production Networks in ASEAN*, edited by Young-Chan Kim, 137–156. London: Springer International Publishing Switzerland.

Kknews. 2017. "Li Renliang: Huoyue Yu Guoji Wutai Shang De Taiyu Zhuanjia" 李仁良: 活躍於國際舞臺上的泰語專家 [Li Renliang: A Thai-language Specialist Active on the Global Arena], May 22. Accessed February 11, 2022. https://kknews.cc/zh-tw/news/y6y48pn.html.

Koh, Ernest. 2013. *Diaspora at War: The Chinese of Singapore between Empire and Nation, 1937–1945.* Leiden: Brill.

Koh, Sin Yee, Chang-Yau Hoon, and Noor Azam Haji-Othman. 2021. "'Mandarin Fever' and Chinese Language-learning in Brunei's Middle Schools: Discrepant Discourses, Multifaceted Realities and Institutional Barriers." *Asian Studies Review* 45, no. 20: 325–344.

Koning, Juliette, and Andreas Susanto. 2008. "Chinese Indonesians and 'the Rise of China': From Business Opportunities to Questions of Identity." In *China in the*

World: Contemporary Issues and Perspectives, edited by Emile Kok-Kheng Yeoh and Joanne Hoi-Lee Loh, 161–184. Kuala Lumpur: Institute of China Studies.

Koning, Juliette, and Michiel Verver. 2013. "Historicizing the 'Ethnic' in Ethnic Entrepreneurship: The Case of the Ethnic Chinese in Bangkok." *Entrepreneurship & Regional Development* 25, no. 5–6: 325–348.

Ku, Samuel C. Y. 2006. "Southeast Asian Studies in China and Taiwan: A Comparative Perspective." In *Southeast Asian Studies in China*, edited by Swee-Hock Saw and John Wong, 118–133. Singapore: ISEAS.

Kuah-Pearce, Khun Eng. 2011. *Rebuilding the Ancestral Village: Singaporeans in China*. Hong Kong: Hong Kong University Press.

Kuhn, Philip A. 2008. *Chinese Among Others: Emigration in Modern Times*. Lanham, MD: Rowman & Littlefield.

Kuik Cheng-Chwee. 2008. "The Essence of Hedging: Malaysia and Singapore's Response to a Rising China." *Contemporary Southeast Asia* 30, no. 2: 159–185.

Kumar, Sree, Sharon Siddique, and Yuwa Hedrick-Wong. 2005. *Mind The Gaps: Singapore Business in China*. Singapore: Institute of Southeast Asian Studies.

Kuntjara, Esther, and Chang-Yau Hoon. 2020. "Reassessing Chinese Indonesian Stereotypes: Two Decades after Reformasi." *South East Asia Research* 28, no. 2: 199–216.

Kuok, Robert, and Andrew Tanzer. 2017. *Robert Kuok: A Memoir*. Singapore: Landmark Books.

Lai, Hongyi, and Lim Tin Seng, eds. 2007. *Harmony and Development: ASEAN-China Relations*. Singapore: World Scientific.

Lasserre, Philippe, and Ching Poy Seng. 1995. *Players in Asia Pacific: The Overseas Chinese, the ASEAN Indigenous Firms and the PRC International Firms: A Profile*. Euro-Asia Centre Research Series No. 35. INSEAD.

Lau, Cheng-Yong. 2015. "The Kra Isthmus Canal: A New Strategic Solution for China's Energy Consumption Scenario?" *Environmental Management* 57, no. 1: 1–20.

Lean, Hooi Hooi, and Russell Smyth. 2016. "The Malaysian-China Economic Relationship at 40: Broadening Ties and Meeting the Challenges for Future Success." In *Chinese Global Production Networks in ASEAN*, edited by Young-Chan Kim, 39–52. London: Springer.

Lee, Edwin. 2008. *Singapore: The Unexpected Nation*. Singapore: Institute of Southeast Asian Studies.

Lee, John. 2016. "The Chinese Diaspora's Role in the Rise of China." *East Asia Forum*, September 14. https://www.eastasiaforum.org/2016/09/14/the-chinese-diasporas-role-in-the-rise-of-china/.

Lee, Kam Hing. 2013. "Malaysia–China Economic Relations: 2000–2010." In *China and East Asia After the Wall Street Crisis*, edited by Peng Er Lam, Mu Yang, and Yaqing Qin, 241–276. Singapore: World Scientific.

Lee, Lai To. 1981. "Deng Xiaoping's ASEAN Tour: A Perspective on Sino-Southeast Asian Relations." *Contemporary Southeast Asia* 3, no. 1: 58–75.

Lees, Lynn Hollen. 2017. *Planting Empire, Cultivating Subjects: British Malaya, 1786–1941*. New York: Cambridge University Press.

Leibold, James. 2007. *Reconfiguring Chinese Nationalism: How the Qing Frontier and Its Indigenes Became Chinese.* New York: Palgrave Macmillan.

Leonard, Mark, Catherina Stead, and Conrad Sweming. 2002. *Public Diplomacy.* London: Foreign Policy Centre.

Leong, Stephen. 1979. "The Malayan Overseas Chinese and the Sino-Japanese War, 1937–1941." *Journal of Southeast Asian Studies* 10, no. 2: 293–320.

Li, Jiangyu. 2020. "Expanding or Accepting: Nation-Work of International Chinese Teachers in a Confucius Institute in Thailand." *Asian Journal of Social Science* 48, no. 1–2: 70.

Li, Mingjiang. 2020. "Southeast Asia through Chinese Eyes: A Strategic Backyard?" In *The Deer and the Dragon: Southeast Asia and China in the 21st Century*, edited by Donald K. Emmerson, 109–132. Stanford: Stanford University Press.

Li, Mingjiang, and Kwa Chong Guan, eds. 2011. *China-ASEAN Sub-regional Cooperation: Progress, Problems and Prospect.* Singapore: World Scientific.

Lim, Alvin Cheng-Hin, and Frank Cibulka. 2019. *China and Southeast Asia in the Xi Jinping Era.* Lanham, MD: Lexington Books.

Lim, Darren J., and Zack Cooper. 2016. "Are East Asian States Really Hedging Between the US and China?" *East Asian Forum*, January 30. https://www.eastasiaforum.org/2016/01/30/are-east-asian-states-really-hedging-between-the-us-and-china/.

Lim, Kean Fan, and Niv Horesh. 2016. "The 'Singapore Fever' in China: Policy Mobility and Mutation." *China Quarterly* 228: 992–1017.

Lim, Linda, and Peter Gosling. 1997. "Strengths and Weaknesses of Minority Status for Southeast Asian Chinese at a Time of Economic Growth and Liberalisation." In *Essential Outsiders: Chinese and Jews in the Modern Transformation of Southeast Asia and Central Europe*, edited by Daniel Chirot and Anthony Reid, 285–317. Seattle and London: University of Washington Press.

Lin, Hsiao-ting. 2011. *Modern China's Ethnic Frontiers: A Journey to the East.* London: Routledge.

Lin, Shaochuan [林少川]. 1994. *Chen Jiageng Yu Nanqiao Jigong* 陳嘉庚與南僑機工 [Tan Kah Kee and the Nanyang Volunteers]. Beijing: Zhongguo huaqiao chubanshe.

Ling, Chunsheng [凌純聲]. 1938. "Tangdai Yunnan De Wuman Yu Baiman Kao" 唐代雲南的烏曼與白蠻考 [A Study of the Wuman and Baiman in Tang Dynasty Yunnan]. *Renleixue Jikan* [Anthropology Journal] 1, no. 1: 57–86.

Ling, Chunsheng [凌純聲]. 1940. "Zhongguo Yu Suowei Taizu Zhi Guanxi" 中國與所謂泰族之關係 [Relationship between China and the So-called Thai Race]. *Qingnian Zhongguo Jikan* [China Youth Journal] 1, no. 2: 331–36.

Liu, Gretchen. 2005. *The Singapore Foreign Service: The First 40 Years.* Singapore: Editions Didier Millet.

Liu, H. [劉宏], Zhang H. M. [張慧梅], and Fan, X. [範昕]. 2016. "東南亞跨界華商組織與'一帶一路'戰略的建構和實施" [Overseas Chinese Business Associations in Southeast Asia and the Construction of the Belt and Road Initiative]. *Southeast Asian Affairs*, no. 4: 1–10.

Liu, Hong, and Els van Dongen. 2016. "China's Diaspora Policies as a New Mode of Transnational Governance." *Journal of Contemporary China* 25, no. 102: 805–821.

Liu, Hong, Xin Fan, and Guanie Lim. 2021. "Singapore Engages the Belt and Road Initiative: Perceptions, Policies, and Institutions." *Singapore Economic Review* 66, no. 1: 219–241.

Liu, Naifu [柳乃夫]. 1903. "Shijie Xin Shi: Xianluo Guo Guoshi Xiaoshi" 世界新史: 暹羅國國勢小史 [A New History of the World: A Short History of Siam]. *Xuanbao*選報 42: 22–23.

Liu, Naifu [柳乃夫]. 1905. "Shijie Tanpian: Xianluo Zhi Xiaofa Riben" 世界談片: 暹羅之效法日本. *Dalu bao* 大陸報 3, no. 11: 3–4.

Liu, Tony Tai Ting, and Tsai Tung Chieh. 2014. "Swords into Ploughshares? China's Soft Power Strategy in Southeast Asia and Its Challenges." *Revista Brasileira de Política Internacional* 57: 28–48.

Liu, Xiaoyuan. 2004. *Frontier Passages: Ethnopolitics and the Rise of Chinese Communism, 1921–1945.* Stanford, CA: Stanford University Press.

Liu, Xiaoyuan. 2015. "Reshaping China: American Strategic Thinking and China's Ethnic Frontiers during World War II." In *Negotiating China's Destiny in World War II*, edited by Hans van de Ven, Diana Lary, and Stephen R. MacKinnon, 161–164. Stanford, CA: Stanford University Press.

Liu, Ying, and Kankesu Jayanthakumaran. 2016. "People's Republic of China (PRC): Thailand Economic Relationship After Signing of Free Trade Agreement in 2005." In *Chinese Global Production Networks in ASEAN*, edited by Young-Chan Kim, 77–96. London: Springer.

Llewellyn, Aisyah. 2018a. "What's Made Indonesian Students Forget the China Taboo?" *South China Morning Post*, April 1. https://www.scmp.com/week-asia/society/article/2139714/whats-made-indonesian-students-forget-china-taboo.

Llewellyn, Aisyah. 2018b. "Student Politics: Indonesians Confront China Prejudice." *The Interpreter*, Lowy Institute, May 31. https://www.lowyinstitute.org/the-interpreter/student-politics-indonesians-confront-China-prejudice.

Lou, Guipin [婁貴品]. 2014. *Fang Guoyu Yu Zhongguo Xi'nan Bianjiang Yanjiu* 方國瑜與中國西南邊疆研究 [Fang Guoyu and Research on China's Southwestern Frontier]. Beijing: Renmin chubanshe.

Low, Choon Ming. 2005. "Reflections of 33 Years in Diplomacy." In *The Little Red Dot: Reflections by Singapore's Diplomat*, edited by Tommy Koh and Chang Li Lin. Singapore: World Scientific.

Luo, Yadong. 2020. *Guanxi and Business*, Third Edition. Singapore: World Scientific.

Ma, Yuhua [馬玉華]. 2006. *Guomin Zhengfu Dui Xi'nan Shaoshu Minzu Diaocha Zhi Yanjiu (1929–1948)* 國民政府對西南少數民族調查之研究 [Study of the Nationalist Government's Ethnological Surveys in Southwest China, 1929–1948]. Kunming: Yunnan renmin chubanshe.

Mackie, Jamie. 2003. "Pre-1997 Sino-Indonesian Conglomerates, Compared with Those of Other ASEAN Countries." In *Ethnic Business Chinese Capitalism in Southeast Asia*, edited by Jomo K. S. and Brian C. Folk, 104–128. New York: Routledge Curzon.

Mahbubani, Kishore. 2021. "The Genius of Jokowi." *ASEAN Post*, October 7. https: //theaseanpost.com/article/genius-jokowi.

Malik, J. Mohan. 2019. "Myanmar's Role in China's Maritime Silk Road Initiative." In *China's Maritime Silk Road Initiative and Southeast Asia: Dilemmas, Doubts, and Determination*, edited by Jean-Marc F. Blanchard, 133–162. Singapore: Palgrave Macmillan.

Manarungsan, Sompop. 2009. "Thailand-China Cooperation in Trade, Investment and Official Development Assistance." In *A China-Japan Comparison of Economic Relations with the Mekong River Basin Countries*, edited by Kagami Mitsuhiro, 290–367. Bangkok Research Centre Report No. 1. Institute of Developing Economies, Japan External Trade Organization (JETRO).

Mandal, Sumit K. 1998. "Pengantar" [Introduction]. In *Hoakiau di Indonesia* [Overseas Chinese in Indonesia], edited by Pramoedya Ananta Toer, 1–30. Jakarta: Penerbit Garba Budaya.

Matten, Marc André. 2016. *Imagining a Postnational World: Hegemony and Space in Modern China.* Leiden: Brill.

Mbembe, Achille. 2019. *Necropolitics.* Translated by Steven Corcoran. Durham, NC: Duke University Press.

McCord, Edward A. 2011. "Ethnic Revolt, State-Building, and Patriotism in Republican China: The 1937 West Hunan Miao Abolish-Military-Land Resist-Japan Uprising." *Modern Asian Studies* 45, no. 6: 1499–1533.

Menkhoff, Thomas, Yue Wah Chay, Hans-Dieter Evers, and Chang-Yau Hoon. 2014. *Catalyst for Change: Chinese Business in Asia.* Singapore: World Scientific.

Merkel-Hess, Kate. 2016. *The Rural Modern: Reconstructing the Self and State in Republican China.* Chicago: University of Chicago Press.

Min, Aung, and Toshihiro Kudo. 2014. "Business Conglomerates in the Context of Myanmar's Economic Reform." In *Myanmar's Integration in the Global Economy: Outlook and Opportunities*, edited by Hank Lim and Yamada Yasuhiro, 138–173. Bangkok: Bangkok Research Centre.

Mitsuru, Hagiwara. 2011. "The Japanese Air Campaigns in China, 1937–1945." In *The Battle for China: Essays on the Military History of the Sino-Japanese War of 1937–1945*, edited by Mark Peattie, Edward J. Drea, and Hans van de Ven, 237–255. Stanford, CA: Stanford University Press.

Mitter, Rana, and Aaron William Moore. 2011. "China in World War II, 1937–1945: Experience, Memory, and Legacy." *Modern Asian Studies* 45, no. 2: 225–240.

Mitter, Rana. 2013. *Forgotten Ally: China's World War II, 1937–1945.* Boston: Houghton Mifflin Harcourt.

Mitter, Rana. 2020. *China's Good War: How World War II Is Shaping a New Nationalism.* Cambridge, MA: Belknap Press of Harvard University Press.

Mizuno, Atsuko. 2016. "Economic Relations Between Myanmar and China." In *The Myanmar Economy: Its Past, Present and Prospects*, edited by Konosuke Odaka, 195–224. New York: Springer.

MoE. 2014. *2014 Report on Concise Statistics on International Students in China* [2014 來華留學生簡明統計]. Department of International Cooperation and Exchanges, Ministry of Education, The People's Republic of China.

MoE. 2015. *2015 Report on Concise Statistics on International Students in China* [2015 來華留學生簡明統計]. Department of International Cooperation and Exchanges, Ministry of Education, The People's Republic of China.

MoE. 2016. *2016 Report on Concise Statistics on International Students in China* [2016 來華留學生簡明統計]. Department of International Cooperation and Exchanges, Ministry of Education, The People's Republic of China.

MoE. 2017. *2017 Report on Concise Statistics on International Students in China* [2017 來華留學生簡明統計]. Department of International Cooperation and Exchanges, Ministry of Education, The People's Republic of China.

MoE. 2018a. *2018 Report on Concise Statistics on International Students in China* [2018 來華留學生簡明統計]. Department of International Cooperation and Exchanges, Ministry of Education, The People's Republic of China.

MoE. 2018b. "Educational Opening Up to Provide Services for the Belt and Road." Ministry of Education, People's Republic of China, June 26. http://en.moe.gov.cn/ Specials/Review/Facts_2147443481/201806/t20180626_341024.html.

Mudimbe, V. Y. 1988. *The Invention of Africa: Gnosis, Philosophy, and the Order of Knowledge*. Bloomington: Indiana University Press.

Mullaney, Thomas S. 2010. *Coming to Terms with the Nation: Ethnic Classification in Modern China*. Berkeley: University of California Press.

Mullaney, Thomas S. 2011. *Coming to Terms with the Nation: Ethnic Classification in Modern China*. Berkeley: University of California Press.

Murashima, Eiji. 2005. "Opposing French Colonialism: Thailand and the Independence Movements in Indo-China in the Early 1940s." *South East Asia Research* 13, no. 3: 333–383.

Murashima, Eiji. 2006. "The Commemorative Character of Thai Historiography: The 1942–43 Thai Military Campaign in the Shan States Depicted as a Story of National Salvation and the Restoration of Thai Independence." *Modern Asian Studies* 40, no. 4: 1053–1096.

Nathan, S. R. 2011. With Timothy Auger. *An Unexpected Journey: Path to the Presidency*. Singapore: Editions Didier Millet.

Nathan, S. R. 2014. "Foreword." In *Tan Siak Kew: Going Against the Grain*, edited by Fiona Tan. Singapore: World Scientific.

National Archives of Singapore. 2010. *Xinjiapo De Nanqiao Jigong: Yi Pi Rexue Huaqiao Hui Zhongguo Kang Ri De Bupingfan Gushi* 新加坡的南僑機工：一批熱血華僑回中國抗日的不平凡故事 [Singapore's Nanyang Volunteers: The Extraordinary Story of Nanyang Drivers and Mechanics who Returned to China during the Sino-Japanese War]. Singapore: National Archives of Singapore.

National Mining Hall of Fame and Museum, Inductee Database. 2019. "Li, Dr. Kuo Ching." http://www.mininghalloffame.org/inductee/li.

Nuechterlein, Donald E. 1965. *Thailand and the Struggle for Southeast Asia*. Ithaca, NY: Cornell University Press.

Nurbaiti, Alya, and Dian Septiari. 2020. "Pompeo Calls on Indonesian Muslims to Oppose China's Uighur Issue." *Jakarta Post*, October 30.

Nye, Joseph. 1990. "Soft Power." *Foreign Policy* 80: 153–71.

Ong, Aihwa. 1997. "Chinese Modernities: Narratives of Nation and of Capitalism." In *Ungrounded Empires: The Cultural Politics of Modern Chinese Transnationalism*, edited by Aihwa Ong and Donald Nonini, 171–202. New York: Routledge.

Ong, Aihwa. 1999. *Flexible Citizenship: The Cultural Logics of Transnationality*. Durham, NC: Duke University Press.

Owyang, Hsuan. 1996. *The Barefoot Boy from Songwad: The Life of Chi Owyang, Entrepreneurs of Asia*. Singapore: Times Books International.

Pan, Lynn. 1990. *Sons of the Yellow Emperor: The Story of the Overseas Chinese*. London: Mandarin.

Pananond, Pavida. 2001. "The Making of Thai Multinationals: A Comparative Study of the Growth and Internationalization Process of Thailand's Charoen Pokphand and Siam Cement Groups." *Journal of Asian Business* 17, no. 3: 41–70.

Parameswaran, Prashanth. 2014. "Thailand Turns to China." *The Diplomat*, December 20. https://thediplomat.com/2014/12/thailand-turns-to-china/.

Parameswaran, Prashanth. 2018. "What's Next for China-Indonesia Military Ties?" *The Diplomat*, July 31. https://thediplomat.com/2018/07/whats-next-for-china -indonesia-military-ties/.

Park, Sa-Myung. 2013. "Southeast Asian Studies in China: Progress and Problems." In *The Historical Construction of Southeast Asian Studies*, edited by Park Seung Woo and Victor T. King, 48–49. Singapore: ISEAS.

Pearson, Margaret, Meg Rithmire, and Kellee S. Tsai. 2021. "Party-State Capitalism in China." *Current History* 120, no. 827: 207–213.

Peterson, Glen. 2012. *Overseas Chinese in the People's Republic of China*. Abingdon, UK: Routledge.

Popkin, Jeremy D. 2005. *History, Historians, and Autobiography*. Chicago, IL: University of Chicago Press.

Powell, Miles Alexander. 2016. "People in Peril, Environments at Risk: Coolies, Tigers, and Colonial Singapore's Ecology of Poverty." *Environment and History* 22, no. 3: 455–482.

PPI Tiongkok [PPIT]. N.d. https://ppitiongkok.org/.

Pradt, Tilman. 2016. *China's New Foreign Policy: Military Modernisation, Multilateralism and the "China Threat."* Cham: Palgrave Macmillan.

Qi, Siang Ng. 2019. "The Scramble for Southeast Asia: ASEAN-Great Power Relations in an Increasingly Contested Region." *OXPOL* (The Oxford University Politics Blog), September 6. https://blog.politics.ox.ac.uk/the-scramble-for -southeast-asia-asean-great-power-relations-in-an-increasingly-contested-region/.

Qin, Qinzhi [秦欽峙], and Tang Jialin [湯家麟]. 1989. *Nanqiao Jigong Huiguo Kangzhanshi* 南僑機工回國抗戰史 [The History of Nanyang Volunteers]. Kunming: Yunnan renmin chubanshe.

Rajaratnam, S. 2005. "Principles of Singapore's Foreign Policy." In *The Little Red Dot: Reflections by Singapore's Diplomats*, edited by Tommy Koh and Chang Li Lin. Singapore: World Scientific.

Rakhmat, M., and W. Aryansyah. 2020. "Rising Anti-Chinese Sentiment in Indonesia." *ASEAN Post*, July 4. https://theaseanpost.com/article/rising-anti-chinese-sentiment -indonesia.

Rawnsley, Gary. 2012. "Approaches to Soft Power and Public Diplomacy in China and Taiwan." *Journal of International Communication* 18, no. 2: 121–135.

Raymond, Gregory. 2019. "Competing Logics: Between Thai Sovereignty and the China Model in 2018." In *Southeast Asian Affairs 2019*, 341–360. Singapore: ISEAS.

Redding, Gordon. 1990. *The Spirit of Chinese Capitalism*. Berlin: De Gruyter.

Ren, Guixiang [任貴祥]. 1993. *Huaxia Xiangxinli: Huaqiao Dui Zuguo Kangzhan De Zhiyuan* 華夏向心力: 華僑對祖國抗戰的支援 [The Centripetal Force of China: The Contributions of Chinese Overseas to Their Motherland's War of Resistance]. Guilin: Guangxi shifan daxue chubanshe.

Ren, Na, and Hong Liu. 2021. "Southeast Asian Chinese Engage a Rising China: Business Associations, Institutionalised Transnationalism, and the Networked State." *Journal of Ethnic and Migration Studies*. (Online first)

Ren, Qi. 2020. "Lippo Group Founder Mochtar Riady: Globalisation without China Is Unrealistic." *Think China*, May 29. https://www.thinkchina.sg/lippo-group -founder-mochtar-riady-globalisation-without-china-unrealistic.

Republika. 2020. "Dahlan Iskan Berpesan Santri di China Teladani Wali Songo." November 14. https://www.republika.co.id/berita/qjjqotn396/dahlan-iskan-berpesan -santri-di-china-teladani-wali-songo.

Research Center for Thai Studies, Guiyang University. Accessed February 11, 2022. http://tgyjzx.gyu.cn/info/1073/1065.htm.

Reuters. 2021. "China to Import More Indonesian Products to Balanced Trade." January 13. https://www.reuters.com/world/china/indonesia-calls-more-trade -barriers-with-china-be-removed-2021-01-13/.

Reynolds, Bruce E. 2004. "Phibun Songkhram and Thai Nationalism in the Fascist Era." *European Journal of East Asian Studies* 3, no. 1: 99–134.

Reynolds, Craig. 1996. "Tycoons and Warlords: Modern Thai Social Formations and Chinese Historical Romance." In *Sojourners and Settlers: Histories of Southeast Asia and the Chinese*, edited by Anthony Reid, 115–147. Honolulu: University of Hawai'i Press.

Riady, Mochtar. 2017. *Mochtar Riady: My Life Story*. Singapore: John Wiley & Sons.

RICH. 2019. "Huaqiao Ikut Rayakan HUT Kemerdekaan RI di KBRI Beijing" [The Returnees Joined in the Celebration of Indonesian National Day at the Indonesian Embassy in Beijing]. *Quarterly*, Embassy of Republic of Indonesia in China, no. 3.

RICH. 2020. "3000 Beasiswa Tiongkok untuk Mahasiswa Indonesia" [3,000 Chinese Scholarships for Indonesian Students]. *Quarterly*, Embassy of Republic of Indonesia in China, no. 2.

Rohman, Abid, et al. 2020. *Laporan Akhir Islam, Indonesia dan Tiongkok: Analisis Potensi Peningkatan People to People Connectivity Antara Indonesia-Tiongkok Perspektif Elite Muslim Indonesia* [Final Report on Islam, Indonesia and China: Analysis on the Potential of Elevating People to People Connectivity between China and Indonesia from the Perspective of Indonesian Muslim Elites]. Joint Research and Development Center between Policy Analysis and Development Agency, Ministry of Foreign Affairs, Republic of Indonesia; and UIN Sunan Ampel Surabaya.

Ruth, Richard A. 2011. *In Buddha's Company: Thai Soldiers in the Vietnam War.* Honolulu: University of Hawai'i Press.

Sai, Siew Min, and Chang-Yau Hoon. 2013. "Chinese Indonesians Reassessed: A Critical Review." In *Chinese Indonesians Reassessed: History, Religion and Belonging,* edited by Siew Min Sai and Chang-Yau Hoon, 1–26. London and New York: Routledge.

Sai, Siew-Min. 2013. "The Nanyang Diasporic Imaginary: Chinese School Teachers in a Transborder Setting in the Dutch East Indies." In *Chinese Indonesians Reassessed: History, Religion, and Belonging,* edited by Siew-Min Sai and Chang-Yau Hoon, 45–63. London: Routledge.

Samphantharak, Krislert. 2011. "The Rise of China and Foreign Direct Investment from Southeast Asia." *Journal of Current Southeast Asian Affairs* 30, no. 2: 65–75.

Santasombat, Yos, ed. 2017. *Chinese Capitalism in Southeast Asia: Cultures and Practices.* Singapore: Palgrave Macmillan.

Santasombat, Yos, ed. 2019. *The Sociology of Chinese Capitalism in Southeast Asia: Challenges and Prospects.* Singapore: Palgrave Macmillan.

Santasombat, Yos, and Lee Kian Cheng. 2017. "Introduction." In *Chinese Capitalism in Southeast Asia: Cultures and Practices,* edited by Yos Santasombat, 1–34. Singapore: Palgrave Macmillan.

Saw, Swee-Hock. 2006. "A Review of Southeast Asian Studies." In *Southeast Asian Studies in China,* edited by Swee-Hock Saw and John Wong. Singapore: ISEAS.

Saw, Swee-Hock, Sheng Lijun, and Chin Kin Wah, eds. 2005. *ASEAN-China Relations: Realities and Prospects.* Singapore: Institute of Southeast Asian Studies.

Sawada, Yukari. 1998. "The Rise of Overseas Chinese Investment in China." In *Challenges for China-Japan-US Cooperation,* edited by Ryosei Kokubun, 132–153. Tokyo: Japan Center for International Exchange.

Schmidt, Blake, and Natnicha Chuwiruch. 2019. "Thailand's Richest Family Gets Richer Helping China." *Taipei Times,* April 29. http://www.taipeitimes.com/News/editorials/archives/2019/04/29/2003714226.

Schwarcz, Vera. 1986. *The Chinese Enlightenment: Intellectuals and the Legacy of the May Fourth Movement of 1919.* Berkeley: University of California Press.

Scott, James C. 2009. *The Art of Not Being Governed: An Anarchist History of Upland Southeast Asia.* New Haven, CT: Yale University Press.

Seagrave, Sterling. 1996. *Lords of the Rim.* London: Corgi.

Seah, Leander. 2017. "Between East Asia and Southeast Asia: Nanyang Studies, Chinese Migration, and National Jinan University, 1927–1940." *Translocal Chinese: East Asian Perspectives* 11, no. 1: 30–56.

Seah, Leander. 2017. "Chinese Identities between Localization and Globalization: The South Seas Society, Chinese Intellectuals in Singapore, and Southeast Asian Studies, 1958–1971." *China Review* 17, no. 3: 87–110.

Seah, Sharon, Hoang Thi Ha, Melinda Martinus, and Pham Thi Phuong Thao. 2021. *The State of Southeast Asia: 2021.* Singapore: ISEAS.

Setijadi, Charlotte. 2017. "Chinese Indonesians in the Eyes of the Pribumi Public." *ISEAS Perspectives,* no. 73: 1–12.

Shambaugh, David. 2015. "China's Soft Power Push: The Search for Respect." *Foreign Affairs* (July–August).

Shambaugh, David. 2021. *Where Great Powers Meet: America and China in Southeast Asia*. Oxford: Oxford University Press.

Sheng, Lijun. 2008. "China and ASEAN in Asian Regional Integration." In *China and the New International Order*, edited by Gungwu Wang and Zheng Yongnian. New York: Routledge.

Shih, Chih-Yu. 2019. "Introduction: Complicating China through Southeast Asia." In *Researching China in Southeast Asia*, edited by Chow-Bing Ngeow, 1–3. New York: Routledge.

Siddiqui, Kalim. 2016. "A Study of Singapore as a Developmental State." In *Chinese Global Production Networks in ASEAN*, edited by Young-Chang Kim, 157–188. London: Springer.

Simanjuntak, D. 2017. "Commentary: Why Anies Baswedan, a New Governor with Big Shoes to Fill, Is Echoing Hardline Sentiment." *Channel News Asia*, October 19. http://www.channelnewsasia.com/news/commentary/commentary-why-anies-baswedan-a-new-governor-with-big-shoes-to-9322756.

Skinner, G. William. 1957. *Chinese Society in Thailand: An Analytical History*. Ithaca, NY: Cornell University Press.

Stanek, Pavel, and Zbynek Skvor. 2019. "Automated Magnetic Field Evaluation for Magnetic Particle Inspection by Impulse." *Journal of Nondestructive Evaluation* 38, no. 3: 1–6.

Steinberg, David. 2021. "China's Myanmar, Myanmar's China: Myths, Illusions, Interactions." In *The Deer and the Dragon: Southeast Asia and China in the 21st Century*, edited by Donald K. Emmerson, 353–376. Singapore: ISEAS.

Straits Times. 1950. "A Most Tragic Suggestion." April 27.

Straits Times. 2021. "Singapore Business Chamber in China Key to Relations Between the Two Countries: Alvin Tan." February 14. https://www.straitstimes.com/singapore/singapore-business-chamber-in-china-key-to-relations-between-the-2-countries-minister-of.

Strangio, Sebastion. 2020. *In the Dragon's Shadow: Southeast Asia in the Chinese Century*. New Haven and London: Yale University Press.

Strate, Shane. 2015. *The Lost Territories: Thailand's History of National Humiliation*. Honolulu: University of Hawai'i Press.

Subrahmanyan, Arjun. 2015. "Education, Propaganda, and the People: Democratic Paternalism in 1930s Siam." *Modern Asian Studies* 49, no. 4: 1122–1142.

Sukma, Rizal. 1999. "'Masalah Cina' Dalam Kerangka Hubungan Indonesia-RRC" ["Chinese Problem" in the Framework of Indonesia-China Relations]. In *Retrospeksi dan Rekontekstualisasi "Masalah Cina"* [Retrospection and Recontextualisation of the "Chinese Problem"], edited by I. Wibowo, 129–146. Jakarta: PT Gramedia Pustaka Utama, Pusat Studi Cina.

Suryadinata, Leo. 2006. "Southeast Asianists in China in the Last Three Decades: A Preliminary Survey." In *Southeast Asian Studies in China*, edited by Swee-Hock Saw and John Wong, 30–53. Singapore: ISEAS.

Suryadinata, Leo. 2007. *Understanding the Ethnic Chinese in Southeast Asia.* Singapore: ISEAS.

Suryadinata, Leo. 2017. *The Rise of China and the Chinese Overseas.* Singapore: ISEAS.

Suryohadiprojo, Sayidiman. 1997. "Pembauran Lewat Wajib Militer" [Assimilation through military conscription]. In *70 Tahun Junus Jahja: Pribumi Kuat Kunci Pembauran* [70 Years of Junus Jahya: Strong Pribumi, The Key Is to Assimilate], edited by Riyanto D. Wahono, 116–120. Jakarta, Indonesia: PT Bina Rena Pariwara.

Suzuki, Ayame, and Lee Poh Ping. 2017. "Malaysia's Hedging Strategy, a Rising China, and the Changing Strategic Situation in East Asia." In *Southeast Asia and China: A Contest in Mutual Socialization*, edited by Lowell Dittmer and Ngeow Chow Bing, 113–130. Singapore: World Scientific.

Tagliacozzo, Eric, and Wen-Chin Chang, eds. 2011. *Chinese Circulations: Capital, Commodities, and Networks in Southeast Asia.* Durham and London: Duke University Press.

Tai, Jeremy. 2015. "The Northwest Question: Capitalism in the Sands of Nationalist China." *Twentieth Century China* 40, no. 3: 201–219.

Tan, Eugene K. B. 2001. "From Sojourners to Citizens: Managing the Ethnic Chinese Minority in Indonesia and Malaysia." *Ethnic and Racial Studies* 24, no. 6: 949–978.

Tan, Eugene K. B. 2003. "Re-Engaging Chineseness: Political, Economic, and Cultural Imperatives of Nation-Building in Singapore." *China Quarterly* 175: 751–774.

Tan, Fiona. 2014. *Tan Siak Kew: Going Against the Grain.* Singapore: World Scientific.

Tan, Gang [唐剛]. 2013. *Kangzhan Shiqi Dahoufang Jiaotong Yu Xibu Jingji Kaifa* 抗戰時期大後方交通與西部經濟開發 [Communications of the Rear Area and the Economic Development of West China during the "War of Resistance"]. Beijing, China: Zhongguo shehui kexue chubanshe.

Tan, Isaac C. K. 2016. "Unrequited Patriotism: Remembering the Stories of the Nanyang Volunteers." *New Zealand Journal of Asian Studies* 18, no. 1: 75–90.

Tan, See Seng. 2021. "Coping with the Dragon: Vulnerability and Engagement in Singapore-China Relations." In *The Deer and the Dragon: Southeast Asia and China in the 21st Century*, edited by Donald K. Emmerson, 197–220. Singapore: ISEAS.

Tang, Shipping, and Jie Zhang. 2006. "The State of Southeast Asian Studies in China: An Institutional Interpretation." In *Southeast Asian Studies in China*, edited by Swee-Hock Saw and John Wong, 54–74. Singapore: ISEAS.

Tang, Xiaobing. 1996. *Global Space and the Nationalist Discourse of Modernity: The Historical Thinking of Liang Qichao.* Stanford, CA: Stanford University Press.

Tay, Frances. 2015. "Making Malaysian Chinese: War Memory, Histories, and Identities." PhD diss., University of Manchester.

Teoh, Karen M. 2010. "Exotic Flowers, Modern Girls, Good Citizens: Female Education and Overseas Chinese Identity in British Malaya and Singapore, 1900s–1950s." *Twentieth-Century China* 35, no. 2: 25–51.

Terwiel, B. J. 1923 (reprinted 1996). "Foreword to the New Edition." In *The Tai Race: Elder Brother of the Chinese, Results of Experiences, Exploration, and Research*, edited by William Clifton Dodd. Bangkok: White Lotus.

Tetsuo, Maeda. 2009. "Strategic Bombing of Chongqing by Imperial Japanese Army and Naval Forces." In *Bombing Civilians: A Twentieth Century History*, edited by Yuki Tanaka and Marilyn B. Young, 135–153. New York: New Press.

Thak Chaloemtiarana. 2014. "Are We Them? Textual and Literary Representations of the Chinese in Twentieth-Century Thailand." *Southeast Asian Studies* 3, no. 3: 473–526.

Theo, Rika. 2018. "Unravelling Indonesian Student Mobility to China: Politics, Identities, and Trajectories." PhD diss., Utrecht University.

Thomas, John N. 1974. *The Institute of Pacific Relations: Asian Scholars and American Politics*. Seattle: University of Washington Press.

Tian, Tong [田彤]. 2006. *Zhuanxingqi Wenhuaxue De Pipan: Yi Chen Xujing Wei Gean De Lishi Shidu* 轉型期文化學的批判：以陳序經為個案的歷史史讀 [Criticisms of Cultural Studies in the Transitional Period: A Historical Interpretation of Chen Xujing]. Beijing: Zhonghua shuju.

Tighe, Justin. 2009. "From Borderland to Heartland: The Discourse of the North-West in Early Republican China." *Twentieth-Century China* 35, no. 1: 54–74.

Tisdell, Clem. 2008. *Thirty Years of Economic Reform and Openness in China: Retrospect and Prospect*. Economic Theory, Applications and Issues Working Paper No. 51. School of Economics, University of Queensland.

Tjhin, Christine Susanna. 2012. "Indonesia's Relations with China: Productive and Pragmatic, but Not Yet a Strategic Partnership." *China Report* 48, no. 3: 303–315.

To, James Jiann Hua. 2014. *Qiaowu: Extra-Territorial Policies for the Overseas Chinese*. Leiden: Brill.

Toer, Pramoedya Ananta. 1998. *Hoakiau di Indonesia* [Overseas Chinese in Indonesia]. Jakarta: Penerbit Garba Budaya.

Tong, Lam. 2011. *A Passion for Facts: Social Surveys and the Construction of the Chinese Nation-State, 1900–1949*. Berkeley: University of California Press.

Tong, Chee-Kiong. 2010. *Identity and Ethnic Relations in Southeast Asia: Racializing Chineseness*. Dordrecht: Springer.

Tong, Sarah Y., and Wen Xin Lim. 2017. "China-ASEAN Economic Relations." In *Southeast Asia and China: A Contest in Mutual Socialization*, edited by Lowell Dittmer and Chow Bin Ngeow, 163–186. Singapore: World Scientific.

Tu, Wei-Ming. 2005. "Cultural China: The Periphery as the Center." *Daedalus* 134, no. 4: 145–167.

Tungkeunkunt, Kornphanat, and Kanya Phuphakdi. 2018. "Blood Is Thicker Than Water: A History of the Diplomatic Discourse 'China and Thailand Are Brothers.'" *Asian Perspective* 42, no. 4: 597–621.

van Bruinessen, Martin. 2013. "Introduction: Contemporary Developments in Indonesian Islam and the 'Conservative Turn' of the Early Twenty-First Century." In *Contemporary Developments in Indonesian Islam: Explaining the Conservative Turn*, edited by Martin van Bruinessen, 1–21. Singapore: ISEAS.

van de Ven, Hans. 2018. *China at War: Triumph and Tragedy in the Emergence of the New China.* Cambridge, MA: Harvard University Press.

Vella, Walter F. 1978. *Chaiyo! King Vajiravudh and the Development of Thai Nationalism.* Honolulu: University of Hawai'i Press.

Viraphol, Sarasin. 1977. *Tribute and Profit: Sino-Siamese Trade, 1652–1853.* Cambridge, MA: Council on East Asian Studies, Harvard University.

Visscher, Sikko. 2007. *The Business of Politics and Ethnicity: A History of the Singapore Chinese Chamber of Commerce and Industry.* Singapore: NUS Press.

Vu, Linh D. 2021. *Governing the Dead: Martyrs, Memorials, and Necrocitizenship in Modern China.* Ithaca, NY: Cornell University Press.

Wade, Geoff, and James K. Chin, eds. 2019. *China and Southeast Asia: Historical Interactions.* London: Routledge.

Wade, Geoff. 2020. "Re-enlisting the Diaspora: Beijing and the 'Overseas Chinese.'" In *The Deer and the Dragon: Southeast Asia and China in the 21st Century*, edited by Donald K. Emmerson, 171–196. Stanford: Stanford University Press.

Wakeman, Frederic, Jr. 1997. "A Revisionist View of the Nanjing Decade: Confucian Fascism." *China Quarterly* 150: 395–432.

Wanandi, Jusuf. 2012. *Shades of Grey: A Political Memoir of Modern Indonesia 1965–1998.* Jakarta, Indonesia: Equinox Publishing.

Wang, Di. 2017. "A College Student's Rural Journey: Early Sociology and Anthropology in China Seen Through Fieldwork on Sichuan's Secret Society." *Frontiers of History in China* 12, no. 1: 2n4.

Wang, Gungwu. 1976. "Are Indonesian Chinese Unique?" In *The Chinese in Indonesia: Five Essays*, edited by James Austin Copland Mackie, 119–210. Honolulu: University of Hawai'i Press, in association with Australian Institute of International Affairs.

Wang, Gungwu. 1981. *Community and Nation: China, Southeast Asia, and Australia.* Sydney: Allen & Unwin.

Wang, Gungwu. 1994. "Southeast Asian Chinese and the Development of China." *Asian Journal of Political Science* 2, no. 2: 1–19.

Wang, Gungwu. 2008. "China and the International Order: Some Historical Perspectives." In *China and the New International Order*, edited by Wang Gungwu and Zheng Yongnian, 21–31. New York: Routledge.

Wang, Gungwu. 2015. "Singapore's 'Chinese Dilemma' as China Rises." *Straits Times*, June 1.

Wang, Gungwu. 2019. *China Reconnects: Joining a Deep-rooted Past to a New World Order.* Singapore: World Scientific.

Wang, Qingyuan [王清遠], and Zhu Zhenming [朱振明], eds. 2020. *Taiguo Yanjiu Luncong* 泰國研究論叢 [Essays on Thai Studies]. Chengdu: Sichuan daxue chubanshe.

Wang, Shilu. 2006. "Southeast Asian Studies in Yunnan: Achievements, Challenges, and Outlook." In *Southeast Asian Studies in China*, edited by Swee-Hock Saw and John Wong, 102–117. Singapore: ISEAS.

Wang, W., and Z. Lin. 2008. "Investment in China: The Role of Southeast Asian Chinese Businessmen." In *China in the World: Contemporary Issues and*

Perspectives, edited by Emile Kok-Kheng Yeoh and Joanne Hoi-Lee Loh, 147–160. Kuala Lumpur: Institute of China Studies.

Wang, Yucun [王漁邨]. 1880. "Xianluo Kao" 暹羅考 [A Study of Siam]. *Huatu Xinbao* [畫圖新報] 1, no. 1: 177.

Wang, Yucun [王漁邨]. 1899. "Xianluo Zhongxing Ji" 暹羅中興記 [A Record of Siam's Resurgence]. *Wanguo Gongbao* 萬國公報 123: 18–21.

Wang, Zheng. 2012. *Never Forget National Humiliation: Historical Memory in Chinese Politics and Foreign Relations*. New York: Columbia University Press.

Wattimena, Tiara Cornelia. 2021. "China's People-to-People Exchange Policy and National Image Building: A Study of Indonesian Students in China." Master's diss., National Sun Yat-sen University, Taiwan.

Weatherbee, Donald E. 2017. "Indonesia and China: The Bumpy Path to a Wary Partnership." In *Southeast Asia and China: A Contest in Mutual Socialization*, edited by Lowell Dittmer and Ngeow Chow Bing, 131–160. Singapore: World Scientific.

Webster, Donovan. 2003. *The Burma Road: The Epic Story of the China-Burma-India Theater in World War II*. New York: Farrar, Straus & Giroux.

Weidenbaum, Murray L., and Samuel Hughes. 1996. *The Bamboo Network: How Expatriate Chinese Entrepreneurs Are Creating a New Economic Superpower in Asia*. New York: Martin Kessler Books.

Welch, Anthony. 2014. "China-ASEAN Relations in Higher Education: An Analytical Framework." In *Emerging International Dimensions in East Asian Higher Education*, edited by Akiyoshi Yonezawa, Yuto Kitamura, Arthur Meerman, and Kazuo Kuroda, 103–120. Dordrecht: Springer.

Wiens, Herold J. 1954. *China's March toward the Tropics: A Discussion of the Southward Penetration of China's Culture, Peoples, and Political Control in Relation to the Non-Han-Chinese Peoples of South China and in the Perspective of Historical and Cultural Geography*. Hamden, CT: Shoe String Press.

Williams, Michael. 1991. "China and Indonesia Make Up: Reflections on a Troubled. Relationship." In *Indonesia: The Role of the Indonesian Chinese in Shaping Modern Indonesian Life*, 149–150. Symposium at Cornell University.

Winichakul, Thongchai. 1994. *Siam Mapped: A History of the Geo-Body of a Nation*. Honolulu: University of Hawai'i Press.

Winichakul, Thongchai. 2020. *Moments of Silence: The Unforgetting of the October 6, 1976, Massacre in Bangkok*. Honolulu: University of Hawai'i Press.

Wong, Danny Tze Ken, and Tan Miau Ing. 2017. "The Development of Chinese Capitalism in Malaysia: The Cases of H. S. Lee and Robert Kuok." In *Chinese Capitalism in Southeast Asia: Cultures and Practices*, edited by Yos Santasombat, 85–102. Singapore: Palgrave Macmillan.

Wong, John. 1984. *The Political Economy of China's Changing Relations with Southeast Asia*. United Kingdom: Macmillan Education.

Wong, John. 1995. "China's Economic Reform and Open-Door Policy Viewed from Southeast Asia." *ASEAN Economic Bulletin* 11, no. 3: 269–279.

Wong, John. 1999. "Southeast Asian Ethnic Chinese Investing in China." *Global Economic Review: Perspectives on East Asian Economies and Industries* 28, no. 1: 3–27.

Wong, John, Zou Keyuan, and Zeng Huaqin, eds. 2006. *China-ASEAN Relations: Economic and Legal Dimensions*. Singapore: World Scientific.

Wongsurawat, Wasana. 2008. "Contending for a Claim on Civilization: The Sino-Siamese Struggle to Control Overseas Chinese Education in Siam." *Journal of Chinese Overseas* 4, no. 2: 161–182.

Wongsurawat, Wasana. 2019. *The Crown and the Capitalists: The Ethnic Chinese and the Founding of the Thai Nation*. Seattle: University of Washington Press.

Wood, W. A. R. 1924. *A History of Siam: From the Earliest Times to the Year A.D. 1781, with a Supplement Dealing with More Recent Events*. Bangkok, Thailand: Chalermnit.

Wu, Xiao An. 2009. "China meets Southeast Asia: A Long-Term Historical Review." In *Connecting and Distancing: Southeast Asia and China*, edited by Ho Khai Leong, 3–30. Singapore: ISEAS.

Xia, Yuqing [夏玉清]. 2015. "Nanqiao Zonghui Dui Zhongguo Kangzhan De Gongxian" 南僑總會對中國抗戰的貢獻 [Nanyang China Relief Fund's Contributions to Wartime China]. *Kang Ri Zhanzheng Yanjiu*, no. 3: 95–106.

Xia, Yuqing [夏玉清]. 2016. *Nanyang Huaqiao Jigong Yanjiu, 1939–1946* 南洋華僑機工研究, 1939–1946 [A Study of the Nanyang Volunteer Drivers and Mechanics, 1939–1946]. Beijing: Zhongguo shehui kexue chubanshe.

Xie, Kankan. 2021. "Experiencing Southeast Asian Studies in China: A Reverse Culture Shock." *Journal of Southeast Asian Studies* 52, no. 2: 170–187.

Xu, Yihua. 2015. "Religion and China's Public Policy in the Era of Globalization." *Journal of Middle Eastern and Islamic Studies (in Asia)* 9, no. 4: 14–35.

Xu, Yunqiao [許雲樵]. 1908. "Ying Yun Huan Xianluo Zhiwai Faquan" 英允還暹羅治外法權 [Britain Abrogates Extraterritorial Rights in Siam]. *Xinwen Bao* 新聞報, March 5.

Yang, Bin. 2009. *Between Winds and Clouds: The Making of Yunnan (Second Century BCE to Twentieth Century CE)*. New York: Columbia University Press.

Yang, Fang [楊芳], and Xu Jie [徐傑]. 2015. "Nanqiao Jigong Dui Xinan Zhanchang Ji Zhongguo Kang Ri Zhanzheng De Gongxian" 南僑機工對西南戰場及中國抗日的貢獻 [Nanyang Volunteers' Contributions to China's Southwestern Front and War with Japan]. In *Jinian Zhongguo Renmin Kang Ri Zhanzheng Ji Shijie Fan Faxisi Zhanzheng Shengli 70 Zhounian Guoji Xueshu Yantaohui Lunwenji* 紀念中國人民抗日戰爭暨世界反法西斯戰爭勝利70周年國際學術研討會論文集 [Conference Essays Celebrating the 70th Anniversary of China's War with Japan and the World's Victory Over Fascism], edited by Zhonggong Zhongyang Dangbu Yanjiushi 中國中央黨部研究室, 434–438. Beijing: Zhonggong dangshi chubanshe.

Yang, Sen [楊森]. 1946. *Yang Zhuxi Yanlun Xuanji* 楊主席言論選集 [Collected Speeches of Yang Sen]. Guiyang: Guizhou shengzhengfu mishuchu.

Yang, Sen [楊森]. 1972. *Yang Sen Jiushi Yiwang* 楊森九十憶往 [Yang Sen's Recollections at 90]. Taipei.

Yang, Sen [楊森]. 1979. *Guizhou Zayi* 貴州雜憶 [Recollections of Guizhou]. In *Yang Sen Zhuanji Ziliao (Xu)* 楊森傳記資料 (續) [Materials on the Biography of Yang Sen, continued], Vol. 4, edited by Zhu Chuanyu. Taipei: Tianyi chubanshe.

Yen, Ching-Hwang. 1986. *A Social History of the Chinese in Singapore and Malaya, 1800–1911*. Singapore: Oxford University Press.

Yen, Ching-Hwang. 2003. "Modern Overseas Chinese Business Enterprise: A Preliminary Study." In *The Chinese Diaspora: Selected Essays* Vol. 1, edited by Wang Ling-Chi and Gungwu Wang, 125–144. Singapore: Eastern University Press.

Yeoh, Emile Kok-Kheng, Chan Sok Gee, Wendy Chen-Chen Yong, and Joanne Hoi-Lee Loh, eds. 2009. *China-ASEAN Relations: Economic Engagement and Policy Reform*. Kuala Lumpur: Institute of China Studies.

Yeremia, Ardhitya Eduard. 2020. "Guarded Optimism, Caution and Sophistication: Indonesian Diplomats' Perceptions of the Belt and Road Initiative." *International Journal of China Studies* 11, no. 1: 21–49.

Yeremia, Ardhitya Eduard. 2021. "Explaining Indonesia's Constrained Engagement with the Belt and Road Initiative: Balancing Developmentalism against Nationalism and Islamism." *Asian Perspective* 45, no. 2: 325–347.

Yeung, Henry. 1999. "The Internationalization of Ethnic Chinese Business Firms from Southeast Asia: Strategies, Processes and Competitive Advantage." *International Journal of Urban and Regional Research* 23: 88–102.

Yip, Seong Chun Linda. 2006. *Bibliography of ASEAN-China Relations*. Singapore: Institute of Southeast Asian Studies.

Yong, C. F., and R. B. McKenna. 1990. *The Kuomintang Movement in British Malaya, 1912–1949*. Singapore: Singapore University Press.

Yoshida, Takashi. 2006. *The Making of "The Rape of Nanking": History and Memory in Japan, China, and the United States*. New York: Oxford University Press.

Yow, Cheun Hoe. 2013. *Guangdong and Chinese Diaspora: The Changing Landscape of Qiaoxiang*. London: Routledge.

Yu, Dingyi [余定義]. 1938. *Xi'nan Liu Sheng Shehui Jingji Zhi Niaokan* 西南六省社會經濟之鳥瞰 [Overview of Society and Economy of the Six Provinces in Southwest China. N.P.: Zhongguo yinhang jingji yanjiushi chuban.

Yu, Hong. 2020. "Connecting Chongqing and Southeast Asia: Challenges and Potential of China-Singapore (Chongqing) Connectivity Initiative." *Think China*, November 10. https://www.thinkchina.sg/connecting-chongqing-and-southeast-asia-challenges-and-potential-china-singapore-chongqing.

Yunnan Sheng Minzhengting Sansan Zi Di 4444 Hao Miling 雲南省民政廳叁三字第4444號密令 [Secret Dispatch from Yunnan Provincial Home Office, no. 4444]. 1940. File 13, p. 7, *Quanzong* 1011, May 15. Yunnan Provincial Archives.

Yunnan Shengzhengfu Mi Wai Zi Di 537 Hao Xinling 雲南省政府秘外字第537號信令 [Secret Dispatch to Yunnan Provincial Government, no. 537]. 1940. File 13, p. 2, *Quanzong* 1011, April 25. Yunnan Provincial Archives.

Zawacki, Benjamin. 2017. *Thailand: Shifting Ground Between the US and a Rising China*. London: Zed Books.

Zeng, Doug. 2019. "Building a Competitive City through Integrating into Global Value Chains: The Case of the Sino–Singapore Suzhou Industrial Park." *China: An International Journal* 17, no. 2: 164–180.

Zhang, Fengqi [張鳳岐]. 1939. "Xianluo Gaiming 'Taiguo' Yu Zhongguo Xi'nan Taizu Zhi Qiantu" 暹羅改名泰國與中國西南泰族之前途 [The Renaming of Siam and the Future of the Thai Race in Southwest China]. *Xin Dongxiang* [New Trends] 3, no. 4: 922.

Zhang, Jing [張靜]. 2012. *Zhongguo Taipingyang Guoji Xuehui Yanjiu* 中國太平洋國際學會研究 [Study of the Institute of Pacific Relations]. Beijing: Shehui kexue wenxian chubanshe.

Zhang, Tingxiu [張廷休]. 1939. "Zai Lun Yi Han Tongyuan" 再論夷漢同源 [Another Discussion of the Common Origins of the Yi and the Han]. *Xi'nan Bianjiang* 6: 501–509.

Zhang, Xizhen. 2006. "Overview of Teaching Programmes and Curriculum Development on Southeast Asia in China." In *Southeast Asian Studies in China*, edited by Swee-Hock Saw and John Wong, 75–86. Singapore: ISEAS.

Zhong, Weichang [仲維暢]. 2009. "Zhongguo Cifen Tanshang Xin Jishu Wei Nanqiao Jigong Shuaixian Yinjin" 中國磁粉探傷新技術為南僑機工率先引進 [Magnetic Particle Inspection Was First Introduced by Nanyang Volunteers]. *Bagui Qiaokan* 八桂僑刊, no. 2: 65–66.

Zhou, Taomo. 2019. *Migration in the Time of Revolution: China, Indonesia, and the Cold War*. Ithaca, NY: Cornell University Press.

Zhou, Ying, and Sabrina Luk. 2016. "Establishing Confucius Institutes: A Tool for Promoting China's Soft Power?" *Journal of Contemporary China* 25, no. 100: 628–42.

岑家梧. 1992. *Xi'nan Minzu Jiqi Wenhua* 西南民族及其文化 [Xi'nan Minzu and Its Culture]. In *Cen Jiawu Minzu Yanjiu Wenji* 岑家梧民族研究文集 [Ethnological Writings of Cen Jiawu]. Beijing: Renmin chubanshe.

Index

About the Authors

Ying-kit Chan is assistant professor at the Department of Chinese Studies, National University of Singapore. He received his PhD in East Asian studies from Princeton University and his BA and MA in Chinese studies from the National University of Singapore. He served as a research fellow at the International Institute for Asian Studies, Leiden University, and was a visiting scholar at the Faculty of Liberal Arts, Thammasat University, and the Center for Chinese Studies, National Central Library, in Taipei. His books include *Alternative Representations of the Past: The Politics of History in Modern China* (2020) and *Contesting Chineseness: Ethnicity, Identity, and Nation in China and Southeast Asia* (2021, with Chang-Yau Hoon).

Chang-Yau Hoon is associate professor at the Institute of Asian Studies, Universiti Brunei Darussalam, as well as adjunct research fellow at the University of Western Australia, where he received his PhD (with distinction) in Asian studies. He specializes in the Chinese diaspora, identity politics, multiculturalism, and religious and cultural diversity in contemporary Southeast Asia. His books include *Chinese Identity in Post-Suharto Indonesia: Culture, Politics and Media* (2008), *Chinese Indonesians Reassessed: History, Religion and Belonging* (2013), *Catalysts of Change: Ethnic Chinese Business in Asia* (2014), *Contesting Chineseness: Ethnicity, Identity, and Nation in China and Southeast Asia* (2021), and *Christianity and the Chinese in Indonesia: Ethnicity, Education and Enterprise* (forthcoming in 2023).